WOMEN IN IRAQ

WOMEN IN IRAQ

PAST MEETS PRESENT

Noga Efrati

COLUMBIA UNIVERSITY PRESS   NEW YORK

COLUMBIA UNIVERSITY PRESS
Publishers Since 1893
NEW YORK   CHICHESTER, WEST SUSSEX
CUP.COLUMBIA.EDU
COPYRIGHT © 2012 COLUMBIA UNIVERSITY PRESS
ALL RIGHTS RESERVED

LIBRARY OF CONGRESS CATALOGING-IN-PUBLICATION DATA

EFRATI, NOGA.
    WOMEN IN IRAQ : PAST MEETS PRESENT / NOGA EFRATI.
        P.   CM.
    INCLUDES BIBLIOGRAPHICAL REFERENCES AND INDEX.
    ISBN 978-0-231-15814-5 (CLOTH : ALK. PAPER) — ISBN 978-0-231-53024-8 (EBOOK)
  1. WOMEN—IRAQ—SOCIAL CONDITIONS.   2. FEMINISM—IRAQ—HISTORY.
3. WOMEN'S RIGHTS—IRAQ—HISTORY.   I. TITLE.

    HQ1735.E47 2012
    305.4209567—DC23

                                                        2011022457

COLUMBIA UNIVERSITY PRESS BOOKS ARE PRINTED ON PERMANENT AND
DURABLE ACID-FREE PAPER.
THIS BOOK IS PRINTED ON PAPER WITH RECYCLED CONTENT.
PRINTED IN THE UNITED STATES OF AMERICA

C   10   9   8   7   6   5   4   3   2   1

REFERENCES TO INTERNET WEB SITES (URLs) WERE ACCURATE AT THE TIME OF
WRITING. NEITHER THE AUTHOR NOR COLUMBIA UNIVERSITY PRESS IS RESPONSIBLE FOR
URLs THAT MAY HAVE EXPIRED OR CHANGED SINCE THE MANUSCRIPT WAS PREPARED.

DESIGN *by* VIN DANG

TO PAUL AND YONATAN

CONTENTS

PREFACE   IX

ACKNOWLEDGMENTS   XVII

INTRODUCTION   *The Historical Setting*   1

1   Occupation, Monarchy, and Customary Law: *Tribalizing Women*   20

2   Family Law as a Site of Struggle and Subordination   51

3   Politics, Election Law, and Exclusion   86

4   Gender Discourse and Discontent: *Activism Unraveled*   111

5   Challenging the Government's Gender Discourse   137

EPILOGUE   *Past Meets Present*   163

NOTES   175

BIBLIOGRAPHY   211

INDEX   225

PREFACE

Saddam Husain's downfall raised the hopes of many Iraqi women for a better future. The U.S.-led invasion of their country in March 2003 had been accompanied by a promise to improve their lives: the George W. Bush administration in particular had pledged to turn Iraq into a free and democratic country in which women's rights are enshrined as a model for the whole region. Galvanized by this fresh sense of freedom, a multitude of women's associations appeared countrywide, representing all segments of Iraqi society.

Early on, however, obstacles appeared as women's political participation in the "new Iraq" became an issue of contention. Only three of twenty-five seats on the U.S.-appointed interim Iraqi Governing Council in July 2003 went to women, and only one woman minister was selected for the provisional government set up immediately afterward. Then, in December 2003, a resounding wake-up call was delivered: the council announced it was abolishing Iraq's Personal Status Law—the family law that had included many provisions favorable to women. Furthermore, under the mounting disorder, tribal courts were convened, and coalition forces, faced with the urgent need to reestablish order across the southern part of the country, gave a nod to tribal law that sanctioned coercive practices pertaining to women. As the invasion turned into full-scale occupation, it became increasingly clear that any promise by the allies to support women's rights was far from realization.[1]

Beyond the crumbling infrastructure and general lack of security, an increase in gender-based violence gravely concerned activists. If anything, developments were pulling women back to the past, they cautioned. It was not only the memory of life under Saddam's regime that fanned their fears. They were haunted, too, by ghosts of a more distant history. A foreign occupation with the declared intent of building a liberal state was not a new notion in their country. Indeed, the British invasion and occupation of Mesopotamia had led to the inception of the Iraqi state in the wake of World War I and determined its structure for years to come. Activists often alluded to this attempt at state building and its harsh long-lasting consequences for women.[2]

Unfortunately, however, most observers and, more important, decision makers failed to appreciate the weight of these warnings. Activists did not often elaborate on this untold history of women in Iraq, and even as scholars began revisiting the period of direct British rule and the British Mandate era in Iraq, their works offered little illumination. In fact, historical studies of women's issues have only rarely extended beyond the Ba'th period (1968–2003).[3] This book contributes to filling this historiographical lacuna and elucidates activists' fears springing from the period of the British occupation and the British-backed monarchy (1917–1958).

Looking back to the monarchy period and beyond enhances our understanding of activists' post-2003 struggle to secure meaningful participation in politics for women, to preserve Iraq's progressive Personal Status Law, and to prevent state acknowledgment of customary law and coercive practices pertaining to women. The pages of history shed light on the struggle from a different perspective as well. Conservative and religious politicians attempting to delegitimize activists' struggle accused activists of unauthenticity and of being detached from Iraq's traditions and past.[4] I demonstrate here, however, that the roots of activists' struggle against coercive customs, unfavorable interpretations of Islamic law, and exclusion from the political sphere reach back to the birth of the state.

This volume is first and foremost a historical work. It is a part of a rapidly growing research field—the study of women and gender in the Middle East. This field has come into its own over the past thirty years:[5] the literature is rapidly expanding;[6] collections of articles are being compiled on topics of increasing specificity;[7] the associated basic concepts are being discussed;[8] and criticism regarding preconceived assumptions and value-laden writing is evolving.[9] To deal with the considerable momentum in the study of women's history in the region and to ease navigation through this field, scholars have categorized works according to various criteria. Judith Tucker and Margaret Meriwether offer a categorization that best helps locate my work within the growing genre of the history of women in the Middle East.[10]

Meriwether and Tucker identify four approaches. The first is the study of "women worthies"—that is, notable women who in the past played a visible role in public activities. This approach includes biographical studies of famous women or a vivid recounting of known historical events that highlights the hitherto unknown (or underappreciated) role played by individual women.[11] The second approach encompasses the study of political and institutional history. It looks at the activities of women in political movements, whether feminist or nationalist or both. Some of the works characterizing this approach were written in an institutional history style that reconstructs the events, leadership, and activities of the subject organization while allowing us to follow the evolution of feminist thought as it developed in practice. Tucker and Meriwether note that applying these two approaches opens a new angle of discussion regarding issues such as the nature of political power and the location of political activities. However, these approaches generally seek to add women, mainly women of the elite, to the pages of history and not to challenge the fundamental bases of history writing.

The remaining two approaches take up this challenge. The study of women in the social and economic history of the Middle East also seeks to add women to history, but as part of an extended picture of the past that exceeds the boundaries of political history or the study of elites. It looks at women as economic actors and as active members of their communities, families, and classes. The final approach centers on women in the cultural history of the Middle East. Tucker and Meriwether emphasize the study of dominant and contesting gender discourses within this framework. The discourse on gender, they explain, attends to the ways in which the dominant culture in a particular place and time has defined maleness and femaleness as points of difference or opposition, with the male always in the position of power and domination. Although it seeks to understand how male-privileged discourses evolved, it also endeavors to bring subversive discourses—that is, the ways in which people endeavor to undermine and contest the discourse of power—to the forefront.

Meriwether and Tucker's categorization is helpful, but it is also problematic in that many of the groundbreaking studies they mention can be placed in more than one category. This problem is due mainly to the fact that most historians they survey published their works in the 1990s and were aware of these different approaches and their limitations. These historians did not hesitate, therefore, to combine different methods in their effort to provide the most comprehensive picture on the subject of their research. Leila Ahmed's *Women and Gender in Islam* and Parvin Paidar's *Women and the Political Process in Twentieth-Century Iran*, for example, fall into the first and second categories, respectively, but the notion of competing discourses was a unifying theme for both.[12]

My book, inspired by these works, similarly fits into more than one category. It can be located within the realm of political history because it deals mainly with the Iraqi political elite and the women's movement under the mandate and the monarchy. Yet the subtle but pervasive force of discourse is also a unifying thread.

In choosing to work with the notion of "discourse," one enters hazardous territory. It is hazardous not only because of the plethora and range of meanings the term *discourse* enjoys, as reflected in scholarly works, but more so because of the risk of entanglement in an unproductive "discourse about discourse."[13] In my research, I sought an understanding of women's position in Iraq under British occupation and the British-backed Hashemite government (1917–1958), but as I worked toward achieving this purpose, discourse gradually began to surface as the best analytical tool for it. Indeed, the sources my international search yielded, more than delineating women's lived experience, allowed me to track attitudes and practices concerning women. These attitudes and practices were reflected in three main contexts: customary law and the controversy over the British-introduced Tribal Criminal and Civil Disputes Regulation (TCCDR), formulated in 1916; family law and the call for the regulation of personal status matters; and election law and the conflict over the nature of the political system. The discourse tool allowed me not only to tie together attitudes and practices, but, more important, to expose them as an expression of a much larger reality.

I then found Michel Foucault's concept of discourse, as understood by Stuart Hall, to be the most suitable for my discussion. Hall explains that discourse provides "a language for talking about—a way of representing the knowledge about—a particular topic at a particular historical moment." But it is not purely a "linguistic" concept. He indicates that discourse is about both language and practice:

> It attempts to overcome the traditional distinction between what one *says* (language) and what one *does* (practice). Discourse . . . constructs the topic. It defines and produces the objects of our knowledge. It governs the way that a topic can be meaningfully talked about and reasoned about. It also influences how ideas are put to practice and used to regulate the conduct of others. Just as a discourse "rules in" certain ways of talking about a topic, defining an acceptable and intelligible way to talk, write, or conduct oneself, so also, by definition, it "rules out," limits and restricts other ways of talking, of conducting ourselves in relation to the topic or constructing knowledge about it.[14]

These aspects of discourse helped me unfold the conflicting ways of thinking about women and how their conduct should be regulated in the nascent state. This book proceeds along this path: it presents the ways Iraqi women were constructed as citizens by the gender discourse of Iraq's rulers from the outset of the British occupation until the overthrow of the British-backed monarchy and traces efforts by the Iraqi women's movement to contest this construct.

The first three chapters describe how and why during the state-building process under the mandate and the monarchy women were constructed as second-class citizens. They outline the way the legal and political systems were shaped first by the British occupation and then by the Iraqi government the British put in place, focusing on the evolution of legislation that defined and influenced women's position in family and society. At the same time, it acknowledges conflicting perceptions, power struggles, and other larger issues of the era as driving forces fueling this evolution.

Chapter 1 addresses the topic of customary law. During World War I, the British imposed the TCCDR for the purpose of ruling over Iraq's vast countryside. The regulation bolstered tribal leaders and tied them to the state by giving them authority to settle disputes between "their tribesmen" in accordance with "tribal methods" and "tribal law." Customary practices were thus not only sanctioned but, because the presumed existence of "age-old tribal practices" provided an important justification for deploying the TCCDR, were also perpetuated. The chapter explains how this regulation, which later became state law, was incorporated into the government gender discourse despite growing criticism from Iraqi intellectuals[15] and reveals the harsh implications for rural women. The chapter further demonstrates that women's well-being was knowingly sacrificed to facilitate the governing of Iraq's vast rural areas.

Chapter 2 looks at the topic of family law. Under the Hashemite monarchy, Iraq had no civil law governing personal status matters (marriage, divorce, child custody, inheritance, etc.). This chapter briefly reviews British policy, which left family matters in the hands of religious leaders in order to tie these leaders to the British-dominated nascent state, and highlights opposition to this course of action. It then expands on state attempts to intervene by way of legislation and examines their ramifications for women. Although the debate over the state's introduction of the Personal Status Law has been inextricably linked to the debate over Iraqi women's standing in the domestic realm, the chapter shows that gender relations were not the only object of dispute; in fact, the conflict between the government and the 'ulama' to a large extent also centered on who had the authority to formulate laws governing personal status, which courts were to be involved, and who should be entrusted with the authority to adjudicate disputes. Meanwhile, women citizens were constructed as subordinate and dependent and were left unprotected from unfavorable interpretations of Islamic law.

Chapter 3 is devoted to women's participation in formal politics. A parliamentary system was an efficient tool for the British to tie urban intellectuals in Iraq to the new state. But to ensure that the power of the British-backed Hashemite government would not be undermined, the Constitution and election system posed considerable obstacles for most men and totally blocked women from entering Parliament. This chapter looks at women's disenfranchisement throughout the Hashemite period. It delineates the huge obstacles that stood in the way of altering the first Iraqi Constitution, emphasizing the entanglement of the efforts to gain political rights for women with the broader struggle to effect change in the existing political order. It argues that the Hashemite government, troubled by the prospect of rocking the political boat, employed a strategy that simultaneously avoided distancing conservative supporters who opposed women's vote and placated the opposition that favored it. In line with its modernity rhetoric, this government strategy required women to exhibit signs of "progress" as a prerequisite to receiving rights. What facilitated this tack was the fact that supporters of women's suffrage shared with those opposing enfranchisement certain assumptions that constructed women as ill prepared for political participation.

Chapters 4 and 5 seek to show how those active in the women's movement under the monarchy contested their government's gender discourse. Chapter 4 claims that there were two main reasons why the full scale of women's response is difficult to trace. The first is connected with circumstances of the time—that is, with the government's reining in of the women's movement. The second, however, is rooted in the nature of the accounts portraying the history of the women's movement, provided by Iraqi women's activists, and their later reproduction in contemporary scholarly literature published in English. It argues that the early history of the women's movement in Iraq remains little known because the two key organizations involved in the movement—the Iraqi Women's Union (al-Ittihad al-Nisa'i al-'Iraqi), which was sanctioned by the regime, and the underground League for the Defense of Women's Rights (Rabitat al-Difa' 'an Huquq al-Mar'a)—produced two competing narratives of the women's movement before 1958. Later scholars reproduced either one account or the other. This chapter unravels these two narratives in order to piece together a more elaborate portrayal of women's efforts at organization. It unveils some of the earliest scenes of activists' challenging their government's gender discourse and follows the process of organization that later facilitated a more direct challenge.

Women's activism in Iraq gained momentum after World War II: it expanded, gained strength, and became institutionalized. Chapter 5 focuses on activists' struggle against their construction as second-class citizens as that construction became increasingly obvious during the 1950s. It registers voices raised by both union and league members against the TCCDR, the lack of government intervention in the realm of personal status, and women's disenfranchisement. In addition, it argues that the challenge that the union and league posed to the government's discourse shaped to a large extent the new gender discourse that emerged in Iraq after 1958 and prevailed well into the second half of the twentieth century.

All too soon after the 2003 U.S.-led invasion, Iraqi women's rights activists began cautioning that developments were pulling Iraqi women back to the days of the British-backed monarchy. The epilogue marks similar threads running through past British and present American policies influencing the fate of two generations of Iraqi women separated by half a century. Under the Americans who came to Iraq armed with a vision of creating a free and democratic state in which women's rights are enshrined, women were returned to pre-1958 conditions, and the floodgates opened to a new wave of tribalization and subordination.

ACKNOWLEDGMENTS

My intellectual journey to Iraq's past would not have been possible without the generous support of the Harry S. Truman Research Institute for the Advancement of Peace at the Hebrew University of Jerusalem and the encouragement of its former head, Amnon Cohen. My deepest thanks also to the academic director, Steve Kaplan, and the Truman Institute staff.

I am indebted to Leonard Polonsky for his continued financial support, which enabled me to pursue and complete this study. My research was also made possible by the Nathan Rotenstreich Fellowship for Outstanding Ph.D. Candidates in the Humanities and by grants from the Friedrich Ebert Foundation, the Jewish Arab Center at the University of Haifa, and the Georg Eckert Institute for International Textbook Research, Braunschweig.

I received invaluable assistance from the staff at the National Archives of India, New Delhi; the Public Record Office and the India Office, London; the Middle East Center Archive, St. Antony's College, Oxford; the School of Oriental and African Studies Library; the Princeton University Firestone Library; the Harvard University Widener Library; the Smith College Sophia Smith Collection; the Tel Aviv University Moshe Dayan Center Library; the University of Haifa Library; and the National Library, Jerusalem.

A number of people shared with me their intellectual wisdom, and I have benefited equally from agreement and disagreement. I owe deep gratitude to Amatzia Baram, who offered me his expertise and spared no time or effort on my behalf. I also thank Gad Gilbar for his support and valuable advice at the earlier stages of this research. I had the pleasure to work with Ruth Roded and benefit from her vast knowledge and insights. I was fortunate to have known the late Joseph Kostiner and enjoy his perceptive and thought-provoking comments.

Many have offered sound advice and insights and given generously of their knowledge. I thank Peter Sluglett, Beth Baron, Nadje al-Ali, Yizhak Nakash, Sara Pursley, Mubejel Baban, Bushra Perto, Frank H. Stewart, Ron Shaham, Michael Eppel, Sylvia Haim, Achim Rohde, Ronen Zeidel, Avi Rubin, Helen Ben Mordechay, Deena Laventer, Lisa Perlman, Paul Binstock, Amiram Efrati, and, last but not least, Hasan Shufani.

I am grateful to my family for their support, especially my husband, Paul, and son, Yonatan, for their never-ending encouragement and understanding.

WOMEN IN IRAQ

INTRODUCTION

THE HISTORICAL SETTING

A brief review of Iraq's development, its regimes, and modes of governance and an outline of the political and socioeconomic realities that emerged from the time the British took over from the Ottoman rulers until a military coup overthrew the Hashemite government in 1958 is essential to understand the context in which the old "new" state of Iraq constructed women as second-class citizens.

Under the Ottoman Empire, the area that now forms the state of Iraq was divided into three provinces,[1] Basra, Baghdad, and Mosul. The Ottomans, who governed these provinces from the sixteenth century, left a legacy that would influence the shaping of the modern state of Iraq. This legacy of institutions, law, political culture, and education was what the British found after arriving in 1914. And yet until the second half of the nineteenth century, Ottoman authorities had failed to extend central control to this area. It was only when the capable Ottoman envoy Midhat Pasha assumed the governorship of Baghdad in 1869 that things changed. In his three years in office, Midhat Pasha launched reforms intended to modernize the bureaucracy, improve overall economic standards and education, and integrate the area into the rest of the empire. Applying the Ottoman Vilayet Law of 1864, Midhat set up a new centralized administrative system and mapped out the borders of the Iraqi provinces, along with that of their various subdivisions. An appointed official governed each administrative division, assisted by a council that for the first time included a number of elected representatives.

Through the application of the Ottoman Land Law of 1858, Midhat also sought to transform the nature of land holdings and settle nomadic tribes. The law did not recognize communal (e.g., tribal) ownership of land, but rather a prescriptive right only of individual cultivators who could prove actual possession and cultivation of a particular plot of land for at least ten years. In some locations, land registration did produce beneficial results. In most regions, however, the peasants were left worse off than before. Due to the shifting and communal nature of agriculture, continuous cultivation was difficult to prove. On the one hand, tribesmen, fearing not only conscription and taxation but also that their prescriptive rights might somehow be revoked, saw no advantage in approaching the authorities to legitimize their rights. On the other hand, those who understood the benefits of doing so—shaikhs, notables, and urban merchants—wasted no time in acquiring titles to large tracts of land. Many of the tribesmen eventually found themselves mere tenant farmers.[2]

Midhat also set the foundations for a secular education system in Iraq. He established free public schools that included a technical school, a middle-level school, and two secondary schools (one for the military and one for the civil service). His successors continued support for general secular education, and by 1915 there were 160 schools listed in the system.[3] In 1908, a law college was founded, which offered the country's only higher education. Graduates of these schools or those returning from schooling in Istanbul formed the core of the urban literate elite. Military academies were a main avenue of mobility for Iraq's lower-middle-class and middle-class families. On the eve of British occupation, Iraqi graduates of these schools were already filling positions in government schools, new secular courts, the army, and administration. Most of Iraq's leaders rose from within this group in the period following World War I.

British occupation of the three Ottoman provinces, Basra, Baghdad, and Mosul, began as a preemptive move in 1914 to protect British interests at the head of the Persian Gulf. These interests had in large part been born out of Britain's concern to protect its trade route to India. They grew as trade with the gulf area developed, but especially with the discovery of oil in commercial quantities in southern Iran in 1908 and with the British navy's decision to convert its fleet from coal to oil fuel. There was considerable hope that oil would be found in Iraq as well. After the outbreak of World War I, when it became obvious that the Ottoman Empire would join with the Central Powers, Britain sent troops to occupy Faw and Basra. The occupation of Basra in November 1914 began a process that ended with the occupation of Baghdad in March 1917 and of Mosul in November 1918. Other areas, however—including the Kurdish highlands bordering Turkey and Iran, the tribal land of the Euphrates stretching from Baghdad south to Nasiriyya, and the two Shi'i cities Karbala and Najaf—were and would remain foci of unrest throughout the mandate period and beyond.

Under British military control was a territory containing a population with diverse ethnic, religious, and tribal loyalties. Some 75 to 80 percent of the population were Arabic speakers, but for 15 to 20 percent Kurdish was the mother tongue. The Arabic speakers, however, were divided not only between Sunnis and Shi'is, but also along several tribal confederacies.

The Arab Shi'a, constituting some 55 percent of the population, lived predominantly in the basin of the Tigris and Euphrates rivers south of Baghdad. The Shi'a started off as a political movement soon after the death of the Prophet, rejecting Muhammad's close associates Abu Bakr, 'Umar, and 'Uthman as his rightful successors. They considered 'Ali ibn Abi Talib, the Prophet's cousin and son-in-law, and his descendants alone as the legitimate successors and leaders, or imams, of the Muslim community. The name "Shi'i," in fact, evolved from "Shi'at 'Ali," meaning "the faction or partisans of 'Ali." In the ninth century, after the disappearance of the twelfth Shi'i imam, the spiritual leadership of the Shi'i community and authority to interpret Qur'anic verse passed to the *mujtahids* (senior religious scholars). Each Shi'i was expected to follow a leading *mujtahid*, which made these religious scholars very powerful. The Shi'a, then, evolved from a political group into a religious sect with several distinctive rituals and somewhat different interpretations of Islamic law.

Under the Sunni Ottoman administration, the only Muslim faith officially accepted was Sunnism. Shi'is of the Iraqi provinces were largely excluded from government positions and institutions. Sunni notables thus maintained a monopoly over the government and judiciary. The Shi'i, or Ja'fari,[4] school of law and Shi'i judges were excluded from the Ottoman shari'a courts, and Shi'is tended to settle their cases by referring to their own religious leaders. By the time of the establishment of the monarchy, however, the Shi'i religious establishment could compete with any government in Iraq over the influence and mobilization of the local population. Therefore, successive governments sought to undermine the power of Shi'i *mujtahids* and institutions.[5]

Sunni Arabs, composing some 20 percent of the population, lived mostly in central and central–northern parts of Iraq, which correlated roughly with a triangle drawn between Baghdad, Mosul, and the Syrian border. They were more urban than the Shi'is, constituting the majority in Baghdad. The Sunnis, however, do not defer to the same degree to their religious leaders—the scholars, jurists, and judges collectively known as *'ulama'*. Since the days of the Ottoman Empire, the Arab Sunnis, despite being a minority, have dominated Iraq.

The Kurds, accounting for about 15 to 20 percent of the population, occupied mainly the mountainous parts of northern and northeastern Iraq. The vast majority were Sunni Muslims who spoke an Indo-European language akin to Persian. A common language, close tribal ties, customs, and a shared history inspired Kurdish nationalist feelings, and, indeed, the abortive Treaty of Sèvres, signed in August 1920 with the Ottoman sultan, promised an autonomous state to the Kurds of Turkey and Iraq. The British also briefly contemplated Kurdish autonomy in Mosul Province, but it failed to materialize. During the monarchy, a number of Kurdish armed revolts occurred; some were quelled only with massive support from the British Royal Air Force. Nonetheless, many Kurds assimilated sufficiently to allow their active participation within the framework of the state. Thus, about 90 percent of Iraq's population in this period were Muslims; Christians, Jews, Mandaeans, and Yazidis formed the rest. Around 80 percent of the population were rural. Most of the nomadic tribes had settled but remained tribally organized and retained their special customs. The country had one major city, Baghdad, which during the monarchy became the political center. Tribal shaikhs, Kurdish chieftains, and notables of the other cities congregated in Baghdad. Failure to have a presence there meant one's interests would not be watched over and ultimately spelled political marginalization.

British occupation brought with it an administration whose immediate desire was to instill order. Largely shaped by the British experience in India, the administration was staffed by the men of the India Office. In other words, the British brought with them the structures of direct British rule, which were associated with the notions of the "white man's burden" and the "civilizing mission." The British divided the country into districts, and political officers were stationed in each, backed by British-staffed departments in Baghdad. The central administration was headed by a civil commissioner, although nominally under military command. The British abolished the Ottoman municipal councils, and in their place political officers maintained order through local notables. In the country-side, the British sought to rule through shaikhs, who were charged with the collection of taxes in their districts and in return had their power and privileges affirmed by the British administration. Tribal leaders had already garnered greater power vis-à-vis their tribesmen after the Otto-man Land Law of 1858 was applied in Iraq in the 1870s. This law allowed shaikhs to register tribal land in their own name. Now the British, in an attempt to secure the loyalty of tribal leaders, whose domains straddled strategic lines, granted them title over lands that they claimed as their own. Thus, vast tracts of land passed into the personal possession of se-lected tribal leaders. The TCCDR further buttressed the shaikhs, giving them judicial authority over members of their tribe. Their rule was now based on powers given them by the British and not on their own author-ity or the support of their tribesmen. True, in the first few years of the monarchy the Iraqi government tried to rescind some of the powers the British had granted the shaikhs, but an informal arrangement gradually emerged between the government and the shaikhs-turned-landowners whereby the government, in return for the shaikhs' support, would large-ly give them a free hand in their local areas in the maintenance of order as well as in administration and taxation matters. British policy ultimately contributed to the transformation of a free cultivating peasantry into a population of serfs tied to the land as sharecroppers.

The policies of what was known as the "Eastern school" were not un-opposed. In the British context, the "Western school," promoted by the Arab Bureau in Cairo, was key in this respect. This group believed that British interests would be better and less costly served by indirect con-trol over friendly Arab governments and that British influence should be maintained through advisers and treaties. Already in March 1917, the British government issued a memo suggesting that an indigenous Arab government under British guidance in Iraq should replace British direct administration. As a result, Ottoman courts and laws were reinstated, re-placing the Anglo–Indian civil code. However, the British bureaucracy continued to strengthen its hold, and few Arabs were appointed to senior positions.

British rule had early on been the cause of considerable opposition inside Iraq. In 1920, a revolt was sparked by the announcement that Britain had been awarded the mandate for Iraq. The revolt was instigated by a coalition of nationalists in Baghdad, Shi'i religious leaders of the Holy Cities, and mid-Euphrates tribal leaders. Although motivated by a variety of factors, these groups shared the desire to shed British rule. The revolt lasted several months, swept over about one-third of the countryside, and cost Britain some five hundred lives and forty million pounds.[6] Although failing to achieve Iraqi independence, the revolt did change British policy. Direct rule was seen as having contributed to the rebellion, and, as a consequence, when Sir Percy Cox arrived in Baghdad in October 1920 to take up his post as the first high commissioner under the mandate, he brought new guidelines: the military administration would be terminated; a constitution would be formulated in consultation with Iraqi elites, and a provisional government with an Arab president and council of state would be established. In short order, Ottoman administrative units and municipal councils were restored. Iraqi officials began to replace British political officers in the provinces. British presence continued, however, in an "advisory capacity." Sunni Arabs, who constituted less than 20 percent of the population, were entrusted with the most important posts. The Shi'is, despite their majority, were noticeably absent—in part because, having previously been excluded from the Ottoman administration, few among them had any administrative experience and in part because of the British attitude in general toward the Shi'is following the revolt. Ottoman-educated Sunni Arabs under foreign patronage were now dominating Iraq.

In 1921 at the Cairo Conference, Britain's plan for Iraq coalesced. It was there, in Phebe Marr's words, that "the three pillars of the Iraqi state were conceived."[7] These pillars were a British-backed Arab monarchy, a treaty that would legitimize British presence in Iraq, and a constitution that, although encompassing the different elements of the population under democratic principles, perpetuated religious, sectarian, geographical, and class- and gender-based divisions and exclusions.

The throne was offered to the Hashemite amir Faisal, third son of the sharif of Mecca. Faisal had headed the short-lived Syrian kingdom (1918–

1920) but was forced to flee following the French occupation in 1920. He enjoyed British protection owing to his role as a leader of the Great Arab Revolt against the Turks during World War I. Faisal was crowned king in 1921. He himself, however, pointed out the weakness of his government's position when he detailed the many conflicting forces within the Iraqi state to which he must appeal, claiming that the government possessed only fifteen thousand rifles compared with one hundred thousand in the hands of the people.[8]

When Faisal left Syria to assume the throne, Iraqis who had served in his short-lived government there and had fought with him in the war returned to Iraq. These repatriated Iraqis, extremely loyal to Faisal, were soon visible at all levels of government and set the cornerstone for Arab Sunni dominance in government. Many among this group would soon attain positions of power. Among them were army officers such as Nuri al-Sa'id, who became Faisal's chief of staff, and Ja'far al-'Askari, who was appointed minister of defense. Also accompanying Faisal from Syria was Sati' al-Husri, an Aleppan, who became a major figure in Iraq's education system.

Because of Iraqi opposition to the idea of a mandate, British relations with monarchial Iraq had been formulated to appear as a treaty between two sovereign states. In the 1922 treaty that was drawn up, however, British authority in financial matters and in international and security affairs clearly indicated the limits on Iraqi sovereignty. The king would be "guided" by Britain on all matters affecting British interests and especially fiscal policy as long as Iraq remained indebted to Britain. A subsequent agreement required Iraq to pay half the cost of maintaining British residency, which perpetuated Iraq's debt and slowed development. Iraq had to demonstrate to the powers dominating the League of Nations that it was ready for sovereignty; until then, it would be advised and assisted by Great Britain. Britain promised to propose Iraqi membership in the League of Nations as soon as possible, regardless of the fact that the duration of the treaty was to be twenty years. In 1924, the Iraqi Constituent Assembly, tasked with passing a constitution and the treaty, seemed less than enthusiastic to ratify the treaty. Sir Henry Dobbs, high commissioner since 1923, then stepped in to clarify the true nature of affairs: if the treaty was not promptly ratified, he warned, Great Britain would fulfill its mandate by other means.[9]

The ratification of the treaty was followed soon afterward by the passage of the Constitution and the Electoral Law. The main bone of contention between the British and the Iraqis concerned the relative powers between king and Parliament. The emerging Constitution, "a gift from the West," as a British judge in Iraq once termed it,[10] granted the king the right to call for general elections, to dismiss the convocation of Parliament, to choose the prime minister, and to confirm all laws. He had the authority to conclude treaties but could ratify them only after parliamentary approval. The Parliament consisted of a Senate, appointed by the king, and an elected Chamber of Deputies. The Chamber of Deputies could force the government's resignation by a simple majority vote of no confidence. Any deputy could propose legislation, if supported by ten others. A bill would become law only after being approved by both chambers.

The Constitution, which remained largely unchanged throughout the monarchy, also determined Iraq's legal system. It perpetuated divisions among Iraqi citizens. It established that state courts would be divided into three classes: civil, religious, and special courts. Although stating that civil courts would have jurisdiction over all Iraqis in all civil and criminal matters, it allowed the establishment of special courts for settling criminal and civil cases relating to the tribes in accordance with their customs. The Constitution divided the religious courts into shari'a courts for the Muslims and Spiritual Councils for other religious communities. In addition, it affirmed that shari'a courts alone were to handle matters pertaining to the personal status of Muslims in accordance with the shari'a provisions particular to each Islamic sect.

The Constitution also provided a base for the election system in Iraq but prescribed that elections for the Chamber of Deputies be regulated according to a special law.[11] The Electoral Law for the Chamber of Deputies, published in 1924, provided for a two-tiered electoral system in which primary electors were to nominate secondary electors, who were in turn to vote for deputies. Only male taxpayers older than twenty could be primary or secondary electors; only male taxpayers older than thirty could become deputies. The law stipulated that after the primary electors had elected secondary electors (one for every 250 primary voters), the latter were to assemble in their respective district headquarters and vote for the deputies. Each district formed an "electoral college," with one deputy for every twenty thousand male inhabitants. Electoral colleges were grouped into three "circles," and no circle was to elect a deputy who was an inhabitant of another circle.[12] The Electoral Law excluded the lower class, men younger than thirty, and women from serving in Parliament; the two-step procedure allowed for considerable government meddling, which made it difficult for urban politicians who opposed the political elite to be elected, and tribal leaders were well represented.

British control and the structuring of state institutions to facilitate its continuation alienated many Iraqis. The young educated elite voiced feelings of both Arab nationalism and a specific Iraqi nationalism.[13] Arab nationalism, primarily a response to colonial rule, held Iraq and all Arab countries as artificial creations. A common history and language, its proponents argued, should unite all Arab countries into a single nation. Iraqi nationalism, however, although not opposing Arab political unity, legitimized the state instead, focusing mainly on Iraq's internal problems, and was by nature more inclusive. Iraq, its advocates believed, was not a creation of colonialism but had roots extending back to ancient Mesopotamia. Beyond these differences, proponents of both forms of nationalism criticized not only their government's ties to Britain, but also the state–society relationship the British promoted. Already in the 1920s, nationalists were expressing their opposition to the treaty, endeavored to amend the Election Law and to erode tribal leaders' power.

In 1929, a newly elected Labour government in Britain declared it would support Iraq's acceptance to the League of Nations in 1932. Britain insisted, however, that a new treaty be negotiated first to determine its relations with Iraq once the latter attained independence. Iraq's prime minister Nuri al-Saʿid was instrumental in the passage of the treaty, which ended the mandate but retained British influence. Silencing broad and vocal opposition both inside and outside the Parliament, he facilitated its ratification in 1930. The treaty placed all responsibility for internal order on the king and put Iraq in charge of its own defense. In return, Iraq agreed to give Britain use of all Iraq's facilities and all assistance in its power in the event of war, including the right to move British troops through Iraq. In addition, it was agreed that the Royal Air Force be allowed to maintain two major bases and that Britain would supply Iraqi army equipment and military advisers. Although the treaty was for twenty-five years, it was stipulated that a new treaty could be renegotiated after twenty years.

In October 1932, Iraq was granted formal independence. British advisers and officials, however, stayed at their posts; the Royal Air Force retained control over the bases at Habbaniyya near Baghdad and Shuʻaiba near Basra; British-owned companies dominated all major sectors of the economy; and British influence on the Iraqi king and government continued. Nevertheless, Iraqi politics were molded more and more by Iraqi forces. The main difference between the politics of the 1920s and those of the 1930s was the army's emergence as a locus of political power, especially following King Faisal's death in 1933 and succession to the throne of his anti-British, pan-Arabist son Ghazi. In 1936, Iraq underwent its first military coup, the Bakr Sidqi coup. The government that emerged revealed the mix of forces at play. General Bakr Sidqi became chief of staff, and members of the left-wing reformist al-Ahali group received most of the economic and social ministries. Hikmat Sulaiman, who favored the authoritarianism of Mustafa Kamal (Atatürk) as well as modernization and secularization along Turkish lines, became prime minister.

The Ahali group had begun coalescing in the early 1930s. They were young reformers who shared dissatisfaction with the "establishment": government manipulation of elections that entrenched the ruling elite and the profound social and economic abuse that it inflicted in support of the landowners. Members bore witness to how major landowners—whether rural shaikhs, state officials, or urban merchants—used their influence to fortify their power. In 1931, landowners had pushed through a consumption tax that further reduced their tax burden. In 1932, the passage of the Land Settlement Law became the main avenue via which the government could confer propriety rights on individuals—mostly the well-connected landlords. In 1933, the landlords were again behind the Law Governing the Rights and Duties of Cultivators. This law made peasant tenants responsible for crop failures and tied them to the landowner as long as they remained in his debt. The fast-growing slums around Baghdad at this time can be attributed more than a little to these measures, enriching and empowering the landlords at the rural peasantry's expense. Reformers in Sulaiman's government at first seemed capable of challenging the socioeconomic and political structure. Seeking to build on the support expressed in demonstrations organized by the nascent Iraqi Communist Party (ICP), underground labor associations, and radical discussion groups, the Ahali group sponsored the Popular Reform Association. Four reformist ministers were on its executive committee. Its agenda included greater democracy, land reform and the annulment of laws detrimental to the peasants, protective labor legislation, a progressive income tax, as well as broad-based education and the emancipation of women.[14] The reformists intentions, however, soon alarmed many, among them Sidqi's supporters in the officer corps, whose vision of an orderly society under an authoritarian regime was threatened by the reformists' ideas. In the 1937 elections, the biggest winners were Bakr Sidqi's nominees together with conservatives, nationalists, and tribal shaikhs, who saw communism behind the Popular Reform Association. The remaining reformist ministers soon resigned, and Sidqi was assassinated a little later.

The next four years saw governments being formed and dissolved according to the military's whims. Circumstances were complicated by the premature death in 1939 of the young king Ghazi. His pro-British cousin ʿAbd al-Ilah was nominated as regent for his four-year-old son, Faisal II. With the outbreak of World War II, a deepening division became apparent between military and civilian politicians who were or were not ready to support Britain against Germany and Italy. The regent and Nuri al-Saʿid supported Britain. Among Britain's most prominent opponents were Rashid ʿAli al-Kailani, a known Arab nationalist, and his circle, supported by a powerful group of officers known as the Golden Square. In April 1941, with strong army backing, al-Kailani became the prime minister. Hoping for support from the Axis powers, al-Kailani refused to honor Iraq's treaty commitments, but the British quickly reoccupied the country and reinstated the regent. Al-Saʿid, who had fled Iraq with the deposed regent, was entrusted with forming a government. Although the regent and al-Saʿid disagreed on many issues, the pro-British leadership they formed reigned over Iraqi politics until the end of the monarchy in 1958.

The reoccupation of Iraq by British forces in 1941 brought with it a wave of restrictions and regulations. War also adversely affected the economy. Wartime shortages created many opportunities for exploitation. The widening gap between rich and poor added to social tensions and was exacerbated by obvious corruption in high places, so the regime's legitimacy suffered further. The middle class, among whom fixed salaries was the norm, saw their economic position erode; the poor simply became poorer. In the 1940s and 1950s, high inflation and shortages led to increasing social unrest, manifested in student demonstrations, workers' strikes, and peasants' flight from the countryside. Historian Hanna Batatu clearly shows the direct relationship between the rise in the cost of living and the uprisings in the last decade of the monarchy.[15]

The war also brought other changes, especially after Germany's invasion of the Soviet Union and the ensuing Soviet alliance with the United States and Great Britain. Change was particularly noticeable in the relationship between the regime and the ICP. Founded in 1934, the ICP became a significant factor in Iraqi politics by the early 1940s. Its oppositionist activities gained momentum in October 1941, when Yusuf Salman Yusuf ("Fahd") became the party's secretary-general. After the Soviet alliance with the United States and Britain, the ICP stopped its public protest against the British. Relations with successive Iraqi governments improved, and the party won greater freedom to organize and publicize its views.

The party's platform, first published in 1944, called for Iraq's "true independence," the establishment of "a genuinely democratic regime," and the "revival of the Constitution." It supported developing a national economy, "delivering the people . . . from the monopolistic hold of foreign companies . . . on our agriculture products," "stopping the plunder of state lands by those in authority . . . or their alienation to tribal shaikhs . . . and the distribution of these lands in small patches to the peasant without charge." It also called for organizing the workers, recognizing their unions, fulfilling and expanding the Labor Law, expanding education, providing health services, and granting equal rights to the Kurdish and other minorities. Women were promised equal political, social, and economic rights.[16] Students, bureaucrats, teachers, and workers, in particular those in the oil, port, and railway sectors, were the party's main support. Many members were Jews, Christians, and Shi'a. After 1945, as tension mounted between the USSR and the Western Allies, the ICP returned to its outspoken criticism of the monarchial regime and British presence. Not surprisingly, although several political parties were granted licenses in 1946, the ICP was not.

Relations with the ICP notwithstanding, however, the aftermath of the war witnessed the regime's proposal to ease political restrictions in order to gain public support. In a December 1945 speech, the regent promised some measures to redistribute wealth, improve social security, and combat unemployment as well as a new election law and the licensing of political parties. Indeed, five political parties were licensed, although three were short-lived. The other two, however, the Istiqlal (Independence) Party and the National Democratic Party (NDP, al-Hizb al-Watani al-Dimuqrati), together with the underground ICP played an important role in shaping the opposition of the postwar years.

The Istiqlal Party—led by Muhammad Mahdi Kubba, Fa'iq al-Samarra'i, and Siddiq Shanshal—was a joint venture of figures who had been drawn to pan-Arabism in the previous decades. Its stance was decidedly anti-British and called for the elimination of British influence and total independence for Iraq. It advocated a merger between central banks in Arab countries, a unified monetary system and customs authority, and, ultimately, the establishment of federated Arab states. Nonetheless, it supported Iraq's "national sovereignty." It favored expanding civil liberties and criticized the parliamentary system, which it believed denied the people proper representation. It called for socioeconomic reforms, emphasizing more equitable land distribution. It also supported improving education and health services, combating unemployment, and settling nomadic tribes. Women were promised education.[17] Although headed by a Shi'a, Muhammad Mahdi Kubba, the main party supporters were Sunni Arabs.

The NDP was also licensed in 1946. It was led by Kamil al-Chadirchi and Muhammad Hadid and brought together many who had been affiliated with the left-wing reformist al-Ahali group in the 1930s. The party's criticism of British military presence and influence in Iraq's affairs was a main staple of its policy. Rather than taking up a pan-Arab agenda, the party advocated independence for all Arab states. It called for social democracy and political reform by parliamentary means. The party advocated civil liberties, land reform, the abolition of monopolies, and a more just distribution of wealth, mainly through tax measures. The NDP also sought to improve health services, to introduce free primary education, and to stamp out illiteracy. It promised women liberation and rights.[18] Because of its focus on domestic reform rather than on pan-Arabism, the NDP appealed more to minorities and the Shi'a. It drew support from the liberal and left-leaning elements of the educated middle class.

The regime's liberalization program, however, did not last. Opponents of reform perceived the newly licensed parties' activities as signposts of an eventual overthrow of the regime. The more liberal and tolerant cabinet under Tawfiq al-Suwaidi was soon forced out, and repressive measures were introduced under the government of Arshad al-'Umari. These measures brought resentment and strikes. Al-'Umari, unable to suppress the opposition, lost the confidence of the regent and the British when he wanted to declare martial law prior to new elections. The regent then again called on Nuri al-Sa'id, who became prime minister at the end of 1946 with instructions to hold new elections. Al-Sa'id was able to negate much of the party-based opposition by offering some of its members ministerial posts. The ICP's activities were also severely curtailed when in January 1947 Fahd and other party leaders were arrested. General elections were held in March 1947 and not surprisingly gave a nod to the status quo. Al-Sa'id, however, declined to form a new government. Instead, Salih Jabr became the first Shi'i prime minister. Having a Shi'i prime minister initially raised the hopes of many, but optimism soon faded when Jabr led a new round of oppression.

At this point, the regent made another move, which he hoped would gain public support—a revision of the 1930 treaty with Britain. However, the opposition wanted the treaty's abolition, not its revision. In January 1948, in the wake of the negotiations between the British and the Iraqi government and the eventual signing of the treaty in Portsmouth, enormous popular demonstrations broke out in Baghdad, and many participants were killed and injured. The regent did not ratify the treaty, and Prime Minister Jabr resigned. The opposition gained confidence, realizing its ability to mobilize the masses in protest against the regime and its foreign connections. But because the old 1930 treaty was still in effect, the British were hardly perturbed.

All through *al-wathba* ("the leap"), the popular uprising against the treaty, anger over developments in Palestine and Britain's role there continued to spark strikes and demonstrations.[19] In May 1948, a token force of Iraqi troops was sent to join with Jordan's Arab Legion north and west of Jerusalem in the Arab–Israeli war. The Iraqi forces, however, returned bitter, believing that their corrupt and subservient government had prevented them from making a true contribution to the Arab cause. Among the returning officers was the future leader of postrevolutionary Iraq, 'Abd al-Karim Qasim.

During the monarchy's last ten years, from 1948 to 1958, some twenty cabinets passed in and out of office. The one person who dominated

Iraqi politics during the final decade of the monarchy, when the regime
was confronted by growing political unrest and increasing demands for
social, economic, and political reforms, was Nuri al-Sa'id. A representative of the interests of the socially dominant landed class, al-Sa'id, even
when not directly in power, was never far removed or long away from it.
Also at this time oil revenues became significant. The government signed
a new oil agreement with the foreign-owned Iraq Petroleum Company.
Oil revenues soared from about 2.0 million Iraqi dinars in 1948 to 37.4
million in 1952, then 68.9 million in 1956, and jumping to just less than
80 million dinars in 1958.[20] Seventy percent of oil revenue was now ear-
marked for development, and a special board was set up to oversee the
funds. Al-Sa'id hoped that this development program would help relieve
the social and political tensions. Capitalizing on the general desire to turn
Iraq into a modern state, al-Sa'id and his associates promised "progress"
through reforms in all aspects of life. Already in 1949, al-Sa'id's Constitutional Union Party (CUP) presented itself as championing a fundamental
and comprehensive "awakening" through a series of far-reaching social,
economic, and political reforms. It pledged to combat poverty and unemployment by modernizing agriculture, encouraging industry, and dis-
tributing government land. It also promised to expand modern education
and to extend health services.[21]

Despite al-Sa'id's rhetoric and the development program funded by
oil revenues, life for most Iraqis changed little. There admittedly were
major undertakings such as the flood-control project north of Baghdad,
completed in 1956, and the area of cultivated land and food production
increased. But little was done to modernize agricultural practices, and
any distribution of uncultivated state lands to the peasants was insignificant. The large landowners' influence over the government and their grip
on the rural economy continued: 3 percent of the landholders controlled
almost 70 percent of the land.[22] In the countryside, many *fallahin* (peasants; sing. *fallah*) lived just above subsistence level, and health services
and education were practically nonexistent. In the cities, new bridges
and government buildings were built, but little industrial development
was undertaken to employ the many rural migrants who were flowing
into the major urban centers. From the end of the 1920s and throughout
the monarchy period, Iraq witnessed a large-scale migration to the cities.
Hunger, sickness, natural disasters, almost total subjugation to landlords
in the countryside, as well as hopes for greater job and income opportu-

nities in the cities spurred this migration. However, the migrants found themselves pushed to the outskirts of the big cities, living in small and crowded mud or reed huts that lacked even basic facilities. The absence of funding for raising the standard of living of these migrants or of the politically volatile urban population in general was clearly visible. Outside Baghdad, only about 40 percent of the municipalities had a potable water supply, most had no electricity, and sewage was largely neglected. The overwhelming majority of the population was illiterate; in 1950, only about 23 percent of the school-age children were in school. Infant mortality rates were high, and there was a prevalence of diseases such as malaria and trachoma.[23]

The mood in Iraq during the 1950s was affected not only by these socioeconomic realities, but also by events in neighboring countries. Oil was nationalized in Iran with the rise to power of the nationalist leader Muhammad Musaddiq in 1951; in Egypt in 1952, Gamal 'Abd al-Nasir, along with a group of young officers, succeeded in overthrowing the monarchy and promised social reforms and freedom from foreign subservience. Many saw these developments as an option in response to issues also confronting Iraq.

Moreover, by the 1950s younger politicians were eager to take the reigns of power and move the country forward at a faster pace. Even members of the political establishment were becoming weary of al-Sa'id's immutable hold. Those who were discouraged with the regime now joined opposition parties in demanding electoral reform, which became common ground for different groups objecting to the status quo. Meanwhile, the ICP, under the leadership of Baha al-Din Nuri, was recovering from the blow it had suffered between 1947 and 1949. During that time, many of the most experienced party members were arrested, most of whom would spend the last decade of the monarchy in prison. Among those incarcerated were Fahd, the party's secretary-general, and two members of the Politburo; they were hanged in February 1949. A consequence of their "martyrdom," however, was that the party became all the more popular.

Political and social stagnation help explain the 1952 intifada (uprising). Though smaller in scale than the massive demonstrations of the 1948 *wathba*, the intifada led to scores of deaths at the hands of the army and police. General Nur al-Din Mahmud, the army chief of staff, was named prime minister, and martial law was declared. Political parties were banned, newspapers were shut down, and a wide net of arrests fell over even some former ministers and deputies. At the same time, however, hoping to dampen tensions, an electoral decree was promulgated that provided for direct elections. But the government once again rigidly controlled the first direct elections, conducted in January 1953 under martial law. Faisal II's coming of age that year made little difference. 'Abd al-Ilah, the former regent, became the crown prince but remained, despite his unpopularity, firmly in control.

Any hopes for change as Shi'i Muhammad Fadil al-Jamali became prime minister at the end of 1953 were soon dashed. Al-Jamali, who had occupied high posts in the Ministry of Education in the 1930s and was foreign minister in 1946, 1947, and 1952, was at the center of a younger group of officials and academics with reformist ideas pertaining to land law, government organization, and the provision of social services. His cabinet included the highest proportion of Shi'a yet seen in an Iraqi government. But al-Jamali and his relatively modest reform package were nevertheless thwarted by conservative resistance.

Hopes were again raised in 1954. 'Abd al-Ilah, seeking a Chamber of Deputies that might undermine al-Sa'id's influence, planned to hold relatively free elections while al-Sa'id was in Europe. The June 1954 elections have been regarded as the freest elections of the entire monarchy period. All licensed parties participated; the campaign was intense, with some 425 candidates vying for 135 seats. It resulted in the powerful CUP's loss of the controlling majority. At this point, however, 'Abd al-Ilah did an about-face, calling al-Sa'id to return from Europe and form the new government. Al-Sa'id immediately repressed all political activities. Opposition parties were banned, associations were brought under tight control, and legislation was introduced that restricted the freedom of the press and the right to hold public meetings. Fresh elections in September produced the so-called unopposed Parliament, in which most deputies retained their seats because there was no opposition to their candidacy. During the next four years (1954–1958), Iraq settled under rule maintained by police and the army.

These repressive tactics led to the stability by which the Iraqi government weathered the 1955 Baghdad Pact and the 1956 Suez crisis. The Baghdad Pact was a regional security agreement; al-Sa'id hoped it could replace the Anglo–Iraqi Treaty in a way that would avoid another popular uprising but retain the alliance with Britain. According to the new agreement, Britain relinquished control over the Habbaniyya and Shuʻaiba air bases but retained its air corridor over Iraq and the use of the bases for refueling. Britain would come to Iraq's aid if attacked and would continue, with U.S. assistance, to train and equip the Iraqi military forces. The Baghdad Pact, which eventually included Iraq, Turkey, Iran, and Pakistan, split the Arab world into two camps—those aligning with the West and those remaining neutral or joining with the USSR. It brought the Cold War to Iraq and Egypt, pitting al-Saʻid and ʻAbd al-Nasir against each other. Using Cairo Radio to reach the masses, ʻAbd al-Nasir found a sympathetic audience in Iraq. In 1956, he announced the nationalization of the Suez Canal. Britain's role in the tripartite attack with France and Israel further eroded the regime's position and generated a crisis in Iraq almost as severe as the *wathba*.

By 1957, the political tensions had subsided somewhat, but many saw al-Saʻid and the regime as living on borrowed time. Opposition factions, now underground, were joining forces. This process had begun earlier, and in May 1954 the NDP, the Istiqlal Party, and the ICP managed to work together and form the National Front. They even won fourteen seats in the June elections. In 1957, the United National Front formed and included the NDP, al-Istiqlal, the ICP, and the Baʻth Party (the Baʻth Party remained quite small until the end of the monarchy).

In addition to the opposition parties' unified front, the specter of discontent was growing within the officer corps. For members of the middle class, the army provided perhaps the best opportunity for advancement. In the 1950s, the most senior officers were still tied to the regime, but younger officers held a variety of oppositionist views. Perhaps as early as 1952, the first revolutionary cell in the officer corps had begun to organize, but by summer 1956 such cells came to the chief of staff's attention, and wayward officers were transferred or demoted. The Suez crisis, however, further spread discontent within the army, and by 1957 the movement had come under the leadership of Brigadier ʻAbd al-Karim Qasim. The formation of the United Arab Republic in February 1958, uniting Syria and Egypt, quickly raised concerns in Iraq and Jordan that their regimes could be threatened by forces favorable to the United Arab Republic. This concern in turn prompted the formation of the Arab Union, composed of the Iraqi and Jordanian monarchies. In May 1958, a revolt in Lebanon against President Kamil Sham'un erupted. Wary of the United Arab Republic and concerned that Lebanon's crisis might spread to Jordan, the Iraqi government ordered troops to reinforce the Jordanian border. The troops, however, were directed to Baghdad. On 14 July 1958, under Brigadier Qasim and his ally Colonel 'Abd al-Salam 'Arif, a military coup swiftly dispatched the Hashemite and al-Sa'id regime. The monarchy period was over.

1

OCCUPATION, MONARCHY, AND CUSTOMARY LAW

TRIBALIZING WOMEN

Customary law, or "tribal custom" as British officials often called it, was a central component of the government gender discourse in Iraq. It became an integral part of this discourse through the Tribal Criminal and Civil Disputes Regulation. Introduced by British occupying forces during World War I and remaining in force until the overthrow of the monarchy, the TCCDR sanctioned settlement of disputes among the rural population in accordance with "tribal methods" and "tribal law." Much has been written about the TCCDR, the way it eased British control over Iraq, and how it reflected the British occupiers' perception of the social structure they found therein.[1] But, interestingly, its implications for women, which stirred much controversy at the time, have received little scholarly attention. This chapter explains how and why this regulation that sanctioned customary law became part of the regime's gender discourse. The discussion points to how British and Iraqi perceptions of state and society influenced implementation of the regulation and then focuses on the consequent ramifications for women. Because of it, rural women were constructed as tribal possessions rather than as citizens of the emerging state, and their welfare was knowingly sacrificed.

A BRIEF HISTORY OF THE TCCDR

At the beginning of the British occupation, the most immediate concerns were imposing order over the vast rural areas, preventing assistance to the Ottoman armies, and securing supplies for the British army. Toward this end and with their understanding of the rural areas as tribal, the British sought to enhance the authority of the shaikhs, whom they saw as the tribes' natural leaders. Appointed shaikhs were given responsibility for maintaining order. Within a shaikh's domain, it was expected that British property would be protected, revenue collected, and aid to Ottoman armies cut off. In return, the shaikhs were not only given support and, if necessary, arms but also awarded title to lands over which they claimed possession. Sizeable tracts of land were thus rendered the private property of British-designated shaikhs, thereby promoting the creation of a class of landlord-shaikhs loyal to the British.[2] Yet many of these figures were, even by British admission, "small men of no account,"[3] and in some places where there were no "shaikhs" or "tribes" they were artificially resurrected: "Petty village headmen were unearthed and discovered as leaders of long dead tribes. Disintegrated sedentary clans . . . were told to reunite and remember that they had been once tribesmen. Tribal chiefs were found for them. Revenue was to be paid on the estimate of this chief. Law was to be administered by this chief."[4]

The TCCDR, issued in February 1916 and reissued in July 1918, was among the measures intended to bolster these shaikhs' position by prescribing their judicial authority over their tribes. Sir Henry Dobbs, at the time revenue commissioner and later high commissioner, drew up the regulation along the lines of the colonial code used on the Indian North-West Frontier, where he had vast experience. In importing the idea of a separate tribal jurisdiction from India, Dobbs was inspired, as were many other colonial administrators, by the methods of Sir Robert Sandeman. When Sandeman in nineteenth-century Baluchistan began inaugurating the policy, which has since borne his name, he also faced what he described as a "tribal organization in a state of rapid decay and the power and influence of the tribal leaders much diminished." To impose order, combat raiding, and settle disputes along the border, he sought to revive this system under "competent chiefs and headmen, advised, controlled, and supervised by experienced British Political Officers."[5] Official recognition was given to tribal chiefs, laws, and customs.

The TCCDR placed tribesmen in a separate system of law. It was designed to arrange for the speedy settlement of their civil and criminal disputes in accordance with tribal customs. The system as a whole, however, was supervised by and subordinate to the British administration. The regulation prescribed that when a British political officer—who was defined therein as an officer appointed to settle tribal affairs—was convinced that at least one of the parties involved in a dispute was a tribesman accustomed to settling his disputes "by tribal methods," it was within his purview to appoint a special council (*majlis*), which would include one or more tribal arbitrators, mainly "chiefs and shaikhs." After receiving the *majlis's* findings, the officer had the authority to dismiss the case or to convict the accused in accordance with the *majlis's* recommendations. He could also remand the case back to the *majlis* for a further finding or refer it to a second *majlis*. The scope of powers conferred by the regulation was extremely broad, as mandated by wartime conditions. Political officers could impose order in rural areas by meting out collective punishments, transferring any "tribal encampment" from one place to another, or expelling any person of "a dangerous character" from their districts. No appeals were allowed, although the civil commissioner or an officer appointed by him could revise decisions or sentences.[6] It is important to note that political officers and later on the Iraqi state officials who replaced them often dispensed with the *majlis* and made the ruling themselves, which was their prerogative according to the regulation.[7]

After an exhausting world war, as it became necessary to devise a policy that would hasten the evacuation of troops from Iraq and reduce expenditures, the British clung to the TCCDR, which had facilitated the cheap, indirect administration of vast territories and the securing of order around the countryside. At the insistence of the mandate authorities, provision for a separate tribal jurisdiction was included in the Organic Law (embodying the Constitution), and in 1924 the TCCDR became state law. The fledgling state now recognized the powers initially conferred on British officials and later transferred to their Iraqi successors. The civil commissioner was replaced by the minister of the interior, and the political officers and their assistants by local government officials—the *mutasarrif*s and *qa'imaqam*s.[8] Citizens of the new Iraqi state were thus divided into two groups with two different legal systems. The rural population was subject to the TCCDR, but the urban population was subject to civil and criminal courts. Urban crime fell under the jurisdiction of the Baghdad Penal Code enacted by the British in 1918 and based primarily on the Ottoman and Egyptian penal codes, which in turn had been framed according to the French Penal Code.[9]

CUSTOMS "FOREIGN TO BRITISH JUDICIAL TRADITION"

The TCCDR, as noted, allowed "tribesmen" to settle their disputes according to "tribal custom," but it did not elaborate on the term *tribal custom* per se. British officials presumed, however, to understand what it was.[10] Many perceived it to be universal, age old, and unchanging. Arnold T. Wilson, acting civil commissioner to Iraq until June 1920, claimed that the regulation "helped us all to a better understanding of the principles underlying tribal customs: these principles varied little from district to district, though in detail there were many differences; they were all based not on Islamic law, but on something much older, human nature, and on local conventions, some of which, it would not be difficult to show, were probably codified by Khamurabi in 2000 B.C. or earlier."[11]

As for customs concerning women, the British described them as particularly uncompromising and harsh. They found evidence for this callous treatment in numerous tenets: women could never inherit landed property; in the settlement of feuds, especially blood feuds, tribes required the guilty party, in addition to paying blood money, to hand over one or more women from his clan to the tribe or family of the victim for the purpose of marriage; a young woman was compelled to marry her paternal cousin or to receive his consent to marry another man—and if overlooked, the cousin was justified in killing the woman or the man she ultimately married; a girl or a married woman—indeed, any woman—who "lapsed from the strict path of virtue" brought a stain to the family honor that could be washed away only by her blood. Aberrations, when noted, were usually explained as exceptions to the rule or as deviation from tribal custom.[12]

British officials lamented that practices pertaining to women were "savage," "barbaric," and "a travesty of justice" and that their implementation through the TCCDR was "foreign to British judicial tradition" and "discreditable."[13] However, British actions were dissonant and often contradictory. Some political officers were reluctant to sanction marriages that involved the handing over of women in dispute settlements (*fasl* marriage) and instead encouraged alternative monetary settlements. But Gertrude Bell, Oriental secretary to the civil commissioner, advised that such interference was incompatible with the valued "local justice" that promoted good conduct and order.[14] In 1927, a disturbing book written by a political officer and his wife (Stuart Edwin Hedgcock and Monica Grace

Hedgcock) exposed the cruel fate of women given in dispute settlements: maltreated and enslaved, they had no recourse to divorce and were in fact bereft of any rights.[15] In 1929, following a report that in al-'Amara the settlement of sixty-two tribal cases involved handing over 125 women from one clan to another, the British president of the Court of Appeal and Cassation protested in his annual report that "it is most discreditable to find scores of women handed over in those disputes in the name of justice."[16] Seemingly in response to this situation but lacking in its resolve, the Ministry of the Interior later that year instructed its officials to "encourage" arbitrators in tribal cases to settle disputes with money rather than with women. This proposal, however, may not have even been a British initiative.[17] In 1929, some limited measures were also taken to annul *al-nahwa*, men's right to prevent the marriage of their female relatives, but here again it would appear that Iraqi officials initiated the move.[18]

Similar ambivalence in British attitudes and actions can be seen in response to the murder of women by their relatives. Some political officers ignored the tribal *majlis* and imposed punishments on perpetrators of such murders.[19] However, the Office of the Civil Commissioner cautioned against such initiatives, basing itself on the opinion of "experienced authorities on the control of semi-civilised tribes on the frontier of India" that such intrusion "tends to undermine the force and the appeal of this method of settlement."[20] An amendment introduced into the 1918 revised TCCDR may have represented an effort aimed at tackling such crimes: section 34(1) imposed up to five years imprisonment or a fine or both on a married woman who had consensual sexual relations with a man who was not her husband (her accomplice went scot-free).[21] If this clause indeed intended to protect such a woman by placing her punishment in the state's hands, it nonetheless failed to ensure that she would not be killed after serving her sentence. In 1923, the Iraqi minister of justice Naji al-Suwaidi suggested a broad revision of the TCCDR. The amendment of section 34(1) stipulated that offences affecting sexual morals and honor be punishable under the Baghdad Penal Code. However, Henry Dobbs, now the high commissioner, strongly objected to the transference of tribal criminal cases to the civil courts. The proposed amendment to section 34(1) seemed inexplicable to him. As we shall see, both he and Kinahan Cornwallis, adviser to the Ministry of the Interior, would in 1926 object to a similar attempt to tamper with the regulation.[22] At the same time,

Edgar Bonham-Carter, the judicial secretary to the Iraqi government, and E. M. Drower, adviser to the Ministry of Justice, supported the referral of tribal criminal cases to the civil courts, there to be prosecuted under the penal code, an act that would have constituted de facto annulment of the TCCDR.[23]

BRITISH PERCEPTIONS: COMPETING OR COMPLETING?

These contradictions concerning the treatment of women may well be the expression of competing British perceptions of how best to govern an alien society. Toby Dodge identifies two conceptions of Iraqi society influencing British rulers in their attempt to create the modern Iraqi state: romantic collectivism and rational individualism. Those adhering to the ideas Dodge classifies as romantic collectivism saw Iraq as premodern and tribal. The "tribe," not the individual, was the lens through which their interpretation of society gained its coherence. They romanticized the tribes as egalitarian and their shaikhs as natural leaders by force of personality. Thus, those upholding these views endeavored to rule Iraq on the basis of what they conceived to be the existing tribal system with its tribal leaders and its distinct tribal law and customs. Advocates of the ideas Dodge classifies as rational individualism, on the other hand, saw Iraq destined for modernization and viewed the individual as the fundamental unit of society. The tribal system was in decline and was no longer seen as an appropriate instrument to govern society. The rational individualists argued that as the tribes settled, they tended to break away from their shaikhs and relinquish their tribal customs, an ongoing process that was to be encouraged; modern Iraq was expected to engage its citizenry equally under the law, through a unified system.[24]

Dodge's model is appealing in that it clarifies certain disparities regarding the treatment of women. Those who sought to rule utilizing the tribal system were convinced that tribal law and customs should be safeguarded. Thus, the Office of the Civil Commissioner warned political officers against imposing their own punishments on men who murder women relatives because such intrusion would undermine the force and the appeal of the tribal method of settlement.[25] Gertrude Bell, although admitting that handing over a woman as part of a settlement in a blood dispute was "foreign to British judicial tradition," accepted its value as a safeguard against the outbreak of tribal animosities. Her support of political officers' noninterference in the decisions of tribal arbitrators encompassed honor murders.[26] In a similar vein, High Commissioner Dobbs and the Interior Ministry adviser Cornwallis vehemently opposed tampering in any way with the TCCDR. In 1926, Dobbs threatened to invoke his powers under the Military Agreement should the Iraqi government attempt to "emasculate" so effective a system of maintaining order in tribal areas.[27] Making offences related to sexual morals and honor punishable under penal law seemed to him inexplicable because "if there is any case in which tribal feeling is keen and tribal custom necessary to follow, it is the case of adultery and the like."[28]

Those who perceived the tribal system in Iraq as in decay, however, felt that the TCCDR should be abolished and tribal law overruled. Iraq should gravitate toward one system of law, they held. Thus, political officers and their assistants, such as Major Hedgcock and Captain H. G. Rivett Carnac in al-'Amara, imposed punishments on men who murdered their female relatives by intervening in decisions of the tribal *majlis* or by trying such cases under penal law.[29] Hedgcock's sympathies regarding the harsh treatment of women were well documented in his book *Haji Rikkan*. Legal experts such as Bonham-Carter and Drower favored the transference of tribal criminal cases to the civil courts, which would allow punishment of "crimes of honor" under the penal code. Such crimes, lamented Bonham-Carter in 1919, were regrettably common and would be difficult to eradicate.[30] Rational individualists, according to Dodge's model, thus seemed more inclined to perceive rural women as individuals whose welfare should be protected from infringement by their extended families. Romantic collectivists, in contrast, tended to see the tribal collective's needs and customs as overriding a woman's well-being.

British reluctance to intervene in practices pertaining to women, therefore, was to a large extent the result of the dominance of romantic collectivism over rational individualism. For collectivists, "the tribe" not "the individual" was the more relevant construct by which to view Iraqi society; thus, they sought to rule Iraq through its tribal system. Their subscription to the notion of distinct "tribal custom" was a major justification for deploying the TCCDR. Interference with practices affecting women challenged this notion and threatened to undermine this effective tool for controlling the countryside.

Yet it would be incorrect to assume that British reticence to intervene in practices pertaining to rural women resulted only from romantic collectivism's dominance. In fact, those touting rational individualism revealed a tendency toward the marginalization of women not unlike that of their colleagues. "Saving brown women from brown men," in Gayatry Spivak's words,[31] although a goal, was not high on their agenda. Higher priority was given to building a progressive legal system within a "civilized government" and to imposing order. When political officers in al-ʿAmara punished men who had murdered their female relatives, their main concern was not the lot of women, but rather that a "civilized government" could not condone brutal acts of murder. In 1919, Captain Rivett Carnac supported imposing capital punishment on three tribesmen who murdered an old man over "a petty quarrel" on the grounds that it would deter such "casual murdering." Yet at the same time he supported commuting to five years imprisonment the death sentence of a tribesman who had murdered his allegedly promiscuous sister. Marking the notion of male honor and male fears of disempowerment, and concerned that overlooking these factors might cause unrest, he explained that "the attitude of the average Arab to the affair may be described as one of apprehension lest by condemning the accused as a common murderer and executing him the law should deter tribesmen from the fulfillment of their obligations and thereby relax the hold they at present have on what is very much to them, the frail sex. But the brutality of the act was great and no civilized Government could let it pass without punishment."[32]

The expediencies of maintaining order were likewise evident in the words of Nigel Davidson, judicial adviser to the Iraqi government in 1921. Davidson favored increasing central government control over the administration of justice to the tribes by encompassing tribal customs within the judicial system. He suggested as a preliminary step compiling a list of customs so that those "contrary to common justice and humanity" could be excluded. However, Davidson took exception to Bonham-Carter's recommendation that all cases regarding ownership of land should be excluded from the tribal *majlis*. Tribal custom could restrict or prohibit women from inheriting land, he said, but this was not "unreasonable as women may marry out of a tribe and so break up the tribal area." Such cases, if heard by civil or shariʿa courts, which might allow such inheritance, could yield judgments whose execution "might entail bloodshed and feuds and the necessity for armed intervention in remote districts."[33] Bonham-Carter and Drower's support for abolishing the TCCDR and transferring tribal murder cases to the civil courts to be tried under the penal code reveals a similar set of priorities. To them, building a progressive legal system required a unified legal system, with the responsibility for punishment solely in the hands of the government and not delegated to tribal shaikhs or anyone else. The elimination of "tribal custom," however, was not an immediate concern. Both men suggested that the civil courts wield the authority given to them by the Baghdad Penal Code to punish tribal offenders according to tribal custom (Article 41). Moreover, Article 216 of the code, promulgated when Bonham-Carter was senior judicial officer, stated that a man who found one of his close female relations in the act of adultery or "illicit intercourse" and killed her forthwith would be punished with imprisonment not exceeding three years. In 1929, while Drower was still the adviser to the Ministry of Justice, a British-prepared draft of a new penal code retained these articles.[34]

The Hedgcocks' book, *Haji Rikkan*, however, places great emphasis on the importance of the individual. Written in the form of tales told to the authors by Haji Rikkan, a marsh peddler and guide, women figures are given names and voices. They determine the fate of wars, influence tribal leaders as wives, and even have the capacity, as demonstrated in one notable instance, to become shaikhs themselves. Common women, although depicted as primitive, ignorant, and unkempt, are nonetheless portrayed as hard workers pursuing and protecting their economic interests as well as at times having the courage to defy their fathers' wishes in order to follow their own hearts. The book touches repeatedly on themes of killing in the name of honor and the use of women as a means for settling disputes. Tragedies unfold, one after another: a father feels compelled to kill his beloved daughter for falling in love with a man from a tribe of lower status; a brother is taunted into murdering his sister; a girl fleeing with her cousin, whom she loves, from a forced marriage begs him to kill her when their escape fails; a grieving father laments the cruel fate of his daughter, who is to be handed over in a dispute settlement. The notion that future issues from settlement marriages would "knit together the enemy households by bonds of common love"[35] is challenged by a mother who mourns her daughter's forced move to another tribe and the loss of sons she had hoped to see through her. The language the authors used in describing the women's plight is explicit. A woman handed over to a hostile tribe is torn from her parents and "becomes the absolute chattel of the stranger to whom she is allotted. However bad her treatment—and it is not likely to be over-good—she cannot demand a divorce." If a woman's reputation is called into question, "it is not unusual for her to be enveigled to some lonely spot, there abused and reviled for her conduct, and stabbed with a dagger or even beaten to death with a spade."[36]

In spite of these grim descriptions, implicit in the Hedgcocks' narration is their resignation to the fact that other considerations took precedence over women's well-being. Referring to the TCCDR as legislation that "makes full allowance for the binding obligation on a tribesman to take a life when his honour is at stake,"[37] the Hedgcocks implicitly sanctioned "honor" murders. Although "appalled" at the "savage act" of a brother slaying his sister, the Hedgcocks accepted Rikkan's circular explanation: the woman must have been guilty, or she would not have been accused. Thus, ancient law required the murder to preserve tribal honor.[38] Also, although disapproving of the handing over of women in dispute settlements, the Hedgcocks accepted the utility of the practice and recommended noninterference: "To Western minds it seems intolerable that the custom of a money payment instead of payment of a woman, sometimes adopted among the tribes, should not be generally enforced. But the Arabs have learned by long experience that the old method of handing over women is by far the most effective for ensuring future amity between the tribes hitherto at feud. More surely than the payment of money, this inter-marriage brings about a lasting and real reconciliation."[39]

British romantic collectivism and rational individualism, then, were not mutually exclusive as far as practices affecting rural women were concerned. Those who put a premium on the building of a modern state allowed the utility of customary law in a society perceived as culturally different. Those convinced of the validity of the tribal system tended to legitimize its laws and to moderate criticism that could undermine it. That "barbaric" customs concerning women stirred so little British reaction followed from the marginalization of women that was intrinsic to both perceptions and that was effected to facilitate the maintenance of law and order. This marginalization was a major factor defining the nature of women's civil status in the emerging state. Under the British Mandate, rural women—the majority of women in Iraq—were not constructed as citizens of a modern state whose rights and liberties should be protected, but as tribal possessions, abandoned and left outside state jurisdiction.

This "tribalization" of rural women was initially an unintended result of wartime conditions. However, when tribal jurisdiction, at the insistence of the mandate authorities, was sanctioned by the Iraqi Constitution, and the TCCDR became state law, "tribalization" became one of the important features of the government's gender discourse.

NEGOTIATING "TRIBAL LAW"

During the mandate period, two main groups in Iraq contested the British position concerning customary law and its integration into the state legal system. The first group came from the ranks of urban intellectuals, and the second from among the shaikhs. At issue mainly was the degree to which the administration of justice in tribes was to be under the central government's control, but within the framework of this larger debate specific issues affecting women emerged.

An important bloc whose opposition to the TCCDR placed it in a position of influence over the construction of rural women comprised urban politicians, state officials, lawyers, and nationalist journalists. In 1923 Naji al-Suwaidi, the justice minister, and in 1926 'Abd al-Muhsin al-Sa'dun, the prime minister, tried in vain to initiate reforms of the TCCDR that would bring the administration of justice to tribes further under the central government's control. Successive Iraqi governments, according to departing High Commissioner Dobbs in 1928, had to be prevented from abrogating the regulation. Nationalist journalists also criticized the TCCDR as a foreign imposition, incompatible with national unity. They asserted that the citizenry should be equal before the law and that the TCCDR contradicted the fundamental principles of democracy and state sovereignty. The TCCDR weakened Iraq's claim to be a modern and progressive state, sanctioned unjust punishments, and failed to decrease crime rates because it offered no deterrent to murder. Moreover, it concentrated two powers in the same office, making the *mutasarrif*s both judges and administrators in tribal areas.[40]

Critics from this group also charged that the TCCDR had legalized certain unacceptable practices pertaining to women. Customs were condemned not only because they were incompatible with the principles of a modern state, but also because they restricted personal liberty and degraded women. As noted, in 1923 Justice Minister al-Suwaidi suggested a broad revision of the TCCDR according to which offences affecting sexual morals and honor would be punishable under the penal law. In 1929, the Ministry of the Interior instructed its officials to urge arbitrators in tribal councils to use money rather than women to settle disputes, and steps were taken to encourage the annulment of the *nahwa* (the right of men to prevent their female agnates' marriage). Ja'far Hamandi, the Shi'i director of legal affairs in the Ministry of the Interior at the time, claimed it was he who convinced the ministry heads to issue the decree urging the settlement of disputes monetarily. Hamandi openly expressed his disapproval of practices that treated women as property and criticized the *nahwa* as a vehicle for restricting personal liberty. During his term as director of legal affairs, the government made agreements with several shaikhs and village leaders to annul the practice.[41] Opponents of the TCCDR such as Muhammad Fadil al-Jamali, a Shi'i who in the 1930s had held high positions in the Ministry of Education, shared Hamandi's views. In his dissertation on Bedouin education written at Columbia University Teachers' College, where he studied between 1929 and 1932, he enumerated grounds for criticizing the TCCDR, among them "that it legalized certain tribal customs, some of which should not be permitted to continue." He underscored in this context the use of women in dispute settlements, remarking that "this means of atonement for murder is certainly degrading to those women handed over to an enemy tribe."[42] Al-Jamali further argued that tribal women in Iraq were perceived as inferior beings and the possessions of men, and he saw it as the state's responsibility to improve their lot. Education was an important step in this direction. In his view, one of the main educational objectives for the tribes should be to raise the status of women and give them "the emancipation which is their right." He stressed that "education should provide the enlightenment and the means with which the tribal women can preserve their freedom and lessen their burden of labor."[43] It is not surprising, then, that when a delegation arrived from the United States, the Monroe Educational Inquiry Commission, to examine Iraq's education system in 1932, it denounced discrimination against rural girls in education.[44] It is believed that al-Jamali instigated the visit.

British officials dismissed outright the urban intellectuals' opposition to the TCCDR. Dobbs accused the intellectuals of being impatient with "gradual development" and hasty in their efforts to destroy the tribal organization and to introduce "a system of centralized and individual control."[45] In 1926, he decisively employed a tactic to discredit the campaign and silence any opposition. He delegitimized its proponents, claiming: "The whole campaign against the tribal system is a plot of the lawyers, who have been cheaply manufactured by the Law School in excessive numbers and now find themselves starving for want of work." In characterizing the campaign as a deception motivated by selfish interests, he dismissed the possibility that it might contain valid criticism. Dobbs proclaimed: "There is no genuine dislike of tribal law and customs as a barbarous system. It is merely a pounds, shillings and pence dislike of an arbitration system which deprived the lawyers of bread."[46] With that, the British turned a deaf ear to any voice that criticized the TCCDR for ramifications it had on the construction of women as citizens in the new state.

Another challenge to the TCCDR came from those it entrusted with dispensing justice—the shaikhs. In 1925, fourteen shaikhs, members of Parliament (MPs), proposed replacing the regulation. Promulgated, as it was, in the service of the British occupation, they argued, it did not ensure the observation of tribal customs. They demanded a new law, basing their request on Article 88 of the Constitution,[47] which provided for "settling criminal and civil cases relating to the tribes in accordance with tribal custom as provided for by a special law."[48] Between 1931 and 1933, a committee of tribal leaders was engaged in a process of drafting an amendment to the TCCDR. According to one account, tribal leaders were critical of the regulation and the "intolerable deviations it contains." King Faisal promised he would instruct the government to issue a new law to replace the TCCDR based on their suggestions. Another account suggested that the king had actually asked the shaikhs to prepare a list of customs, excluding those that were "improper." In any case, a detailed proposal was submitted to the king, but he died before he could take action. These same shaikhs or their relatives resubmitted an identical draft to the British ambassador in 1944.[49]

The shaikhs' proposed law, the "Tribal Code," set broader criteria for its application than did the TCCDR. It included all "Beduin tribes of Iraq," not only those recognized by the government, as the British regulation stipulated. It covered tribal clans and individual tribesmen detached from their respective tribes and living in the city, provided that they still maintained relations with their tribes. It was also to be applied in any dispute arising between a tribesman and a townsman. In an effort to distance the state from tribal affairs, "tribal magistrates" were to be put at the head of the tribal judicial system in place of state administrative officials. They were to be elected by tribal representatives and leaders as well as by the tribesmen themselves. The minister of the interior, the *mutasarrif*s, and the *qa'imaqam*s were expected only to supervise the election of magistrates. State officials would be prohibited not only from interfering in cases lying within the jurisdiction of tribal arbitrators, but also and in stark contrast to the regulation from arresting tribesmen involved in such cases.

Unlike the TCCDR, however, which left shaikhs and tribal arbitrators free to prescribe tribal custom, several chapters in this proposal delineated certain aspects of tribal law. Chapter VI, for example, contained several articles directly or indirectly dealing with customs affecting women. These articles challenged numerous British perceptions of tribal law pertaining to women. Whereas the British tended to assume that the killing of a woman for "sexually inappropriate behavior" was a foregone conclusion, the tribal leaders' proposal suggested otherwise. It stipulated that a woman "compelled to commit adultery" was not considered guilty of an offence providing she reported it to her family within two days of the act. Thus, a woman who divulged to her family that she had been raped could save herself from death. It also allowed marriage as an alternative following the seduction of a virgin. Although this solution compounded the misery of rape victims, it did provide a solution for eloping couples. The code also attempted to deter incidents of rape by meting out punishments to rapists. At the same time, however, the draft prescribed that relatives' murder of a woman for adultery would not be punished and that the murderer would not be questioned or required to furnish evidence to corroborate the charge of adultery. As for the handing over of women as part of a settlement in blood disputes, whereas the British assumed that tribes favored this choice for subduing animosities, the proposal mentioned no such option. Under the title "Murder and Blood Money," the proposal stated that "blood-money in respect of a murdered person shall in general consist of 70 dinar." A somewhat vague clause also restricted the *nahwa* (sanctioning it only in a case of a man marrying a woman "of a condition unbecoming of his family").[50]

The British officials found the proposal presented to King Faisal "too fantastic" to deserve further consideration, certainly not any legislative discussion. When it was resubmitted in the 1940s, officials noted tribal leaders' efforts to limit state intervention in their affairs and commented that the proposed code left the government so little authority in tribal matters that even contemplating its acceptance was out of the question. The fact that the proposal exhibited a more moderate version of customary law and paved the way for legislation dealing with customs that were perceived as "foreign to British judicial tradition" without causing resentment either escaped officials or was considered inconsequential. In fact, in 1944 one senior official, apparently C. C. Aston, political adviser to the Iraqi government, simply dismissed the chapter in which tribal leaders allowed legislation emphasizing the monetary settlement of blood disputes, restricted men's intervention in their female relative's marriage, set deterrents to acts that might lead to honor murders, and enabled the marriage of lovers who had eloped—saying merely that this section of the code was "inconsistent with tribal practice."[51]

This British response should be viewed against the background of an account of customary law published in 1941 by Fariq al-Muzhir Al Fir'awn, an MP and a shaikh of the Shi'i al-Fatla of the middle Euphrates. Although his declared intent was merely to document the main principles of tribal customs, some tribal leaders, whose letters appeared in the introduction to his work, emphasized the account's value in providing a basis for rulings under the TCCDR by clarifying "tribal custom" and "tribal methods." Indeed, tens of such letters of appreciation prefaced his work, expressing thanks to the author for collecting and accurately presenting tribal customs. The book confirmed British portrayal of tribal law as age old, unchanging, and universal as well as, with regards to women, uncompromising and harsh. The fate of a woman who was kidnapped or had eloped was, according to Fir'awn, death. A similar fate almost always awaited a woman accused of extramarital relations, despite the fact that the accuser was required to prove his allegations. The handing over of women for purposes of marriage was required not only as part of the settlement of blood disputes, but also in the settlement of disputes resulting from slander, sexual harassment, kidnapping, and elopement. A man's right to prevent the marriage of his female agnate was sanctioned, as was the act of murder if his warning went unheeded.[52] Fir'awn's book was received as a "full-dressed essay on tribal customs."[53]

The relative leniency of the "Tribal Code" concerning women might be seen as a means to an end. Willingness to modify customs criticized by the British, the king, and Iraqi urban intellectuals could serve shaikhs seeking to extend their influence and minimize state intervention in their affairs. It is also possible, however, that this relative leniency regarding women was in fact a reflection of the reality in the Iraqi countryside. There is evidence to indicate that customs prevalent in rural areas under the mandate and the monarchy were dynamic and diverse. *Al-nahwa* seemed to be dying out. The British attributed initiatives to annul it at the end of the 1920s to zealous government officials. However, there are reports that such annulments occurred in rural communities in southern Iraq following specific incidents that exposed severe abuse of this right and aroused dissatisfaction with the practice.[54] Shakir Mustafa Salim, who studied the marsh village of al-Chibayish in the early 1950s, reported that *al-nahwa* was not employed among that population after such an incident in the 1930s and that people later often made written agreements to assure that their kin would not prohibit their daughters' marriages.[55] Extramarital relations did not automatically mandate a death sentence. Reports by political officers revealed that in some places murder for adultery was the exception rather than the rule. An agreement signed by several shaikhs of the 'Amara District in 1936, stated that in the case of kidnapping the perpetrator would be required to pay compensation, and the kidnapped woman should be returned to her family. That she would not be killed upon returning to her family would be ensured by a guarantee. She could marry her kidnapper if she were unmarried and so wished. Furthermore, an unmarried woman who tried on her own initiative to seduce a man who was not interested in her would also be returned to her family and her life protected, at least after the first time she committed such an act.[56] Observers acknowledged a diversity of views regarding the settlement of blood disputes, stating that the handing over of women was not universally accepted and noting dissatisfaction with the custom where practiced.[57] Numerous sources indicated that a woman who was raped at home or while about her "legitimate" business would not be considered guilty of an offence if she reported the rape to her family as soon as she possibly could.[58]

Whether clauses concerning women in the "Tribal Code" were a better reflection of the nature of customs prevalent in the Iraqi countryside or whether they were the result of a strategy serving the shaikhs' agenda is unclear. What should be emphasized here, however, is British reaction. The British had been presented with a golden opportunity to deal through state law with customs concerning women that were perceived as "discreditable." The tribal leaders' move in proposing the code not only indicated that intervention would not lead to resentment and disorder but would actually open the gate for bringing customary law into the arena of parliamentary debate. But the British refused to do away with the TCCDR, which allowed them such firm control over the "tribal system." In the 1930s, the "Tribal Code," which was intended to replace the regulation, was summarily dismissed; in 1944, when tribal leaders resubmitted the proposal, the British again rejected it, commenting that "the dear old regulation of Sir Henry Dobbs has survived all attack and continues to be the cornerstone of the administrative building [in Iraq]."[59]

Tribal leaders' dissatisfaction with the regulation, however, coupled with Article 88 of the Constitution, which provided for settling criminal and civil cases involving tribesmen according to tribal custom "as provided for by a special law," most certainly impacted the construction of women. The combination of dissatisfaction and the existence of a constitutional venue for change induced a process of codification that carved in stone "tribal custom" affecting women. These codification efforts, expressed both in the "Tribal Code" and Fir'awn's book, eliminated the diverse possibilities that had come about on the ground and that appear to have worked in women's favor. Whereas on the ground, for example, there seems to have been a process of spontaneous annulment of the *nahwa*, even the more lenient "Tribal Code" sanctioned it in the case of a man marrying a woman "of a condition unbecoming of his family." Fir'awn not only endorsed the *nahwa*—that is, one man's warning to another who wanted to marry the first man's female relative—but also the act of murder if the warning was not heeded. It is noteworthy that Fir'awn's book not only encouraged the reversal of changes that seemed to have been occurring but also allowed the reintroduction of long-gone customs: among the tens of letters that prefaced his book, many lauded him for reviving customs that had been almost lost or forgotten.

The British official position during the mandate period and beyond, then, thwarted any attempt—by British administrators, Iraqi urban politicians, state officials, lawyers, nationalist journalists, and even tribal leaders—to interfere with the TCCDR or with customs affecting women. The TCCDR was still seen as the proper tool of control, and "tribal practices" were a main justification for deploying it. It is not surprising that the more lenient "Tribal Code," which reflected the dynamic nature of rural practices, was rejected. Fir'awn's work, more unfavorable to women, was hailed because, by confirming that Iraq was a tribal society with distinct and age-old tribal customs, it lent legitimacy to the TCCDR. Thus, British tribalization of rural women in Iraq encompassed not only women's construction as tribal, subject to separate "tribal law," but also British involvement in determining "tribal law" affecting rural women as harsh and uncompromising.

THE URBAN "GIRL" MADE TRIBAL

British officials saw Iraqi society as divided between the rural/tribal and the urban, each requiring a separate legal system. Although the TCCDR, designed to bring order to the vast rural areas, played an important part in tribalizing rural women, the cities fell under the jurisdiction and protection of civil courts and laws, tailored to meet the urban environment's different needs.[60] This division, however, was not absolute. Much attention has been given to the use of the TCCDR against urban oppositionists, sentencing them to internal exile and removing them from Baghdad under section 40.[61] However, more subtle is the way the urban population could be treated as tribal under an urban legal system that ostensibly was designed to meet their special needs. In the cities, civil laws and courts also acknowledged tribal custom and tribal motives. The Baghdad Penal Code, drawn up by the British in 1918, allowed courts at their discretion, "if satisfied that the accused is a member of a tribe, which has been accustomed to settle its disputes in accordance with tribal custom," to substitute in whole or in part penalties "customary under tribal custom" in lieu of the ordinary penalty (Article 41). Regarding "honor" murderers, the code also stated that a man who found one of his close female relations in the act of adultery or "illicit intercourse" and forthwith killed her would be imprisoned for not more than three years (Article 216). When a murderer could not prove such a sequence of events, and his act fell within the category of willful premeditated homicide, at the court's discretion penal servitude for life could be substituted for the death penalty if in the court's opinion the circumstances merited leniency (Article 11). Finally, no death sentence could be carried out unless confirmed by the king, and the king could remit such a sentence by special pardon. The Iraqi Court of Appeal and Cassation, which had a British president until 1934, could recommend that a request be made to the Ministry of Justice on behalf of "honor" murderers to persuade the king to reduce their sentences.[62]

The significance of these courses of action was demonstrated following the highly publicized murder of the Interior Ministry director-general after his marriage to the daughter of former prime minister 'Abd al-Muhsin al-Sa'dun.[63] In November 1931, 'Abdulla Falih al-Sa'dun, a leading tribal figure, entered the office of Director-General 'Abdulla al-Sani' and shot him dead. He justified his action as part of his customary right to oppose the marriage of his cousin, the former prime minister's daughter, to an "unfit" husband. The groom came from a "tribe of low standing" and was murdered "to remove the smirch" of the marriage "from the Saduns' escutcheon."[64] The father of the bride, 'Abd al-Muhsin al-Sa'dun, although a member of the family that had dominated the Muntafiq confederation of tribes, had received a modern education in Istanbul, taken a Turkish wife, and become urbanized. He shunned tribal law and favored reforms that would bring the administration of justice under control of the central government.[65] He had apparently planned his daughter's marriage before his death in 1929. His brother, 'Abd al-Karim al-Sa'dun, arranged the marriage, saying he was fulfilling 'Abd al-Muhsin al-Sa'dun's wishes and that he had the agreement of the late prime minister's wife and daughter. But the Sa'dun family opposed the union; they had earlier sent warnings to the groom and had appealed to both the British adviser to the Ministry of the Interior and King Faisal to forbid it—to no avail. Even after the wedding, the threats and warnings continued, now in an effort to induce divorce. The murderer, a prominent member of the family, argued that it was the groom's refusal to divorce his cousin that had necessitated his actions. His motives were tribal, and thus he demanded to be tried under the TCCDR rather than under the Baghdad Penal Code.[66] Tribal law would have exonerated him, whereas the penal code clearly stated that the homicide of a state official while on duty should be punished by death. Tempers were running high: a leading tribal figure had murdered a high-ranking representative of the state, and there was no consensus regarding the appropriate consequences of his actions. At issue was the extent to which tribal customs, in this case the *nahwa*, should be recognized in the cities. The implications of this particular custom for women as individuals, however, were not at issue. The paternal cousin's right to demand his relative in marriage as well as his right to prevent by any means a marriage to someone else, whether consented to by the woman in question and her family or not, were mentioned only as a justification for the murderer's act. "'Abd al-Muhsin al-Sa'dun's daughter" or "the girl," as she was frequently referred to, was rendered passive and submissive, a pawn whose interests, thoughts, and feelings concerned no one.[67]

The British saw 'Abdulla Falih al-Sa'dun's demand as one that threatened to upset the urban–rural power distribution they envisioned for the country. Not only had a state official been murdered in his office, but the murder was an act of disrespect and defiance toward the king, who had, even if indirectly, sanctioned the marriage. Some were of the opinion that the final decision in this case would be a critical indication of whether a strong government or the tribes would ultimately dominate Iraq. Kinahan Cornwallis, adviser to the Ministry of the Interior, was adamant that the penal code be applied and threatened to resign if it was not. He insisted that he was capable of handling any tribal unrest that ensued from the execution of 'Abdulla Falih al-Sa'dun. Meanwhile, delegations of shaikhs arrived in Baghdad, and petitions were sent from all over southern Iraq in an effort to have al-Sa'dun tried under the TCCDR. Veiled threats of revolt were made. Shaikhs saw the support given to a member of a former slave family[68] to marry into the Sa'dun family and the intention to try a prominent figure such as 'Abdulla Falih al-Sa'dun by criminal law as a blatant attempt to break the tribes' power.[69]

In December 1931, al-Sa'dun was sentenced to death according to the Baghdad Penal Code for the premeditated murder of 'Abdulla al-Sani'. Less than a month later, however, the king commuted his sentence to fifteen years imprisonment and later to ten years. The reduction of the sentence was pursuant to a request by the minister of justice and was justified by the fact that the motive for the murder was "purely tribal." Finally, in May 1933, less than two years after committing the act, al-Sa'dun was released.[70] Faisal's actions fell within the boundaries of the king's prerogative as the highest legal authority and did not undermine the legitimacy of the verdict under penal law. Contemporary observers saw his actions as the wisest course to pursue in defusing the crisis.[71] However, this path also rendered ʿAbd al-Muhsin al-Saʿdun's daughter, an urban woman, a tribal possession. Her tribe had reached out and with a bullet ruled that she had no right to independent decision. The king, no doubt with British approval, reluctantly capitulated. He may have prevented tribal law from ruling the state, but not from ruling the lives of its citizens, even at the highest echelons of urban society.

The Saʿdun case was unique in its high profile, but the use of Articles 11, 41, and 216 of the Baghdad Penal Code as well as of appeals to the king were quite common means to obtain leniency, especially in cases of murders whose claimed motive was to "wash away the shame" women brought upon their families.[72] "Tribal motives" as extenuating circumstances, permitted at every level of the British-engineered urban legal system, bestowed legitimacy on the actions of "honor" murderers. Even in the cities, then, women could find themselves constructed as tribal possessions, their urban status an illusion. The murderers were constructed as protectors of tribal integrity and women, the victims, as threats to that integrity, and their rights as citizens usurped.

"INDEPENDENT" IRAQ AND THE TRIBALIZATION OF WOMEN

Following Iraq's formal independence, British presence was still very tangible. Iraqi politics nonetheless was increasingly shaped by distinctively Iraqi forces, especially with the rising political power of army officers. Iraq underwent a series of military coups. The internal power balance that the British had intended for Iraq was being disturbed at a critical stage that saw the approach of war in Europe. Finally, the military coup d'état of 1941 brought British reoccupation of the country, and the monarchy was reinstalled with the aid of British guns. The reoccupation brought with it tighter control in the political arena. Policies strengthening the countryside were reembraced, with the TCCDR an integral part of this strategy. As mentioned, the British still saw the TCCDR as serving its purpose as "the cornerstone of the administrative building"[73] and even as "one of the most valuable legacies of the British regime."[74] Iraqi governments wary of the army as well as of nationalist revolutionary urban forces further propped up the shaikhs and clung to the TCCDR. The regulation was still employed for maintaining order and bolstering the shaikhs' position. Not only did it give them judicial authority over "their tribesmen" as previously, but now it also facilitated the empowerment of their position as landlords. Under the Law Governing Rights and Duties of Cultivators of 1933, a cultivator could be evicted from the land if found guilty of "an act leading to the disturbance of peaceful relations between himself and others with a view to obstructing the management of the farm. . . . [H]e shall be punishable by eviction from the farm by orders of the administrative official concerned according to the provisions of the Tribal . . . Disputes Regulation."[75] From the 1930s through the 1950s, successive ministers of the interior voiced the official government stand against abolition of the TCCDR.[76]

At the same time, however, opposition to the regulation was mounting among those excluded from the government or marginalized in the rigidly controlled Parliament. Opponents charged that the TCCDR was a legacy of the British occupation, designed to serve its interests, and that it reflected British misconceptions of Iraqi society. It created a division between the rural and urban populations, strengthened "feudal influence," and prevented reform. The regulation was contrary to the principles of a modern and democratic state. Not only did it make citizens unequal before the law, but it also undermined the judiciary's power by granting state officials the power to judge and deprived the rural population of proper legal procedures, such as the right of appealing to a higher court. Opponents believed that tribe members and leaders were ready to forgo harmful customs, and they sought instead to liberate the tribesmen and transform them into full citizens. They argued that the government, in refraining from abolishing the TCCDR and in using it against its opponents both in the city and countryside, demonstrated greater interest in imposing order and maintaining the status quo than in the country's progress.[77]

Opposition to the TCCDR also encompassed the plight of women as an important theme. For some, this issue was a powerful vehicle to advance arguments against the regulation and the government rather than a concern in itself. The TCCDR hindered Iraq from becoming a progressive modern state, and the degrading way it allowed women to be treated served as proof.[78] Many opponents, however, were also concerned with women as individuals and with the implications this state law had for them. The regulation's treatment and subsequent construction of women, who should have been citizens of an independent modern state by now, were in their view unacceptable.

Writers and journalists openly deplored the lot of women under the regulation. The renowned poet Ma'ruf al-Rusafi (1875–1945), for example, harshly attacked the government for supporting "barbaric" and "pre-Islamic" (*Jahili*) customs through the TCCDR. He condemned the practices of handing over women in the settlement of blood disputes, of buying and selling women like "sheep and cows" for the purpose of marriage, and of excluding them from inheritance. Guardians of married women, he protested, would force husbands to divorce their wives to obtain a higher *mahr* (pl. *muhur*; according to Islamic law, a sum of money, property, or other benefit given by the husband to the wife as an obligation of marriage). If the women's husbands were absent, the guardians could give their wards in marriage again without bothering first to have them divorced, simply out of greed for another *mahr*. Because women were perceived as property, men who had many daughters thought themselves rich. To demonstrate the role the TCCDR played in preserving such practices, al-Rusafi described firsthand the proceedings of several cases brought before Iraqi administrative officials to be tried under the regulation. In one, a man had attempted to seduce the sister of another man. The *qa'imaqam* instructed the seducer to give his sister as a wife without *mahr* to the brother of the woman he tried to seduce. Al-Rusafi questioned this ruling, inquiring of the *qa'imaqam* what transgression the criminal's sister had committed that would justify her being handed over in this way for a crime perpetrated by her brother. The *qa'imaqam* admitted that a woman handed over in this manner enjoys no respect—indeed, she is disdained, humiliated, and put to work like a slave—but he stressed that "tribal law" demanded such a verdict.[79] Al-Rusafi's concern was genuine. He was among the first in Iraq to oppose the seclusion of women and to advocate education for girls. He came out against forced marriages and supported women's right to choose their husbands. In March 1922, the newspaper *al-Istiqlal* published his poem criticizing the treatment of women and denial of their rights. In response, a fatwa (religious legal opinion) was issued against him, and there was even an instance where he only narrowly escaped a physical attack, but he was undeterred.[80] Nazik al-Mala'ika (1922–2007), another prominent poet, offered more veiled criticism. Her poem "Washing Off Disgrace" lamented the brutal murder of a young woman in the name of honor. The poem was seen as expressing a new generation's aversion to the archaic practices preserved in society.[81] However, her description of the murderer as he sat in a tavern boasting of his deeds and cleaning his dagger also bemoaned the fact that he could get away with it. Her criticism, subtle though it was, clearly conveyed the notion that women lived in fear and submissiveness because there was no law to protect them from their kin.[82] Many other poets and authors writing about honor murders exposed the evils allowed by the TCCDR even if they did not mention it by name.[83]

A major political group in the early 1940s that explicitly criticized the TCCDR and the customs it sanctioned as obstacles for women citizens of a modern state was the ICP. Yusuf Salman Yusuf ("Fahd"), a Christian Arab and the party's secretary-general from 1941 until his execution in 1949, raised the subject on the occasion of International Women's Day, 8 March 1944. He explained the significance of the day as a time for reflecting on past achievements and contemplating future tasks in women's struggle against their subjugation. Iraqi women, he said, were burdened by the legacy of a bygone era and deprived of their most basic rights. He emphasized that antiquated regulations, sometimes called "tribal law," compounded the misery of rural woman, who were virtually enslaved to their impoverished peasant fathers and husbands. With the help of this "tribal law," he said, they could be killed or be handed over as part of a blood-dispute settlement. Yusuf linked the harsh conditions of both rural and urban women's lives to the dire situation of the country as a whole, claiming that a common enemy prevented both women and their country from being liberated. Iraq had lost its sovereignty to imperialism, which, Yusuf asserted, fortified its position by allying with reactionary forces and reinforcing backward customs. He thus urged women to struggle for both feminist and nationalist goals.[84]

Dr. Naziha al-Dulaimi (1923–2007) took up the theme of rural women's subjugation under the TCCDR in 1950. Al-Dulaimi, an Arab Sunni gynecologist and a card-carrying Communist, served as the leader of the League for the Defense of Women's Rights, which was founded in 1952 and worked underground until 1958, after which it became legitimate. Her book *Al-Mar'a al-'Iraqiyya* (The Iraqi Woman) analyzed the situation of women of different classes. Her knowledge of women's circumstances was gained from her work as a physician in various parts of Iraq.[85] Al-Dulaimi charged that women among "the *fallahin* stratum" had lost their freedom as human beings. They had become a means of production and reproduction. Perceived as property, they could be bought and sold in marriage, used as recompense for murder and humiliation, and cast aside through divorce and even murder under the pretext of "washing away the shame." The TCCDR, she concluded, was a contributing factor in their oppression.[86]

WOMEN'S "DOUBLE SERVITUDE"

Iraqi intellectuals opposing the TCCDR pointed out many of its adverse effects. However, under the monarchy another more indirect but no less important influence on rural women surfaced. This influence was the outcome of the evolving relationship between shaikhs-turned-landlords and tribesmen-turned-serfs. The significance of women's tribalization becomes even clearer when seen in conjunction with this reality.

In the course of the nineteenth century, the bulk of nomadic tribes in the Iraqi provinces became sedentary. Population estimates suggest that between 1867 and 1905 the nomadic element had fallen from 35 to 17 percent. By 1905, almost 60 percent of the total population was engaged in some form of sedentary agriculture.[87] Cultivated areas of central and southern Iraq in the early nineteenth century, although legally belonging to the state, were maintained according to a variety of customary rights: mostly communal but at times extending to individual cultivators. By the end of the century, however, a large part of this land was already registered in the names of leading families.

As noted in the introduction, because of the changes brought about by the Ottoman Land Law of 1858, tribesmen found themselves in the position of serfs while the shaikhs, former tax farmers, and city merchants became large landowners.[88]

When the British occupied Iraq, their interests resulted in additional tracts of land being made the shaikhs' private property. British land policy was at times confused or contradictory, but the idea of favoring the shaikhs, advocated by Henry Dobbs, gained dominance. In 1926, Dobbs asserted that it would be impossible to deal directly with individual cultivators for revenue purposes because of poor communications and unsettled conditions. The machinery of the Iraqi government would be inadequate to undertake such a policy. For the convenience of administration and preservation of social order, he suggested that large parcels of land be granted to powerful individuals for as long as possible. Shaikhs should be recognized as the landowners with responsibility for the payment of land revenues. They, in turn, were given land and tax exemptions. When the shaikhs were challenged by cultivators, the British did not refrain from using force in coming to their defense.[89]

Under the monarchy, a close relationship between political power and land ownership was forged: shaikhs-turned-landlords were "elected" to the Parliament while the king, successive prime ministers, ministers, and other government officials obtained large landholdings. Government policies and legislation not only made the acquisition of land easier for people of influence but also enshrined their powers over their tenants. Under the 1933 Law Governing the Rights and Duties of Cultivators, *fallahin* could easily be evicted. If indebted to the landlord, they were forbidden to leave his employ. The *fallahin*'s dependence on monetary advances from landlords made it virtually impossible to break out of the circle of debt other than by abandoning the land.[90] The TCCDR was interwoven with the process that empowered the landlord-shaikhs and turned the *fallahin* into semiserfs. In giving shaikhs judicial authority over "their tribesmen," it made them responsible for settling land disputes. Under the Law Governing Rights and Duties of Cultivators and through the use of TCCDR provisions, cultivators could be evicted from the land.[91]

Fallahin sank deeper and deeper into a quagmire as landlords' economic and political position rose higher and higher. In central and southern Iraq, sharecropping was the most common form of agricultural production. *Fallahin*, depending on the region in which they lived and on whether they supplied seeds, tools, or draught animals, in general received a 30 to 50 percent share of the crop. Various dues payable to the shaikh would further reduce their share. In the end, little was left to the actual tillers of the soil. Cultivators usually could not provide the seeds or the other requirements of cultivation, thus repeating an unending cycle of indebtedness.[92]

Scholars have already provided an elaborate picture regarding the harsh living conditions of *fallahin* in the Iraqi countryside. Poverty, illiteracy, and disease were central features of their lives, and the state did little to relieve the situation. However, the academic discussion has to a large extent been gender biased. Peasant women, the *fallahat*, shared the men's misery and worries but experienced differently the prevailing conditions. Cultivators, both men and women, often lived in small mud or mat huts with no running water, had an inadequate diet and insufficient clothing, and suffered from diseases such as malaria, trachoma, bilharzias (also known as schistosomiasis, a disease caused by parasitic worms), and ankylostomiasis (hookworm). The effects of these diseases on women, however, as noted by observers in the mid-1950s, were more pronounced due to childbearing and lactation.[93] Certain complications could be particularly harsh for women. Malaria, which was the most widespread, caused premature birth, miscarriage, and stillbirth.[94] Exacerbating this situation was the scarcity of medical staff and health services in rural areas. As late as 1954, most of the country's doctors were concentrated in Baghdad. In eight out of fourteen provinces, there were fifteen or less government doctors for a population of 200,000 to 380,000. Moreover, most of the qualified midwives also worked in Baghdad, whereas in six provinces there were less than twenty midwives for the same population.[95] Due to the lack of qualified midwives and medical facilities, complications from childbirth often led to maternal mortality or severe gynecological problems. Infant mortality in rural areas was high: women would suffer the loss of a child in one out of three births. In the rare cases where Maternal and Child Health Centers were opened in rural areas, infant mortality dropped considerably.[96]

The rural population was also stricken with illiteracy, and rates were higher among women. Only after the Monroe Educational Inquiry Commission denounced discrimination against girls in agricultural villages in 1932 were schools for these girls opened. However, even then the number of rural girls attending school lagged behind the number of rural boys and urban girls.[97] As late as 1957, the illiteracy rate among rural women was 99 percent in comparison with 86 percent among rural men and 79 percent among urban women.[98]

Beyond the generally harsh conditions of the Iraqi countryside and their particular impact on women, accounts repeatedly related that women worked harder and longer than men. *Fallahat* in southern Iraq plowed the soil, sowed the seeds, weeded, and harvested and threshed the grain. Observers claimed that women could be seen pulling a plow alongside their animals when the task proved too difficult for the beast alone. Women rose early to milk and feed the cattle, clean their pens, and gather thistles for fuel or sale. Women also stayed up late to prepare food for their families or to get ready for the next day's journey to the market, where they would sell their produce. Some even worked nights in public mills, husking rice for a small wage. Women often carried milk and dairy products, eggs, and firewood a considerable distance to sell them in the nearby town or city. They tended the house, cooked the meals, and reared the children. According to many accounts, women's fathers and husbands saw them as an economic asset. From the early age of seven or eight, they were required to tend the flocks and help with all household chores. Some girls between the ages of seven and fifteen were sent to work in construction and road paving. Women's earnings were summarily handed over to their husbands or fathers. Polygamy, it was claimed, was practiced as a means to enlarge the *fallah*'s labor force.[99]

Women activists in the 1950s, such as Naziha al-Dulaimi, designated the situation of the *fallahat* in Iraq as "double servitude": women were subservient to men, who were in turn subservient to landlords.[100] Marriage was a transaction in which a tool was bought by the husband and sold by the father. Additional tools could be acquired through polygamy or easily discarded through divorce. Like beasts of burden, women might, without recourse, bear the brunt of their husbands' anger, be beaten, or be otherwise maltreated. They understood that opposition or reluctance might have harsh consequences. Divorce could leave them destitute. Far worse, as we know, they could be easily disposed of through murder. Such an act, al-Dulaimi said, was readily explained away under the pretext of "washing away the shame," which was officially recognized as justification for murder.[101] Although Iraqi urban intellectuals emphasized the harsh realities and "backwardness" of the countryside usually in service of their critique of the government, the importance of al-Dulaimi's account lies in its understanding and graphic portrayal of the ramifications of the TCCDR in constructing Iraq's rural female citizens. The tribalization of women had abandoned them beyond the boundaries of state protection and allowed men unbridled power over their lives.

THE 1951 AMENDMENT OF THE TCCDR

Iraqi governments after British reoccupation were more often than not headed by the powerful and influential Nuri al-Saʿid. Al-Saʿid had fled Iraq with the deposed regent during the 1941 anti-British coup, but upon its suppression he returned and was entrusted with forming a government. Wary of the army as well as of nationalist and revolutionary urban forces, Iraqi governments after World War II held the TCCDR close and propped up the shaikhs. The number of shaikhs in Parliament rose after 1941 through the manipulation of elections, and their economic position was improved.[102] Yet as criticism of the TCCDR intensified, encompassing not only opposition groups but members of the mainstream political establishment, the government in 1951 amended it.

Al-Sa'id's government in 1951 had no intention of doing away with the regulation even though the first clause of the amendment created the impression that steps were indeed being taken toward its eventual abolition. Another clause stated that the regulation would no longer be applied to crimes committed within the jurisdiction of the larger provincial municipalities. Application of the regulation might also be halted in smaller municipalities at the discretion of the interior minister.[103] This clause also seemed to address criticism concerning the implications of customary law for women in that "honor" killings committed within these jurisdictions would now be punishable under penal law. Perpetrators would be classified as criminals and held accountable for their crimes. Affirming this intent, the government rejected the demand by a group of shaikhs that "honor" cases be excluded from the amendment and not settled within the jurisdiction of regular civil courts.[104]

The government, in parliamentary debates, rejected claims that the regulation was a stumbling block on Iraq's way to becoming a progressive modern state. Prime Minister al-Sa'id argued that a state's progress was not necessarily hampered by the existence of laws that were specific to particular communities—the United States, with its different laws in different states, demonstrated that. Moreover, he explained, conditions were not yet ripe to annul the regulation. He and other supporters of the TCCDR maintained that all Iraqis were of tribal origin; although some had changed their ways and become urbanized, others were only now making progress. Declaring that traditions and customs could not be annulled with a stroke of the pen, he reasoned further that tribesmen were not yet ready to accept state law. Disorder and bloodshed would ensue. The TCCDR, structured to handle tribal crime with its different character and motives, was acceptable to the tribes and still the best way to settle their disputes. According to al-Sa'id, the regulation was also necessary because in remote tribal areas there were no state institutions or courts. Moreover, in order to confront the armed elements opposing the government and its representatives in these areas, the disciplinary actions the TCCDR allowed were essential. He argued that only when opposing tribal elements were brought under state control and mentalities had changed could the regulation be annulled. Such changes, however, could happen only gradually as roads, schools, and health clinics opened and modern villages were built. For the time being, he concluded, the proposed amendment was more compatible with Iraq's anticipated gradual development because it enabled the interior minister to exclude regions from being subject to the regulation as they progressed.[105]

These justifications given by the government and its supporters for amending rather than abolishing the TCCDR illuminate the rationale behind the position regarding customs affecting women. In remote rural areas where the government perceived itself to be weak, the expediencies of maintaining order mandated that it refrain from tackling customs affecting women. In an effort to moderate criticism regarding the handing over of women as a means of dispute settlement, government supporters in the parliamentary debates stressed the role of marriages in averting hostilities between rival tribes. In these remote areas, they claimed, tribes, clinging to their customs, would resist the intrusion of state law. A long and gradual process of development and enlightenment had to precede government intervention in such practices. In Nuri al-Sa'id's view, expressed clearly in these deliberations, before these customs could be seriously confronted, ignorance, poverty, hunger, and sickness among tribesmen had to be done away with, roads had to be built, and schools had to be opened to "raise the level of these people."[106] In contrast, in provincial centers the government felt able to impose its will. In these centers, penal law could be applied by state courts, and tribesmen, brought under state influence, were considered capable of understanding government intervention. Thus, "honor" killings could be deemed a crime.

In 1951, the amendment was ratified, and the TCCDR, despite strong opposition, remained in force. The government claimed that it had taken a big step forward, especially in light of previous governments' inertia. However, as most critics were quick to point out, the amendment's scope was limited, and in any case most Iraqis continued to be subjected to the TCCDR. Disciplinary actions allowing collective punishments, internal exile, and so on were left untouched. Beyond this, the possibility of reducing the geographical area in which the regulation applied was not new; it had already been prescribed in its original British text.[107] Moreover, any implications the amendment could have for women were illusory. The small number of women now added to those covered by the Baghdad Penal Code were offered no greater protection. The penal code allowed, as mentioned earlier, trial according to "tribal law," aside from treating "honor" murderers with leniency. In other words, despite proclamations of progress, nothing had changed for the vast majority of rural women.

Pro-British Iraqi governments, then, continued the process of tribalizing women in Iraq, adopting British perceptions and rhetoric wholesale. Without the TCCDR, a weak state aspiring to rule vast rural areas, populated with a threatening and "uncivilized" tribal society, could not succeed; tribal organization had to be preserved "until a better system is ready to take its place," as former high commissioner Henry Dobbs once stated, and such a system would come about only through "gradual development";[108] hasty abolition or blunt interference in age-old customs would bring only opposition and disorder. Dealing with the consequences of the TCCDR for women remained at the bottom of a long list of priorities. The expediencies of imposing order and maintaining the status quo in a society perceived and constructed as tribal were repeatedly favored over women's well-being. Such considerations actually required that detrimental customs affecting women be sanctioned because, it was argued, any intrusion into these customs would cause resentment among the tribes and undermine methods that were regulating their affairs. Despite an amendment that was presented as responding to developments on the ground, the Iraqi governments, like the British before them, clung to the TCCDR, thus constructing Iraqi female citizens as tribal possessions abandoned beyond the boundaries of state protection. In institutionalizing customary law and in unambiguously permitting the murder of women without punishment, the government gender discourse allowed men unbridled power over women's lives and provided them with the ultimate means of coercion.

2

FAMILY LAW AS A SITE OF
STRUGGLE AND SUBORDINATION

In the new state of Iraq, Islamic law was another important component of the Hashemite government's gender discourse. An unfavorable interpretation of this law became part of that discourse mainly through efforts to set laws that would be applied in the shari'a state courts and govern legal procedures pertaining to family relations, including marriage, divorce, child custody, and inheritance rights.

This chapter looks briefly at British policy that left these rules pertaining to family matters in the hands of religious authorities despite opposition to this course of action. It then focuses on state attempts to intervene by way of legislation. The debate surrounding the state introduction of a personal status law, although clearly a negotiation of gender relations, was to no lesser degree a mere facade. In fact, there was an underlying power struggle over who should be entrusted with the authority to adjudicate disputes, which courts were to be involved, and who had the authority to determine those rules that would govern personal status issues in Iraq. Meanwhile, the emerging government gender discourse further constructed women citizens as subordinate and dependent and left them unprotected from harsh treatment by kin and husbands and from uncompromising rulings by religious clerics.

PERSONAL STATUS UNDER BRITISH RULE, 1917-1932

The British occupation of Baghdad in 1917 saw the collapse of the Ottoman legal system. Several days before the British troops arrived in the city, Baghdad's courts ceased to function as Turkish judges and judicial staff fled, taking recent court records with them. In rebuilding the judicial system, Britain's stated post-1917 policy was to maintain the Ottoman court system and laws to the greatest extent possible. Civil and criminal courts were reestablished, as were religious shariʿa courts, which were charged with handling matters of personal status among Iraq's Muslims. Shiʿi qadis (shariʿa judges) who had been excluded from the state courts under Ottoman rule were gradually made part of the legal system.[1]

The British, as noted, divided the population in Iraq into two groups with two different legal systems. The rural population was subject to the TCCDR, but the urban population was subject to the civil and criminal courts. Islamic law often conflicted with customary law, but shariʿa courts were aimed at mainly the urban population, and most of them functioned in parallel with civil courts; in 1931, the British reported that fifty shariʿa state courts operated in Iraq, forty-seven of them where there were civil courts.[2] Islam in British rhetoric was often synonymous with backwardness,[3] and Islamic law, especially as regards women, was inconsistent with Western concepts. However, British motivation for employing shariʿa courts, as with the TCCDR, had to do with the expediencies of ruling. Edgar Bonham-Carter, the former head of the Sudan Legal Department who was brought to Iraq in 1917 to serve as senior judicial officer, saw many advantages in the courts' reestablishment to fielding matters of personal status among Muslims with their own judges and laws. One important reason for maintaining the shariʿa courts, he said, was that it gave a share in the administration of the country to the influential and respected ʿulamaʾ class, from which the qadis were drawn, and thus ensured its loyalty and support. Although Bonham-Carter believed certain principles of Islamic law to be incompatible with "Western ideas," he advocated noninterference:

> [W]hen, as head of the Sudan Legal Department, which comprised a large number of Muhammadan Courts, I received a petition from a litigant dissatisfied with the application to his or her case of a principle of Muhammadan Law, which is not in accord with Western ideas, such as the law of divorce or the right to the custody of children, I always felt that my position and that of Government was a much stronger one, than, if as a British Judge I had given the decision myself. The argument that the petitioner was a Muhammadan, and desired to have his or her case settled in accordance with Muhammadan

Law, and that it had been so settled was unanswerable, and left the petitioner, even if still dissatisfied, without any feeling of rancour against a British official or the Government.[4]

Dissatisfaction with decisions regarding divorce and child custody doubtlessly came mainly from women. Yet Bonham-Carter saw "Muhammadan law," like "tribal law," as the law of the land, and, although harsh, from a government perspective its use brought many advantages. Other priorities once again led the British to marginalize women's issues.

Bonham-Carter's policies, it is worth noting, did not pass without criticism both from within the British judicial administration and among Iraqi intellectuals. Some British officials not only doubted the wisdom of incorporating the 'ulama' into the administration of the country, but even went so far as to claim that the Qur'an had been misinterpreted by Sunnis and Shi'is alike—particularly in matters of personal status. These officials believed that they had a better knowledge of Islamic law than did local Muslim commentators. One such official was Thomas Lyell, who had been a magistrate in the Baghdad District just after the occupation began in 1917 and later served as assistant director of land registration. In his book *The Ins and Outs of Mesopotamia*, he set out to expose the English reader to "the real character, beliefs and preferences of the people of Mesopotamia, or Iraq" by analyzing the Prophet's teachings in the Qur'an regarding such matters as social customs and by highlighting additions to and departures from "the orthodox Sunnat—or Traditions" on the part of both the common people and their religious leaders. Lyell claimed that in matters of marriage and divorce Iraqi practice had departed radically from what had been set forth by the Qur'an—a result of ignorance and misinterpretation. For instance, Qur'anic license to practice polygamy has been attributed to sura 4, verse 3, which, in Lyell's translation, states: "And if you fear that you cannot act equitably towards orphans, then marry such women as seem good to you, two and three and four; but if you fear that you will not do justice between them, then marry only one, or what your right hand possesses; this is more proper that you may not deviate from the right course."[5] In interpreting this verse as allowing men to take up to four wives, Lyell asserted, both Sunnis and Shi'is had failed to acknowledge the specific context in which it had been written—following a battle in which many of the faithful had been killed, creating the need to look after the surviving women and children. Polygamy had thus been sanctioned for the sake of orphans rather than for the sake of men. Moreover, whereas the Sunnis interpreted this verse as allowing men to take up to four wives, the Shi'is, he claimed, interpreted "what your right hand possesses" as license to practice concubinage. Therefore, "the households of Iraq tribal chiefs, more especially the wealthy land-owning Syeds, are astonishing and immense."[6] According to Lyell, the Shi'is did not stop there: because the verse condoned polygamy only for men wealthy enough to provide for multiple wives, they sanctioned temporary marriages (mut'a), enabling the poor to "enjoy a life of uncontrolled libertinism" as well. The Qur'an, he asserted, had been misinterpreted not only with regard to marriage, but also with regard to divorce. Although permitting a man to divorce his wife, the Qur'an did not sanction the "promiscuous divorce" that he claimed prevailed in Iraq; rather, it saddled divorce with restrictions and limitations that, if enforced, would have made it an abundantly rare occurrence. Lyell depicted Iraqi marriage and divorce customs, in particular those practiced by the Shi'is, as demeaning to women and degrading to the institution of motherhood.[7]

Lyell's criticism, however, was not motivated by a desire to improve women's status through state intervention in the realm of personal status. Rather, it was chiefly intended to advance the main thesis of his book—that the Muslims in Iraq were unfit to govern themselves and that it would be wrong for the British to evacuate the country partially or completely. He wrote: "It will surely not be disputed that family life is the base of all social development, and therefore of ordered Government and national consciousness. The people, who have had these [marriage] systems in force for hundreds of years, are now asked by enlightened Europe what kind of Government they desire, on the ground that they have the right to govern themselves as they wish. If they would only first learn to govern themselves individually, these idealistic aspirations might not seem so absurd." He went on to warn: "To have relieved them from the tyranny of the Turk[s] would be a small matter, if we leave them under the tyranny of their own 'Holy Men,' with full opportunity to promulgate their revolting doctrines of temporary marriage, and concubinage, resulting in an ever-increasing degeneracy and ineptitude."[8]

Lyell's criticism, which justified British direct rule in Iraq by invoking the degeneracy of "Other" men and the plight of "Other" women, a tactic Leila Ahmed terms "colonial feminism,"[9] was rejected in the aftermath of the 1920 revolt. In London, an understanding emerged that the price of direct rule in Iraq was becoming unbearable; this understanding led to further efforts to find an alternative. In October 1920, a provisional government replaced the occupying army's civil administration; departments of the old administration now became ministries headed by Iraqi ministers.

The revolt led to severe criticism of many of the departments within the old administration. However, Bonham-Carter took as an endorsement of his policies the fact that little, if any, criticism pertaining to the causes of the rebellion had been directed against the urban judicial system he had established. As a result, as adviser to the Ministry of Justice, he called for the maintenance of the policy of noninterference with regard to "institutions or laws with which the people were familiar."[10]

In March 1925, the Iraqi Constitution stated that the shari'a courts alone were to handle matters pertaining to the personal status of Muslims in accordance with the shari'a provisions particular to each of the Islamic sects. Further, in each locality the *qadi* had to be a member of the sect adhered to by the majority of the inhabitants of the place in which he was appointed. Nigel Davidson, legal secretary to the high commissioner and a participant in the drafting of the Constitution, supported these provisions, citing the religious orientation of most of the Iraqi populace. Although stating that Islamic law, to be administered by shari'a courts, lagged far behind "the march of civilization" and was "responsible for the deplorable status of women," he believed that because religious law was sacred to the people of Iraq, it would inevitably figure in the country's constitution.[11]

Iraqi urban intellectuals also contested the British incorporation of religious law into the state legal system during the mandate period. Toward the end of this period, a British report to the League of Nations on the "progress of Iraq during the period between 1920 and 1931" noted that "public opinion" in Iraq favored placing all matters of personal status under the jurisdiction of the civil courts to be governed by a special civil law along the lines of the Turkish judicial system. In 1926, the Turkish republic had adopted the Swiss Civil Code as a basis for its civil law. The Turkish law abolished polygamy, allowed women to initiate divorce, and maintained maternal custody rights following divorce. It imposed a minimum age for marriage and recognized women as men's legal equals in matters of inheritance and as witnesses in court. Since then, Turkish civil courts rather than shari'a courts had handled matters of personal status.[12] In the 1920s, Iraqi proponents of change with regard to women's social and economic status called for a similar civil code for family matters, "in keeping with the spirit of the times," to be administrated by state courts.[13] The British, however, dismissed this "public opinion" among the urban intellectuals, claiming that it did not represent society as a whole; they portrayed the idea of abolishing shari'a courts as not only constitutionally unfeasible, but also premature because the prestige these courts enjoyed was still strong.[14]

The mandate period saw religious courts in all places where there were civil courts, but separate qadis were not always appointed. Iraqi-trained civil judges increasingly came to be looked at as sufficiently competent to field matters of personal status; in fact, the 1929 Judges and Qadhis Law showed a preference for graduates of the secular Iraqi Law School over fuqaha' (experts in the science of religious law) to serve as qadis.[15] Until the period ended, however, there was no official requirement that matters of personal status be settled in state courts. Moreover, the 1923 Shara' Courts Law required that state judges seek the legal opinion of the 'ulama' in certain cases, especially when cases to be decided in accordance with Shi'i law were brought before Sunni judges and vice versa.[16] Hence, to a large extent, personal status matters remained outside the state's supervision and in the hands of religious leaders, facilitating—yet by no means necessitating, as we shall later see—rulings unfavorable to women.

WOMEN IN THE DRAFT CODE OF PERSONAL STATUS

The end of the British Mandate saw several government attempts to introduce legislation governing family matters and to further state control over matters of personal status. Scholarly works citing codification efforts preceding the 1959 Personal Status Law give the impression that the 1947 draft Code of Personal Status was the only attempt at legislation made during the monarchy period,[17] but in fact there were several attempts even prior to that. In late 1931, the Iraqi government resolved that the Ministry of Justice was to form a committee to "collect and reedit shari'a doctrines" pertaining to personal status and then select and codify those provisions that "suit the demands of the present time."[18] When a first draft was completed in 1933, it drew much resentment and opposition from religious circles: Shi'i clerics, for instance, charged that the introduction of such legislation was contrary to the principles of Shi'i doctrine; if passed, they feared, it would adversely affect the religious influence of the *'ulama'* and *mujtahids*.[19] Although this opposition prevented the proposal from moving forward, the subject was not abandoned altogether. In the latter half of the 1930s, the Ministry of Justice continued to work on a draft with the intent of submitting it to Parliament.[20] In January 1945, another committee was formed for the same purpose; by May of that year, the committee had forwarded its draft to the Ministry of Justice. The proposal was presented to the Chamber of Deputies in 1946, and a memorandum on the matter was read just before the government fell in May 1946.[21] In 1947, the Chamber of Deputies' Committee for Judicial Affairs urged that the draft be enacted by Parliament and promulgated as law. However, in light of a change of government, the election of a new Parliament, and opposition to the draft on the part of religious circles, the draft was ultimately shelved.[22] But the matter was not dropped. On the contrary, in 1949 the codification of a personal status law was presented as one of the reforms sought by the CUP, headed by the powerful Nuri al-Sa'id.[23] The matter was raised again in 1952, with several amendments, when the Chamber of Deputies' Committee for Judicial Affairs recommended that Parliament accept it. In early May, the proposal was brought to Parliament for debate, but due to clerics' fierce opposition, it was once again shelved, this time indefinitely.[24] After that date and until the overthrow of the monarchy, no serious further efforts appear to have been made.

In the absence of legislation, these proposals represent the only detailed expression of government gender discourse concerning issues of personal status prior to 1958. These proposals were indeed important. They did not get buried in parliamentary red tape; they were taught in the state law school; thus, their construction of women in the domestic realm became embedded in future judges' minds. A comprehensive study of the proposals' content and in particular of the provisions concerning gender roles and the making and breaking of the marriage contract is most relevant to the topic at hand, especially with regard to the draft Code of Personal Status formulated in the mid-1940s.[25]

Like efforts to codify Islamic law with regard to personal status in neighboring countries, the Iraqi law proposal was designed to provide for the unique needs of the country for which it was written.[26] Based mainly on two schools of Islamic jurisprudence, Sunni Hanafi and Shi'i Ja'fari,[27] the proposal consisted of 177 articles, 91 of which applied to all Iraqi Muslims; the remaining 86 applied to Sunnis and Shi'is differently. Yet to fully understand Iraqi government's construction of female citizens in the realm of personal status prior to 1958, it is not enough to focus on these articles and study the matters the bill addressed. Many issues were left unaddressed, and the proposal, acknowledging these lacunae, stipulated that, where no appropriate provision was specified, judgments were to be rendered in accordance with the principles of the school of Islamic law to which the litigants subscribed. This stipulation left the door open for unfavorable interpretations by state judges.

State judges could consult any religious authority or legal text of their choosing. Interestingly, texts that were explicitly or implicitly designed to guide them by covering issues the bill did not address began to appear. Two such books, one mainly elaborating on Sunni law and the other on Shi'i law, shed light on the significance of government failure to address issues and the ramifications of this failure for women. The first book, published in 1949, was penned by Professor Husain 'Ali al-A'zami (1907–1955), a graduate of several distinguished Sunni religious schools who headed the Shari'a Department at the Iraqi Law School and later served as its dean. Based on the author's lectures to first-year students on marriage and divorce, the book presented and discussed the draft Code of Personal Status as it was expected to become law, focusing on Sunni Hanafi doctrine regarding issues not explicitly covered by the proposal.[28] The second book was written by Shaikh 'Abd al-Karim Rida al-Hilli (1887–1963). Joseph Schacht, a leading scholar of Islamic law, described its first edition as a private codification of the "Twelvers" (Ja'fari) Shi'i law, inspired by the code compiled by Qadri Pasha.[29] A second edition appeared in 1947, while the proposal was under consideration in Parliament. Al-Hilli, a Najaf-educated scholar who taught and wrote about Islamic philosophy in his hometown of al-Hilla, did not discuss the bill openly. However, the declared aim of his second edition was to provide state qadis, lawyers, and law students with a clear and easy-to-use summary of Shi'i Ja'fari law concerning matters of personal status. It should be noted that at the time only Sunni jurisprudence was taught systematically at the Iraqi Law School; as a result, no Shi'i equivalent to al-

A'zami's book existed.[30] These textbooks demonstrate that government failure to address issues could often expose women to extremist interpretations; they also indicate that the government often turned a blind eye to rules that were favorable toward women under Sunni Hanafi and Shi'i Ja'fari law.

Finally, to note underlying interests that shaped the bill's spirit and its construction of Iraqi female citizens, we must place the bill within the context of the controversies of its day. Demands for government intervention and reforms came mainly from urban intellectuals, who aspired to change the social order and gender relations in Iraq. Many were concerned about abuses in the realm of personal status resulting from state sanctioning of tribal law. Rejecting the division of urban and tribal populations with separate legal system and laws, they demanded state law that would affect all Iraqis. Some saw Islamic law as the proper framework for reforming gender relations; others preferred secular law. Resistance to state efforts at codification came mainly from within religious circles, upon whose field of expertise codification threatened to encroach.

GOVERNMENT JUSTIFICATION FOR LEGISLATION

As in other countries in the Middle East during this period, efforts to codify Islamic law concerning matters of personal status in Iraq were openly coupled with a desire on the state's part to exert its authority in this field. Neighboring countries used various methods to effect reformist legislation: legislators turned to the Qur'an and hadith to seek interpretations better suited to contemporary needs (*ijtihad*), adopting provisions from the various schools of Islamic law as they saw fit (a process known as *takhayur*). Some even combined elements of various schools of Islamic law into a "patchwork" (*talfiq*). Reform could also be implemented through purely procedural means rather than through changes to the substance of the law: for example, the government could preclude the courts from hearing certain cases. Islamic legal concepts such as *maslaha* (consideration for the public interest) were often used to provide legitimization for reforms. By way of such devices, governments could not only move to advance their own interests but also strengthen women's position vis-à-vis their husbands and male kin, constructing women as more equal and autonomous citizens.[31]

Iraq was no exception in this respect, but despite persistent calls to introduce changes concerning women's position in the realm of personal status, efforts at codification appear to have been fueled to a large extent by the government desire to bring these matters under its own control. The government's stated aim was to bring issues of personal status closer into line with the needs of a modern state. A brief memorandum that accompanied the proposal explained why the drafting of such a law was a necessity, suggesting rather bluntly that anarchy in matters of personal status was a threat to social order. The memorandum pointed to the need to draw up a code of law to apply to all Muslims; until that time, laws in this realm had taken the form of *fatawa* (religious legal opinions), announced at different times and under different circumstances, resulting in rules that were ill determined and difficult to understand. Moreover, the current arrangement failed to suit modern needs, the memo stated, "especially now that the intervention of the state in the registration of marriage and births, etc., has become essential, unless the widest scope is to be given to false testimony in establishing those rights to which marriage and paternity give rise."[32]

It nevertheless remained to be seen how state efforts at codification and control over the personal status arena would impact the construction of Iraq's female citizens.

THE MAKING OF THE MARRIAGE CONTRACT

A woman's position in married life begins to take shape already at the time her marriage is contracted. Here it is determined whether she is entering the marriage of her own free will, whether she is a minor or an adult at the time, and whether she is intended to be her husband's sole wife. The first part of the draft Code of Personal Status, devoted to formulating the marriage contract, was designed to address these issues.

MATRIMONIAL GUARDIANSHIP AND CONSENT TO MARRIAGE The proposal allowed a woman's matrimonial guardians, usually her father or paternal grandfather, to contract a marriage on her behalf. The first article in this regard stated that a marriage contract was to be concluded by way of an offer made by one of the contracting parties and acceptance of that offer by the other party, irrespective of who—the woman, her husband-

to-be, or a guardian—had initiated the offer.[33] The proposal only mini-
mally protected adult women's independence in marriage. Although this
part of the proposal implicitly acknowledged an adult woman's right to
contract her own marriage, nowhere was this right clearly stated. Moreover, Sunni guardians were given the right to reject a woman's choice of
spouse. They were allowed to demand that a marriage contracted in their
absence be dissolved if the husband was found not to be "equal" (*kufu'*) to
his wife; here, equality was defined only with regard to property—namely,
a husband's ability to provide a *mahr* and maintenance befitting his wife's
socioeconomic background.[34] The limitations of these provisions become
clear when we look at al-A'zami and al-Hilli's writings. Al-A'zami taught
his students that under both Ja'fari and Hanafi doctrine no one had the
right to force an adult woman into an unwanted marriage and that arranged marriages still required the woman's consent. Al-Hilli concurred,
emphasizing in addition that an adult woman's consent must be not only
noncoerced, but also unequivocal.[35]

The situation with regard to minors was entirely different. The draft
law did not in any way require that a minor girl consent to her marriage.
It suggested some feeble efforts to prevent child marriage but stopped
short of addressing minors' rights in the annulment of arranged marriages. Unlike in neighboring countries, the Iraqi bill saw sanity and puberty
rather than age as the factors determining a woman's capacity to marry.[36]
Moreover, the bill clearly stated that a guardian may give a minor ward in
marriage. However, courts were prohibited from registering the marriages of minors except in cases of need (*darura*) or benefit (*maslaha*), the establishment of which was left to the *qadi*'s discretion. As discussed more
fully later, this provision could easily have been circumvented because
the proposal did not require that marriages be registered in court. It was
also by no means clear what the consequences were to be of a guardian's
contracting a marriage on behalf of a minor girl in cases involving neither
"need" nor "benefit."[37] Interestingly, whereas both al-Hilli and al-A'zami
clearly pointed out and expanded on a girl's right as soon as she came
of age to request from the court the annulment of a marriage arranged
by anyone other than her father or her paternal grandfather (*khiyar al-
bulugh*), the draft was rather vague on the issue. It declared that in all
cases that a wife is given an option to claim dissolution of a marriage, she
must exercise this option without delay—that is, as soon as she knows of

the circumstances as an adult or as soon as she reaches puberty if she is a minor. It is noteworthy that although the proposal stated that if a minor wife pleads ignorance of the marriage or of her option to have the marriage dissolved, her appeal would be accepted, but it actually relied on a minor's ignorance by never stating the circumstances upon which she could demand an annulment.[38]

Another article in the bill addressed sexual relations with minors: it provided that a husband not be given access to his minor wife until she was capable of engaging in conjugal life.[39] However, this prohibition did not preclude sexual relations with a minor who was "capable"; moreover, the matter was to be brought before a judge only when the parties contracting the marriage were in disagreement in this regard. Because the bill did not instruct judges as to how to determine a minor wife's ability to engage in sexual relations or specify the age at which that ability might emerge, supplementary texts may help shed light on the ramifications of such a provision. Al-Hilli and al-A'zami agreed that in cases of disagreement between the father and the husband of a minor girl regarding the latter's readiness to engage in sexual relations, the judge was to instruct "trustworthy" women to examine her and come to a decision. According to al-Hilli, a husband was permitted to have intercourse with a girl once she had reached the age of nine and was able to "bear" it. Although Al-A'zami did not address the matter specifically, an opinion may be inferred from his discussions on women's right to maintenance. He distinguished between minors "desired by their husbands," ready to have intercourse, and thus entitled to maintenance and those who were "undesired," incapable of having intercourse, and thus not entitled to maintenance. By citing girls under the age of seven as examples of the latter, he implied that sexual intercourse with a girl from that age could be condoned.[40]

Over the years, as the different proposals and draft laws were made public, calls could be heard for the government to protect women—and especially girls—from their kin and to secure such basic personal rights as the freedom to choose a spouse. By the 1930s and 1940s, the condemnation of child marriage and of forced marriage in the countryside was particularly vocal. Concerns were voiced in the press with regard to the impact of the state's noninterference in these matters on both women and society as a whole. As one writer put it, "How does society benefit from the marriage of a man to a girl young enough to be his great-grand-daughter?" Imagine the fate of a family consisting of an eight-year-old wife and a husband whose age might range from adolescence to eighty, wrote another; this writer went on to point out the social consequences and physical dangers of child marriage. He also criticized the portrayal of minors as sexual objects in the 1945 draft bill, although his sympathies lay more with the judge who had to determine whether a girl was ready for conjugal life than with the minor girl who would have to abide by the ruling. Both writers demanded that a legal minimum age be set for marriage, with exceptions to be made only in special cases to be defined by law. Islam, they contended, held the validity of a marriage contract to be dependent on the woman's consent. Yet women were still subject to a variety of coerced unions, such as marriage to cousins and "exchange marriages," resulting in an unhappy married life and much misery. Coerced marriages were thus detrimental to society: without happy husbands—and wives—society's happiness as a whole suffered.[41] Women activists, as we shall see in chapter 5, likewise voiced their indignation, focusing their attention on the countryside.

Legislators were well aware of these calls for change; at the same time, they could not have been unaware of the voices opposing state interference with Islamic law in these matters each time they were on the agenda. For instance, a proposed supplement to the Shara' Procedure Law, discussed in Parliament in 1937, suggested that the minimum age for marriage be set at fifteen for women and eighteen for men, but it was rejected on the grounds that Islam imposed no age requirement for marriage but rather sanctioned it for any woman who had reached puberty.[42]

POLYGAMY The post–World War II proposal did not explicitly condone polygamy; at the same time, it took no steps either to restrict husbands in these matters or to adopt precedents from neighboring countries allowing wives to divest themselves of such marriages.[43] By citing preexisting marriages to more than four women as one of the "temporary impediments" to a valid marriage, the proposal likewise implicitly recognized polygamy.[44]

If the proposal did not take issue with polygamy, it was not due to a lack of criticism. There had long been calls to revisit the issue of polygamy because of its ramifications for both women and society. As early as 1910, the poet Jamil Sidqi al-Zahawi (1863–1936) had criticized men for taking second wives who were younger and better looking than their first wives, challenging them to imagine the inverse situation.[45] Arab nationalist state officials, too, frowned on the practice, not so much because of the way in which it constructed women, but because it allegedly prevented families from producing a "healthier" and more viable nation. One such official was Dr. Sami Shawkat, who served as director-general of education in the 1930s. Shawkat advocated strengthening Iraq's population in terms of both "quantity" and "quality," maintaining that merely bearing children was not enough; their health and education had to be ensured as well, which created a need for mothers who were not only educated and healthy, but also content. Although polygamy may serve to enlarge the population, it impedes family happiness and unity and is thus detrimental to children's happiness and welfare, Shawkat maintained; only in exceptional cases, he felt, could polygamy be justified.[46] State-employed jurists also advocated restrictions on polygamy, seeing monogamous relationships as more progressive and beneficial to society. For example, when the jurist and scholar Prof. al-A'zami censured the proposal, the issue of polygamy lay at the root of his criticism. Taking a tack from such modernist reformers as the Egyptian Muhammad Abduh, who claimed that polygamy was not countenanced by the Qur'an except in extenuating circumstances, al-A'zami asserted that monogamous marriage better reflected the spirit of the shari'a. Although it is true that the shari'a allowed polygamy, it also placed severe limitations on the practice. Sura 4, verse 3 (translated earlier in this chapter), he said, indicated that the mere possibility that a man might treat his wives unequally was a reason not to take more than one wife. Equal treatment of multiple wives, he claimed, was beyond men's ability, especially insofar as the "inclination of the heart" (mail al-qalb) was concerned. As verse 129 of the same sura notes: "Ye are never able to be fair and just as between women, even if it is your ardent desire."[47] Al-A'zami condoned polygamy only in exceptional circumstances: for example, when a man's wife was infertile or suffered from a severe chronic illness or when there was a social need, such as when women in a given society outnumber men as a result of war.[48] Finally, women activists decried polygamy as degrading to women, perpetuating their construction as property. As early as the 1920s, Asma' al-Zahawi, president of the Women's Awakening Club (Nadi al-Nahda al-Nisa'iyya), voiced upper-class women's dismay over polygamy. Naziha al-Dulaimi later claimed that in the countryside the fallahin saw polygamy as a means of enlarging their labor force, and the shaikhs viewed it as a means of flaunting their wealth.[49] Asiya Tawfiq Wahbi, president of the Iraqi Women's Union, suggested that women be given a choice with regard to polygamous marriage by way of a clause in their marriage contracts. Inspired by reforms in neighboring countries that adopted the Hanbali rather than Hanafi view concerning the inclusion of conditions in the marriage contract, she advised women to stipulate that their husbands were not to take further wives and that they retain the right to end the marriage should their husbands do so "without justification."[50]

Calls for the state to address the issue of polygamy thus came from both within and beyond government circles. At the same time, however, there were those who felt the custom was on the decline and that public opinion would bring about change, making legislation unnecessary.[51] Indeed, state statistics indicated that in 1947 only 8 percent of married men had more than one wife; by 1957, the figure had dropped to less than 4 percent.[52] This perception, especially when viewed together with predictable opposition on the part of clerics to government interference, may explain the proposal's avoidance of the issue. Indeed, when the government eventually moved to curtail polygamy in 1959, the issue became a major point of contention with the *'ulama'*.[53]

TEMPORARY MARRIAGE (MUT'A) The draft law did not mention marriage for a limited duration, a practice sanctioned only by the Shi'is, so it thus implicitly sanctioned that type of marriage.[54] Despite a lack of statistical data on temporary marriage, available evidence fails to substantiate Lyell's aforementioned claim that temporary marriage enabled lower-class Shi'i men to "enjoy a life of uncontrolled libertinism." For example, according to Shakir Mustafa Salim, inhabitants of the Shi'i marsh village of al-Chibaish viewed short-term marriage contracts, for a period of several days or even one night, as tantamount to adultery.[55] Temporary marriage also could not have been widespread as a means of taking a fifth wife; as noted, only 8 percent of married men were polygamous in 1947, and, of those, 90 percent had only two wives.[56] It may be that the proposal's silence on this issue again reflected a desire to avoid a confrontation with Shi'i *'ulama'* over a principle seen as applying only to a small number of people. Moreover, it should be noted that of those few men who, according to the available evidence, used temporary marriage as a means of marrying more than four wives, quite a few were members of a group that the government had propped up as its political mainstay: namely, Shiʻi tribal shaikhs.[57]

REGISTRATION OF THE MARRIAGE CONTRACT   Although the draft as presented up to this point did nothing to change women's standing vis-à-vis their husbands and male kin—it failed to impair the ability of a woman's male kin to force her into marriage, to establish a minimum legal age for marriage, or to introduce restrictions on polygamy—it nonetheless had the potential to bring about such change by requiring that marriage contracts be registered.

The proposal provided that marriage contracts be registered in the shariʻa courts, including such details as the names of the spouses and their parents, their place of residence and occupations, their ages and the amount of the *mahr* to be pledged. It prohibited courts from registering the marriages of minors except, as noted, in cases of "need" or "advantage," the assessment of which was left to the judge's discretion. It also required that couples present a medical certificate showing that both parties were free of tuberculosis, elephantiasis, and venereal disease as well as a document from the *mukhtar* (village headman) or from two persons of good standing in their locality stating that there were no legal impediments to the marriage.[58] Some of these details naturally had purely bureaucratic value, including census and financial data, or pertained to issues of public health and welfare. The mere promise to protect certain rights by way of registration likewise served as an incentive for people to make use of the state courts, thus promoting state control over the lives of its citizens. Nevertheless, for women, such registration was significant in that it could protect them from child marriage, enable them to determine their future husbands' true marital status (i.e., by revealing preexisting marriages), allow them to learn of the true state of their intended husbands' health, and help them secure such matrimonial rights as *mahr*, maintenance, and inheritance. Yet the proposal also included a clause stating that marriages may be affirmed by other means. In other words, the bill offered no real deterrent for those wishing to avoid registering their marriages and afforded no real protection for women coerced into marrying.

A no less significant ramification for women, however, emerged almost parenthetically with regard to the criteria according to which courts were to determine the validity of a marriage. The proposal stipulated that a marriage contract not be regarded as valid in court unless concluded in the presence of two adult witnesses. The use of the masculine dual form of the word for witnesses (*shahidan*) indicates that women and men were not viewed equally in this matter. Al-A'zami reinforced this notion: although not altogether rejecting women's ability to act as witnesses, he left no doubt as to their relative position, asserting that the witnesses must be either two men or one man and two women.[59]

This look at the proposal thus far reveals certain clear tendencies. Personal rights—such as the right to consent to marriage, to decide when and whom to marry, and to secure a monogamous marriage—were not protected. The bill allowed for forced marriages at almost any age and did not highlight minors' option to annul the marriage when they reached puberty. Although it offered protection of some rights for women who registered their marriage contracts in court, even women who did so could find themselves forcibly married at a young age in cases of "need." In other words, the government draft law on personal status ignored calls for reforms based on more favorable interpretations of Islamic law and failed to tackle male-dominated customs that harmed women.

GENDER RELATIONS AND ROLES IN MARRIAGE

The bill's construction of female citizens becomes clearer in the sections pertaining to marriage, in which husbands and wives' rights and duties are laid out. The issue of child custody, too, is intimately connected to married women's position. The proposal devoted much attention to what it referred to as the "rights of husbands and wives" resulting from the marriage contract. It is evident from this section that legislators had conceived of a very specific type of marriage, entailing clear gender obligations and roles. In this section, the proposal focused on *mahr* and maintenance, which were considered a wife's right and a husband's obligation; although the reciprocal duties of wives and rights of husbands were not directly mentioned, they were alluded to quite clearly.

THE MAHR The proposal considered *mahr* to be a woman's right in marriage and discussed it in intricate detail. It distinguished between, on the one hand, the "specified" *mahr* (*al-mahr al-musamma*), the sum stipulated in the marriage contract to be paid by the groom to the bride, and, on the other hand, the unspecified, "proper" *mahr* (*al-mahr al-mithli*), equal to the figure set for another agnate woman of a social background similar to that of the bride or, where no such woman existed, equal to the figure that had been fixed for other residents of her locality. It also provided that the *mahr* be paid fully or partially as a "prompt" *mahr* (*mahr mu'ajjal*) or as a "deferred" *mahr*, to be fully or partly deferred and paid either after a specified period or upon divorce or widowhood (*mahr mu'ajjal*).

The proposal not only clearly established the wife's right to *mahr*, be it "specified" or "proper," but also stressed that *mahr* was a woman's sole property. Moreover, problems concerning the *mahr* that might arise under different circumstances were addressed, as were ways in which a woman could substantiate her claim to her *mahr* to her deceased husband's heirs.[60] These provisions made the woman a party to her marriage contract instead of an object for sale. They also provided her with some property (through the "prompt" *mahr*), certain safeguard against divorce, and some economic support in the event of divorce or widowhood (through the "deferred" *mahr*). However, even here, for something that was presented as a woman's right and was so clearly intended to be protected, we find that legislators failed to incorporate provisions from Sunni Hanafi or Shi'i Ja'fari laws that could have further protected women. One conspicuous example is that of "exchange marriage" (*nikah al-shighar*), a practice in which two guardians exchanged their wards in marriage, with each woman serving as the other's *mahr*. It is noteworthy that suits concerning this type of marriage ultimately reached Iraq's urban shari'a courts.[61]

Here, as indicated by both al-Hilli and al-A'zami, legislators could have found a basis in Hanafi and Ja'fari law for considering such marriages void or at least for demanding that a proper *mahr* be paid to each bride.[62] Such provisions would have strengthened women's position as autonomous individuals rather than as the mere possessions of their guardians. The possibility of making the woman a party to the negotiations over her marriage contract and allowing her to stipulate conditions regarding her *mahr* was likewise ignored. According to al-A'zami, a woman could marry with a "specified" *mahr* of lesser value than her "proper" *mahr* in exchange for some benefit bestowed from her husband to her relatives or herself—for example, a promise not to take other wives, not to remove her from her place of residence, or not to make her perform certain household chores. If the husband fulfilled such conditions, he would be obligated to provide only the *mahr* that was specified; if not, he would have to pay the "proper" *mahr*.[63]

MAINTENANCE   One duty the proposal clearly assigned to the husband and viewed as a woman's right in marriage was maintenance. The proposal stated that from the onset of her married life, a woman was entitled to maintenance consisting of three components: food, clothing, and accommodation. The amount of a Shiʿi wife's maintenance was to be calculated in accordance with her economic status; for Sunni wives, maintenance was based on the computed average of the two spouses' economic status. If a husband delayed payment or refused to provide maintenance, his wife was entitled to sue him. Moreover, the maintenance debt of a husband whose wife had "submitted herself" to him began on the day on which he had stopped paying. This debt, the proposal stated, was to hold even if the amount of maintenance had not previously been determined by a ruling or agreement and was to be forgiven only at such time as the husband paid or the wife waived payment. Arrears in maintenance were not to be waived in the event of divorce or the death of either party. Moreover, in a departure from both Hanafi and Jaʿfari doctrine, Article 44, to be discussed later in greater detail, stated that if a husband had no known property out of which a writ of maintenance could be executed, yet he made no declaration as to being destitute and persisted in failing to support his wife, a judge may immediately grant his wife a divorce.[64]

The proposal also stated that if a husband left his wife without support, moving to another locality or going missing, the court was to declare the wife's right to maintenance, effective from the day of her request, provided that she sign a sworn declaration that she had not previously received maintenance, was not already divorced, and had not been "disobedient" (*nashiza*).

The proposal stipulated that a woman was not entitled to maintenance if she had been "disobedient." or "unavailable to her husband." A woman who was ill or a minor not ready for conjugal life was not entitled to maintenance. A woman who failed to move into her husband's home, left her husband's home without his consent and without "lawful justification," or refused to travel with him (provided the destination would not place her in danger) was likewise not entitled to maintenance.[65] In total, although the proposal established maintenance as a married woman's right, it also took care to make this right dependent on her being "obedient."

Al-A'zami and al-Hilli went to great lengths to define "obedience," expounding the bill by providing clear guidelines for sanctioned behavior. Both concurred with the proposal that a wife who left her husband's home without his permission and without "lawful justification" for doing so was not entitled to maintenance. Yet they also made it clear that a husband might restrict even "lawful excursions," those for the purpose of, say, visiting family members. Such visits could be limited to once per week in the case of the wife's parents or once per month or year for other relatives; the actual interval was left to the husband's discretion. Women also needed their husbands' permission to sleep at relatives' homes, to participate in family events, and to visit female nonrelatives. Moreover, both al-A'zami and al-Hilli implied that going to work was not a lawful justification for a woman to leave the house—indeed, that wives who went to work without their husbands' permission were not entitled to maintenance. Also emphasized was a woman's duty to make herself "available" to her husband; al-Hilli clearly stated that a woman who denied her husband his conjugal rights while in his home was to be considered "disobedient" and so forfeited her right to maintenance.[66]

At the same time, dissatisfaction with the type of marriage circumscribed by the proposal mounted among Iraqi urban intellectuals. There were calls to base marriage on companionship and mutual love and understanding rather than on economic and financial obligations (on the husband's part) and obedience (on the wife's part). Some perceived the requirement of obedience as a form of enslavement.[67] It is worth noting that already in the 1920s young couples expressed disdain with the notion of *mahr* by setting the sum of one dinar for both the prompt and deferred *mahr*.[68] Women activists raised broader criticism: Naziha al-Dulaimi, for example, sought not only equality and mutual respect between partners in marriage, but also economic independence for women. She claimed that the peasant woman's enslavement by her "owner," the urban woman's dependence on her provider, and the maltreatment endured by both would be resolved only at such time as the former was allowed to take a real part in the "process of production" and the latter was allowed to work outside of the home.[69] The growing dissatisfaction with the construction of women as nonautonomous, economically dependent beings, however, little influenced the obedience–maintenance dependency delineated in the draft Code of Personal Status.

CHILD CUSTODY   As the bill turned to matters of child custody, the dominant–subordinate gender relations just discussed in terms of maintenance–obedience began to be expressed as motherhood's dependency on submissiveness. In "Rights of Husbands and Wives," legislators clearly assigned men the role of breadwinner and required women to remain, to the greatest extent possible, in the home; aside from the requirement that women be available to their husbands, the draft did not discuss women's other roles within the home. Yet even in the absence of further details, al-A'zami wrote as if women's roles in the home under the proposal were clear-cut, natural, and just. He explained to his students that a husband's natural role was to bear his family's financial burden, whereas a wife's was to maintain her home, raise children, and perform other conjugal and motherly duties.[70]

"Rights of Husbands and Wives" largely glossed over the subject of women's roles as mothers, but the part concerning child custody addressed this issue; here, the raising of and custody over one's children was considered a woman's right—but also a right that could be taken away. Although the proposal gave mothers preferential rights with regard to the custody and upbringing of their children both in marriage and following divorce, it also indicated that the end of a marriage could mean the end of motherhood as well. A divorced woman's right to have custody of her children was by no means secure or inalienable. The proposal required that a divorced woman fulfill certain requirements in order to be considered "fit" for custody (the same requirements did not apply to divorced men); the most conspicuous of them was the requirement that the woman not remarry. Here, the stricter Ja'fari opinion was adopted, according to which subsequent marriage of any kind disqualified a woman from being able to retain custody of her children. It is unlikely, however, that the equivalent provision in the Hanafi context would have greatly improved women's situation. Under Hanafi law, a woman who remarried could retain custody of her children only if her second husband was forbidden in marriage to the children in her custody; this could be the case, for example, if the husband were the children's uncle. More important, the proposal further restricted a woman's right to custody by stipulating that the period of custody in case of divorce was to be determined by the provisions of the sect to which the husband adhered. Textbooks published at the time further clarify the matter. Under Jaʿfari law, explained ʿAbd al-Karim Rida al-Hilli, a mother had the right to the custody of her son prior to weaning—that is, until the age of two—and of her daughter until the age of seven, but he also brought a minority opinion extending mothers' custody until the age of seven for sons and nine for daughters. According to Hanafi law, al-Aʿzami claimed, the mother's right to custody continued until her sons were seven and her daughters were nine, at which time the children passed into their father's care.[71] Although the proposal permitted judges to extend the period of maternal custody in cases where doing so was clearly in the child's interest, this permission was a far cry from assuring that women's natural rights with regard to their children's upbringing were upheld.

The proposal was once again far from a response to the calls for change and demands not to deprive mothers of their children following divorce. Intellectuals such as the poet Nazik al-Malaʾika decried fathers' ability to tear children away from their mothers as the harshest, most unreasonable type of deprivation. Women's organizations protested as well, urging that the custody of children in divorce be given to the parent best suited to raise them. Activists such as al-Dulaimi noted that the threat of divorce, with its subsequent loss of custody, allowed husbands to exploit and abuse their wives and to coerce them into silence and obedience.[72]

The proposal's treatment of women's rights under the marriage contract and the issue of child custody thus reinforced and expanded on the same construction of women discussed in the previous section. By laying the foundations for a marriage in which husbands could absolutely restrict their wives' social and economic freedom, the proposal essentially created two classes of citizens: husbands as providers who must be obeyed and wives as dependants who must be obedient. This dominant–subordinate construction was further cemented in the proposal's discussion of child custody. The state would not secure a woman's right to raise her children, which essentially aided husbands in suppressing their wives' potential defiance by allowing the threat of divorce and the "loss of motherhood" to hang above their marriage like a bleak black cloud.

INHERITANCE

The proposal was meticulous with regard to women's right to inherit as wives, daughters, sisters, mothers, aunts, and so forth under both Sunni and Shi'i law.[73] These provisions may be seen as improving women's position vis-à-vis their male kin as compared to customary law; it was claimed that tribeswomen in Iraq could not inherit, and, moreover, that they themselves could be considered inheritable property.[74] However, although allowing a woman to strengthen her position by accumulating property through inheritance, the proposal also reiterated the general principle that a woman was to receive only half the inheritance a man would receive under the same circumstances.

This discrimination between men and women was again at odds with the demands for change and grave feelings of dissatisfaction among women in Iraq. Already at the turn of the century, the poet Jamil Sidqi al-Zahawi decried the injustice regarding inheritance for Muslim women.[75] However, only after the 1958 coup did women's long-harbored feelings of deprivation burst forth and become an impetus for change. Senior members of the League for the Defense of Women's Rights, which began as an underground organization in 1952 and received official recognition in December 1958, later recalled the multitude of bitter complaints they heard from women in those days. Mubejel Baban explained why her organization demanded legislation giving men and women equal shares in inheritance: "We heard so many complaints from so many women. You know, if a husband dies he leaves only one-eighth to his wife if she has children. If she doesn't have children, she gets one-fourth, and the rest goes to his family. This is according to the Sunnis. With the Shi'is, it's much better, more progressive. . . . So the complaints we got from the women: you have to do something about it. We knew we were going to be touching something that is written in the Qur'an, but people asked us to do something about it. We had to deal with it."[76] Many people, however, supported the Islamic system of inheritance. Interpreting the proposal's intentions, al-A'zami explained that the provisions regarding inheritance took into account the "natural differences between men and women."[77] For al-A'zami, these differences meant that men must assume the role of providers and women the role of mothers and homemakers. Thus, it was only reasonable that men should receive a greater share. As in the case of maintenance, in accepting such a balance in gender relations, the proposal further constructed women citizens as economically dependent beings.

DIVORCE

A substantial portion of the proposal was devoted to the subject of divorce, detailing both the husband's rights in repudiating his wife without recourse to a court of law and the wife's options regarding the dissolution of her marriage, chiefly by way of legal procedures. In what seemed to be an effort to put men and women on more equal footing, husbands' rights in divorce were restricted and wives' rights expanded in a manner that often deviated from both Hanafi and Ja'fari law.

HUSBANDS' RIGHTS   The proposal stated that repudiation without recourse to a court of law (*talaq*) was a husband's right. At the same time, however, it restricted this right. It determined the following: that the formula of repudiation uttered by a husband not fully aware of his actions (due to drunkenness, sleep, or insanity) or acting under compulsion shall have no legal effect; that suspended or conditional divorce (i.e., a pronouncement that makes the divorce contingent upon the occurrence of some future event or sets it to take effect at some future time) shall have no effect if intended only as a threat or an attempt at coercion; and that metaphorical expressions that may be construed as alluding to divorce shall not have that effect unless it was the desired outcome. It also prescribed that divorce formulae accompanied by a pronouncement or the gesturing of a number shall effect only a single and therefore revocable divorce. Thus, if a man said to his wife, "I divorce you three times" or "I divorce you" while holding up three fingers, the resulting divorce was single and revocable rather than triple and final. The proposal also restricted a husband's ability to use divorce as a means of disinheriting his wife, stating that a wife whose husband divorced her while on his deathbed shall inherit from him for a full year from the date of her divorce (among Shi'is) or for as long as she was in her "waiting period" (*'idda*)[78] (among Sunnis).[79]

The extent of husband's privileges in divorce, however, remained evident because the proposal went on to designate *talaq* as a man's right and discussed the distinction between revocable and irrevocable repudiation. The proposal stated that revocable repudiation (*talaq raj'i*) allowed the husband to take back his divorced wife during her "waiting period" and resume marital relations—not only without the need for a new *mahr* or contract, but also without her consent. Even after irrevocable repudiation (*talaq ba'in*), following the waiting period, a man was allowed to resume marital relations with his former wife provided he drew up a new contract, paid a new *mahr*, and obtained her consent. Only after three such irrevocable repudiations was a man prohibited from remarrying his former wife; yet even then the proposal provided a mechanism by which a man could remarry the same woman, stipulating that the two may resume marital relations so long as the former wife had been remarried to someone else in the interim, the marriage had been consummated, and the former wife had subsequently been divorced or widowed from her second husband. The proposal thus rejected the precedent of neighboring countries and did not declare the remarriage of the divorced parties to be valid only if the intervening marriage had not been concluded with the express intention of facilitating the original couple's remarriage. Moreover, the proposal stated that once the intervening marriage had been dissolved and the original couple had remarried, the husband was entitled to three further repudiations.[80]

At many points, the proposal departed from ordinary Hanafi law and contradicted the consensus among Sunni *'ulama'* in Iraq at the time. Letters signed by groups of clerics in the contemporary press decried the attempt to invalidate the divorce of a drunken man, claimed that suspended or conditional divorce was valid even if intended by the husband only as a threat or an attempt at coercion, and rejected the notion that a pronouncement of divorce accompanied by a number effected only a single divorce.[81]

OPTIONS FOR WOMEN   Articles in the proposal pertaining to a woman's options for ending her marriage reflected some expansion of the possible grounds for judicial divorce, many of them contradicting the opinions of Hanafi and Ja'fari *'ulama'* in Iraq and, indeed, as demonstrated later, drawing their fire. The proposal stated, for instance, that a woman could demand the dissolution of her marriage if she discovered her husband to be impotent. It also allowed her to demand a separation if her husband suffered from a disease that made married life to him dangerous, such as elephantiasis, leprosy, tuberculosis, or venereal disease, or if he was found to be insane; most Hanafis and Ja'faris did not see such circumstances as grounds for separation.[82] In these cases, however, the proposal stated that dissolution was not automatic. In the case of impotency, the wife's request for a separation would be accepted after a year of court-ordered respite, during which time the husband had remained impotent and his wife's request had remained resolute. In the case of communicable diseases or insanity, a woman's request to dissolve her marriage would be granted only if a medical committee determined the case to be untreatable.

Other articles in the proposal allowed a woman to demand the dissolution of her marriage if she had been deprived of maintenance by her husband. As noted, the proposal prescribed that if a woman's husband had no known property out of which a writ of maintenance could be executed, made no statement as to being destitute, yet continued to refuse to support his wife, a judge could grant her a divorce at once rather than compelling her husband to fulfill his obligations, as required by both Hanafi and Ja'fari doctrine.[83] After making the necessary inquiries, a judge was likewise allowed to dissolve the marriage of a woman who had been deprived of maintenance while her husband was absent, in hiding, missing, or incarcerated for more than a year. Even where maintenance had been provided, a judge could rule a dissolution in certain cases, such as if a husband had disappeared and four years of investigations had elapsed with no sign of his whereabouts; if he had gone missing in the course of a military expedition in a non-Muslim country and had not been heard from one year after the contending armies and their prisoners had returned home; or if he had been sentenced to at least seven years in prison. Again, these grounds for dissolution generally stood in contradiction to both Hanafi and Ja'fari law.[84]

The proposal delineated two further routes via which women could end their marriages. The first was by way of *khul'*, a divorce in which the wife gives some compensation to her husband (e.g., all or part of her *mahr*). Although stating that money was not an essential part of the *khul'* procedure for Sunnis, the proposal allowed both Sunni and Shi'i husbands to demand compensation greater than the sum of the *mahr*. It did not require that the *khul'* take place in court; for the Shi'is, it required two competent witnesses.[85] More important from our point of view was the second route, which was based on marital discord and a failed attempt at arbitration. On the basis of Sunni Maliki doctrine, Article 52 of the proposal provided that if discord or a conflict had erupted between

spouses and one of them took the matter to court, the judge was to appoint family arbitrators to try and broker a reconciliation. Where reconciliation proved impossible, the arbitrators were to submit a report to the
judge. On the basis of this report, if the husband was found to be at fault,
the judge could grant a divorce; if the wife was found to be in the wrong,
he may declare *khul'* on the basis of the return of her *mahr* or a portion
thereof.[86] In effect, this article opened the gate for a woman to obtain a
separation through state courts for the most common reason—marital
discord—thus allowing her to terminate an unhappy or unwanted union.

It is interesting to note, however, that although legislators deviated
from both Hanafi and Ja'fari opinions of the time to expand the grounds
upon which a woman could seek a divorce, they failed to mention an option noted by al-Hilli and discussed at length by al-A'zami—that a husband might grant his wife the power to end her own marriage (*tafwid
al-talaq*).[87] Such irrevocable authorization, given at the time of the marriage contract or afterward, allowed wives to end their marriages at will,
absolving them of the need for recourse to the courts. This option was
not unheard of in Iraq; among the young intelligentsia, marriage contracts indeed granted wives the power to end their own marriage if they
so chose.[88]

Legislators could not have been unaware of the calls for substantial
state intervention to effect more equal and just divorce. As early as the
1930s, the press published calls to the government to place severe restrictions on men's rights in divorce so as to guarantee that this option
not be used hastily, thus averting the consequent misery and remorse.
All matters of divorce, it was urged, could better be handled by shari'a
state courts. In the 1940s, the press criticized the fact that the proposal required the registration of marriages but ignored the need to register divorces.[89] Women activists, too, expressed grave concern. The Iraqi
Women's Union appealed to Parliament to enact a law placing restrictions on divorce. Naziha al-Dulaimi, a proponent of equal rights in divorce for both spouses, was particularly troubled by the ease with which
a man could divorce his wife. She claimed that divorce was the inevitable
lot of the peasant woman who had become weak, incapacitated, or unable to work or if her "owner" had simply gotten tired of her. The threat
of divorce compelled women from the "peasant and working classes" to
endure hard labor, beatings, and humiliation; otherwise, they could find
themselves homeless, hungry, poor, and devoid of any rights, even with

regard to their own children.[90] Some of the proposal's provisions seemed to respond to these concerns, but they hardly came close to placing men and women on a similar footing.

The section on divorce completes the expression of the dominant–subordinate gender relations that constructed women as second-class citizens throughout the government's draft Code of Personal Status. A single woman was constructed as the possession of her male kin rather than as an individual capable of making free and rational choices. Upon marrying, she was made dependent on and subservient to her husband. If she was a mother, her subordination was further cemented because one of the possible consequences of divorce was the immediate loss of her children to their father and his family. Although certain provisions restricted men in divorce and expanded the grounds for which a woman could seek judicial dissolution of her marriage, as in the case of polygamy and inheritance, men's privileges were preserved. Despite the limitations imposed, men were still free to divorce their wives almost at will, for any reason, and without the need for recourse to the courts. True, some of the grounds for judicial dissolution had been broadened, but women still had no equivalent ability to initiate divorce; their will with regard to resuming marital life after being revocably divorced was similarly ignored. Men's privileges in divorce cemented the dominant–subordinate gender relations. In limiting women's economic resources by requiring that they obtain their husbands' approval to work outside of the home and by deeming them to be less entitled to inheritance than men, the proposed law made divorce for a woman tantamount to losing her home, financial support, and children.

It is noteworthy that this harsh construction of women's position vis-à-vis their kin and husbands was not necessitated by Islamic law. Al-Aʿzami and al-Hilli's works clearly indicate that more favorable rulings were available. It was rather the result of state officials' preferring some rulings over the others. Judith Tucker has pointed out in reference to other countries in the Middle East that in picking and choosing the rulings for states' codes, those who framed them "were engaged in the fundamental transformation of Islamic law from a shariʿa of vast textual complexity and interpretive possibilities to a modern legal code of fixed rules and penalties."[91] In Iraq under the monarchy, this process threatened not only to initiate the loss of diverse interpretive possibilities, but also to bring about a code in which the substantive aspects did not work in women's favor.

Why did the government's proposal rely on rulings that put its female citizens in such an unfavorable position as regards their kin and husbands? A compelling explanation might be found in Mounira Charrad's work about women's rights in postcolonial Tunisia, Algeria, and Morocco. Charrad argues that the nature of the state–tribe alliances and the degree of the state's autonomy or independence from kinship groupings after colonial rule are crucial factors in determining the conservative or liberal tendencies of their personal-status codes. She identifies three distinct paths to state formation and family law. In the first, the newly formed state emerges from colonization in close alliance with tribal kin groupings and adopts a conservative family law (as in the case of Morocco). In the second path, the state develops in partial alliance with tribal kin groupings and stalls between alternatives before finally enacting a conservative family law policy (as in the case of Algeria). In the third path, the national state evolves in relative autonomy from tribal kin groupings and promulgates a liberal family law, expanding the legal rights of women (as in the case of Tunisia).

Islamic family law, Charrad claims, "legitimizes the extended male-centered patrilineage that has served as the building block of kin-based solidarities within tribal groups in the Maghrib." She focuses on the extent that personal status legislation remained close to Maliki law, but many of the aspects she presents can be found in the Iraqi government proposal. She notes that because no minimum age for marriage or clear consent on the part of the bride was required for a marriage to be valid, the door was left open to compulsory and child marriage. This option gave legal prerogatives to male kin over the marriage alliance and the choice of a wife. Under these conditions, marriage could be used to the benefit of the kin group either through the extended patrilineage itself or through a controlled exogamous alliance. Charrad also points to the fragility of the conjugal unit and the ease with which the marital bond could be broken, as demonstrated, for example, by the husband's privileges in divorce. This fragility conveys the message that the nuclear family does not constitute the significant locus of solidarity. Blood ties, however, are emphasized as enduring, demonstrated in the case of the temporary maternal custody over children, especially boys.[92] We can read all of this into the Iraqi proposed legislation and more: the proposal refrained from mentioning temporary marriage despite the fact that the Sunnis would not permit it, possibly because some wealthy Shi'i tribal leaders used temporary marriage as a means of taking more than four wives. It can also be claimed that the proposal worked toward the fragility of the conjugal unit by giving women more grounds to demand dissolution of their marriage based on the Maliki law.

It is thus tempting to argue that because the Iraqi ruling elite emerged from the mandate period in close alliance with tribal kin groupings, the state was about to adopt a conservative personal status legislation that protected extended male-centered patrilineage. This argument however, is problematic. First, personal status legislation was intended to serve mainly the urban population. As shown in chapter 1, at the time when the proposal was discussed, the government still saw the TCCDR as the most appropriate system for the rural population. It was the institutionalization of customary law rather than the codification of Islamic law that was meant to serve and preserve the tribal system. Moreover, some articles in the proposal that seemed to tackle concerns raised by urban intellectuals actually conflicted with those trends Charrad saw supporting the model of the family as extended patrilineage. For example, in prohibiting courts from registering the marriages of minors, male kin's prerogatives over marriage were somewhat restricted; in permitting judges to extend the period of maternal custody in cases where doing so was clearly in the interest of the child, the child's welfare was given preference over that of the patrilineage; in prescribing that divorce formulae accompanied by a pronouncement or the gesturing of a number would be considered only a single and therefore revocable divorce, the proposal actually worked against the fragility of the conjugal unit. In addition, it contained some articles that were clearly in conflict with customary law, most notably those allowing women to inherit land. It is also noteworthy that in determining that divorce by a husband acting under compulsion shall have no legal effect, the proposal went against one of the practices associated with the *nahwa*.

But the main problem in applying Charrad's model to the Iraqi case is that state–mosque relations seem to have had more influence on the shape of personal status legislation than did state–tribe relations. The circumstances that led to the proposal's demise make this point especially evident.

THE PROPOSAL'S DEMISE:
DIVORCE AS THE FOCAL POINT FOR A POWER STRUGGLE

Both Sunni and Shi'i *'ulama'* vociferously protested the draft Code of Personal Status. Since the mid-1940s, clerics had issued appeals and letters to the prime minister, the minister of justice, heads of Parliament, and MPs decrying the proposal. They focused on divorce, fiercely criticizing provisions that restricted husbands' rights or that expanded options for women. Some went so far as to call these provisions a violation of the proper social order. The president of the Ja'fari Division of the Court of Cassation, Muhammad Sadiq al-Sadr, sent one such letter to the minister of justice in January 1948.[93] Al-Sadr singled out the provisions regarding divorce as examples of regulations that the Ja'fari Court of Cassation would not apply so long as they did not conform to the shari'a. Thirteen Sunni *'ulama'*, headed by Amjad al-Zahawi, Qasim al-Qaisi, and Najm al-Din al-Wa'iz,[94] sent a letter to the prime minister, heads of Parliament, and the minister of justice. They, too, based their opposition to the proposal mainly on its provisions regarding divorce; they claimed that the proposal was unconstitutional. It contained articles, they charged, that were inconsistent with what Muslim jurists, in particular those who adhered to Hanafi doctrine ("the school of jurisprudence followed by the majority of Sunnis in Iraq") espoused, whereas the Iraqi Constitution required that matters of personal status be administered in the shari'a courts in accordance with those shari'a provisions particular to each of the major Islamic sects in Iraq.[95]

Neither letter, however, was intended to provide a thorough analysis of the contradictions between the proposal and the accepted schools of jurisprudence in Iraq. They provided only a few examples of this alleged inconsistency, on the basis of which the authors claimed that the proposal should be rejected. These examples were easy enough to find in the provisions concerning divorce, which borrowed elements from schools of law other than the Ja'fari and Hanafi. The Sunni *'ulama'* strongly protested the provision voiding suspended or conditional divorce, claiming that jurists allowed such divorce even if intended only as a threat or an attempt at coercion on the part of the husband. The assertion that formulae of divorce uttered by the husband accompanied by a number, verbal or gestured, effected only a single and thus revocable divorce likewise flew in the face of the existing consensus among jurists, they claimed.

Another concern, this time shared with Shi'i clerics, regarded women's increased ability to obtain a separation through judicial proceedings. One of the first examples given by al-Sadr of provisions his court would not implement pertained to permission given to judges to grant a woman a divorce if her husband had no known property, made no statement as to being destitute, yet persisted in failing to support her. This article, he claimed, was contrary to both Hanafi and Ja'fari doctrines, which dictated that a husband who was able but unwilling to support his wife was to be compelled to do so—if need be, by means of incarceration—but that a woman whose husband was truly incapable of supporting her could be granted permission to secure her own maintenance, for example, by taking a loan in his name. Al-Sadr was concerned with the encroachment on husbands' rights by way of court-enforced repudiation. This article, he said, was borrowed from Egyptian legislation dating from 1920, which was based on Sunni Maliki doctrine. There was nothing to be gained, he claimed, by adopting such legislation in Iraq, where Hanafis and Ja'faris, who are in the majority, maintain that repudiation is the husband's sole right. Al-Sadr went on to voice his objection to the article in the proposal that provided for the appointment of family arbitrators in cases of marital discord, and allowing a judge, based on the arbitrators' recommendation, to make a decree of *talaq* or *khul'*. Al-Sadr claimed that both Hanafi and Ja'fari doctrine limited the arbitrators' ability to broker a reconciliation in these cases, whereas the proposal, inspired again by the Maliki school of jurisprudence, allowed arbitrators in essence to effect *talaq* or *khul'*. He added that in this article and the one preceding it legislators had been concerned with the injury (*darar*) caused to the wife by her husband as a result of marital discord or the latter's failure to provide maintenance. However, the need to prevent injury cannot supersede the husband's right to divorce, he pronounced.

Both letters criticized the articles of the proposal regarding absent or imprisoned husbands, claiming they were essentially incompatible with both Hanafi and Ja'fari law, which endeavored to postpone judicial divorce to the greatest extent possible. Al-Sadr voiced his preference that most of the cases mentioned on this topic in the proposal be referred to the top religious authority—the leading *mujtahid*—and that judgment be rendered in accordance with the resulting fatwa. Likewise, he preferred that judgment with regard to the granting of divorce because of such ailments as tuberculosis and venereal disease be based instead on the opinion of the leading religious authority. At the end of his letter, al-Sadr asserted that giving women a freer hand in divorce posed a threat to the proper social order. He said that there was no benefit in the proposal's articles concerning women's rights in divorce. *Talaq*, which was a husband's God-given right, should not be delegated to the courts, especially at a time when many state judges were unfamiliar with the precepts of the shari'a in matters of personal status. Easing such provisions would destroy the essence of family life, he said, warning of a "grave danger" to society.[96]

Although the proper social order and gender relations constituted the focal point of the debate, al-Sadr's comments reveal that they were not necessarily the primary issue at hand. As scholars have noted, at the heart of the opposition from the *'ulama'* lay their rejection of the state's growing control over the legal system and its encroachment on matters that had traditionally been in their hands. Clerics were apprehensive that codifying shari'a provisions would further accelerate the unification of the civil and shari'a courts because it would allow any state-trained judge to administer the law without taking recourse to expert religious opinion.[97] In 1931, in twenty-four out of forty-seven locations civil judges also took the role of *qadi* when necessary; by the 1950s, only a few specially designated *qadi*s remained. In most places, civil judges were authorized to rule in personal status matters, consulting with *'ulama'* only as necessary. Not only were state-trained civil judges seen as competent to deal with matters of personal status, but the Judges and Qadhis Law preferred graduates of the Iraqi Law School over *fuqaha'* (religious law experts) for the post of *qadi*. The result was a threat to *'ulama'* power, prestige, and income.[98]

It is also important to note in this context that some articles seemingly attuned to calls to improve women's legal standing perhaps had a more central purpose. Provisions promoting the registration of the marriage contract, the possible extension of maternal custody rights, the restriction of men's ability to execute a "hasty divorce," and the expansion of women's options to end their marriages can be seen both as a first step toward improving women's legal position and a response to demands raised by the Iraqi Women's Union, the main legal women's organization active at the time, as discussed in chapter 5. However, the benefits of registration, the potential to extend maternal custody, allegations of "hasty" divorce, and the ability to initiate the dissolution of marriage for a variety of reasons served as incentives to make use of state courts and to enhance the process of the government's taking over the realm of personal status. Perhaps it was to this end that the government was willing to risk raising clerics' ire by turning to other schools of Islamic jurisprudence for provisions that enabled women to end their marriages through legal procedures in the state courts rather than offering them a simple way to initiate divorce that was acceptable to both schools of jurisprudence but did not require recourse to the state court system.

J. N. D. Anderson, a leading scholar of Islamic legal history, was no doubt right when he claimed in 1953 that the Sunni 'ulama' feared that a codification of shari'a provisions would speed up the merger of the civil and shari'a courts and that Shi'i 'ulama' saw the code as a direct encroachment upon their *mujtahids*' prerogative.[99] However, when considering state–mosque negotiations, it must also be noted that the codification of the shari'a was not the only option floating about. Turkey, as mentioned, had done away altogether with shari'a courts and laws. Clerics countered by invoking powerful and impassioned arguments. They claimed that placing personal status matters in the hands of the state courts would threaten the proper, God-prescribed social order and gender hierarchy. This view presented the 'ulama' not as the protectors of their own interests, but as defenders of the "proper" social order. By comparison, the government's argument that placing personal status issues in the hands of state courts would bring order in a way "more suitable to modern requirements" simply lacked the same emotional impact.

In May 1952, the draft Code of Personal Status, the culmination of government efforts dating back to the 1930s, was brought before Parliament, and it seemed that the government expected to see it passed. It is logical to assume that against the background of growing opposition to the government and demands for reforms in between the 1948 *wathba* and the 1952 intifada and amidst the revolutionary winds blowing from Iran and Egypt, the government felt it necessary to push for reform and expected that the 'ulama', apprehensive of a regime change and secular reforms, would agree; after all, a regime change and adoption of secular personal status law would make them dispensable. The government, however, faced fierce opposition—not only from the Sunni camp in the form of the May 1952 letter, but also from prominent Shi'i authority Ayatulla Muhsin al-Hakim. Al-Hakim sent one of his sons to inform the deputies of his opposition to the draft law and his desire to see it rejected. According to al-Hakim, when his opposition became known, the deputies followed suit, expressing their opposition to the bill and forcing the government to send it back to the Judicial Committee.[100] In fact, during the first Chamber of Deputies session after the Sunni clerics' letter and al-Hakim's sweeping opposition were known, the head of the Judicial Committee asked the Chamber of Deputies to return the proposal to the committee "due to the fact that many members asked to express their opinions and due to the comments made by some of the 'ulama' regarding it."[101]

The conservative construction of women in the proposed personal status law must then be understood against the background of this struggle. The government, which saw its raison d'être in the creation of a modern state and was urged on by opposition calls to intervene in the realm of personal status, felt that the time was ripe to make some changes. It tried to sweeten the pill of encroaching on 'ulama' expertise by indicating that state intervention in family matters and response to demands for reform would remain in the realm of Islamic law and by prescribing consultation with the 'ulama'. Moreover, by refraining from requiring registration of marriage and divorce in state courts, the government indicated its acknowledgment of all procedures made by the 'ulama' outside its courts. The harsh construction of women citizens was part of the government's attempt to minimize conflict and subvert the anticipated argument of the 'ulama' that gender hierarchies would be endangered and the social order threatened.

The government, however, was not ready for the vehemence of 'ulama' response, nor was it willing to risk a full-fledged conflict. The proposal was abandoned, and between 1952 and 1958 there seems to have been no effort to pass it or any similar proposal. Women were left unprotected from harsh treatment by male guardians and husbands and from uncompromising rulings by religious clerics who constructed them as subordinate and dependent. In abandoning its attempts to introduce a personal status code, the government had only reemphasized the marginalization of Iraq's female citizens.

3

POLITICS, ELECTION LAW, AND EXCLUSION

Government gender discourse, as it emerged from the legal system of the new Iraqi state, left female citizens unprotected. Turning to the political system, we find that government discourse marginalized them even further, excluding them from formal politics altogether. The Constitution and Electoral Law during the mandate, which set the rules of the game for the formal political arena, prescribed that female citizens of the nascent state would not receive the right to vote. This prescription remained unchanged until the monarchy fell.

This chapter explains why women were disenfranchised throughout the Hashemite period. It delineates the huge obstacles that stood in the way of altering the first Iraqi Constitution, emphasizing the entanglement of the efforts to gain political rights for women with the broader struggle to effect change in the political order. Both opponents and supporters of women's suffrage weighed in on the issue. The government, concerned by the prospect of rocking the political boat, employed a strategy that would avoid distancing its conservative supporters who opposed the idea while simultaneously placating the opposition that favored it. In line with its modernity discourse, government strategy required women to exhibit signs of "progress" as a prerequisite to receiving rights. What facilitated this tack was the fact that supporters of women's suffrage shared with those opposing enfranchisement certain assumptions that constructed women as ill prepared—not yet ready—for political participation and reception of full citizenship rights.

THE ELECTORAL SYSTEM AND WOMEN'S EXCLUSION

The Western-style political system designed by the British for Iraq was delineated by the Iraqi Constitution. The Constitution had been drafted and redrafted starting in 1921 but was not promulgated until March 1925. Iraq was to function as a constitutional monarchy, with a king, cabinet, two legislative chambers, and democratic rights for the populace. In practice, for decades the constitutional system allowed Britain, the royal family, and Sunni former Ottoman officers effectively to control formal politics. The Constitution gave the British-backed king the power to select or dismiss the prime minister, appoint members of the Senate, and call general elections.

From the outset, Iraqi women were denied not only the option to hold elected office, but even the fundamental right to vote. Although the Constitution stated that all Iraqis were equal as pertained to both rights and obligations, two other articles in the document restricted this provision to men only. Article 36 required that the Chamber of Deputies be composed on the basis of one deputy for every twenty thousand male inhabitants; Article 42 stipulated that any Iraqi male who had reached the age of thirty and who was not disqualified by certain provisions stated in the Constitution could be elected as a deputy.[1] The Electoral Law for the Chamber of Deputies, published in 1924, interpreted these clauses to mean that only males could be electors and deputies.[2]

There is no evidence that British officials involved in the different stages of preparing the Constitution and election laws entertained any possibility other than male-only suffrage.[3] This should come as no surprise: in Britain itself, women's suffrage was instituted only at the end of World War I; even then, it was limited to women older than thirty who met minimum property qualifications. Full electoral equality was attained in Britain only in 1928. Moreover, even Gertrude Bell, who was among the British officials who joined the civil administration of Mesopotamia in 1916 and later became Oriental secretary to the civil commissioner in Iraq, was active in the British antisuffrage movement in the first two decades of the century. According to her biographers, Bell saw herself as equal to any man, but she was convinced that most women were not. Ignoring that the privileges she enjoyed were given only to an elite few, she blamed women for their own lack of achievements. Although she would reportedly be amused later in life by her earlier stance, she and her colleagues had believed that gender roles should be fundamentally different: women were supposed to rear children; men were supposed to run the country. Only men, they believed, "had the sound judgment to rule the colonies, to determine foreign policy and to decide matters of the constitution; therefore only men should have the right to cast a ballot."[4]

Bell may have eventually changed her mind regarding women's vote in Britain, but there is no evidence that she sought such a change in Iraq. On the contrary, when the British authorities opened a school for girls in Baghdad in January 1920, Bell made a speech in Arabic in which she made it clear that the new school's goal was not to produce socially, economically, or politically active female citizens, but rather "to create proper mothers."[5] These remarks were well aligned with the notion of British colonial administrators in Iraq and neighboring countries regarding women, especially mothers, who, it was believed, needed to undergo a "transformation." To the British administrators, women were not destined to influence politics as an electoral force, but to affect it by constructing the proper mindset among the country's male subjects. Lord Cromer (Evelyn Baring), the British consul-general in Egypt, a personal friend of Bell and a fellow opponent of women's suffrage in Britain, stated that "the position of women in Egypt, and in Mohammedan countries generally is, . . . a fatal obstacle to the attainment of that elevation of thought and character which should accompany the introduction of European civilization, if that civilization is to produce its full measure of beneficial effect." He thus concluded that "the obvious remedy would appear to be to educate the women."[6] British reports touching on women's education in Iraq similarly stated that "obscurantist mothers" could do more to depress the family than "enlightened fathers" could do to "elevate it."[7] The moral, political, and economic transformation sought by the British in Muslim countries, as Timothy Mitchell notes, required a transformation of the household. Through the creation of "proper mothers," the political power hoped to "penetrate that 'inaccessible' space" of the household and commence working "from the inside out."[8] In practice in both Egypt and Iraq, however, British authorities did not pursue an extensive promotion of women's education or training for mothers.[9] The education system characterizing mandatory Iraq was preoccupied more with creating educated mothers of the future cooperative elite than with educating all Iraqi mothers.[10] The British notion of women as unfit for the preparation of the country's future citizens, let alone full participation in state affairs, and the singling out of modern education as a means of transferring women from the realm of "backwardness" to the realm of "progress" had lasting effects, however.

That the election laws left women out of the Iraqi formal political arena was only one manifestation of an electoral system that actually facilitated the exclusion of all but an elite few from the seats of power.

The Electoral Law, as mentioned earlier, excluded the lower class, men younger than thirty, and women from serving in Parliament; division of the country into three electoral circles, with weight given to rural areas, made it difficult for urban politicians who opposed the political elite to be elected. Moreover, the two-step procedure allowed for a considerable amount of government meddling in the election process: the government not only provided lists of candidates to the secondary electors but also subverted any attempt to oppose its nominees.[11]

This electoral system naturally met with protest; the demand for women's political enfranchisement immediately became entangled in a broader struggle. As early as the 1920s, an effort was made to revise the Electoral Law to prevent government interference in the election process. Critics decried not only the overrepresentation of certain groups in Parliament, such as the shaikhs, but also the underrepresentation of others. The legal provisions depriving women of political rights had been challenged from the moment the draft of the Constitution was discussed by the Constituent Assembly in 1924. When the assembly began its work, Paulina Hassun, publisher of *Laila*, the first women's magazine to appear in Iraq, appealed to Assembly members in her magazine, calling on them not to overlook the importance of women's rights. Participation in democratic life, she emphasized, was not a right that belonged to men alone.[12] According to one account, during the Assembly discussions, Member Amjad al-'Umari demanded that the word *male* be erased from both the Constitution and the Electoral Law in preparation for the possibility that women be allowed to vote in the future.[13]

It is also noteworthy that some simply ignored the prohibition set by the Electoral Law. C. J. Edmonds, who served as political officer and later as adviser to the Iraqi Ministry of the Interior, recalled in his book on northeastern Iraq: "Near Rowanduz there was another lady, well-known to Political Officers, named Fatima Khan who, after the death of her husband, administered a group of eight villages; she transacted every kind of business with the Government herself and was regularly chosen by the villagers to vote on their behalf at the parliamentary elections, although the law said quite clearly that only males were entitled to take part either as primary or secondary electors."[14]

From the 1930s through the mid-1940s, criticism that the Electoral Law had permitted the government's too rigid control of the elections and did not allow adequate representation of the people continued, as did the demand to include the lower classes and women in formal politics. In 1934, a group of women applied to the Ministry of the Interior for a permit to organize a women's club "to encourage women in the exercise of their rights political and otherwise."[15] Another account points to a similar endeavor the following year, this time by a group of "Communist and Democratic" women. Both the ICP and the leftist al-Ahali group announced their support for women's political rights in their publications.[16] During this period, parliamentary committees were appointed to mull over substituting direct for indirect elections, dividing the country into smaller electoral districts, giving representation to trade unions, and announcing the date of elections and candidates' names publicly in advance. Nevertheless, no amendments were introduced.[17]

After the end of World War II, however, the government and Crown Prince 'Abd al-Ilah, regent of Iraq for King Faisal II, realizing how unpopular they had become for their cooperation with the British during the war, enacted a policy of liberalization. During the short term of Prime Minister Tawfiq al-Suwaidi, who was chosen to implement the new policy, the establishment of new political parties was permitted and a new Electoral Law was introduced. The law annulled the division of the country into three electoral circles, replacing them with one hundred electoral districts, thus making it easier for urban politicians to get elected. Voters were no longer required to be taxpayers, although candidates were still required to deposit a sum of one hundred Iraqi dinars, which could be forfeited if too few votes were obtained. The law retained the system of two-stage elections, but only one hundred primary voters were now needed to elect a secondary elector. Although the issue of women's political rights was raised in parliamentary debates concerning the new law, the principle of male suffrage was maintained, and the number of deputies an electoral circle could elect was still to be determined according to the number of male inhabitants.[18] The new law did not prevent government intervention. In the 1947 elections, for example, district governors were summoned to the capital and provided with a list of candidates who should be elected.[19] Opposition mounted; during the 1948 *wathba*, the popular uprising that followed the signing of the Portsmouth Agreement to prolong the Anglo–Iraqi Treaty, one opposition party's demands was free elections. The active participation of many women in the demonstrations and strikes of the *wathba* prompted opposition leaders to proclaim their support for women's suffrage.[20]

Starting in the early 1950s, middle-class women became a pressure group demanding political rights. The Iraqi Women's Union, the main women's organization that was authorized by the government, petitioned senior state figures and met with MPs and government officials, often the prime minister himself; it published its demands in the press and initiated special activities to promote their cause. (I discuss activists' efforts to gain political rights more thoroughly in chapter 5.)

At the beginning of 1951, thirty deputies presented a motion in the Chamber of Deputies to enact a new Electoral Law based on direct elections. In response, twenty-eight other deputies proposed revising the existing law "on the basis of past experiences and new circumstances."[21] After four parliamentary sessions in which the idea of granting women the right to vote was raised, the first motion was rejected.[22] In mid-1952, minor changes were introduced to the 1946 law; nevertheless, the growing demand for free, direct elections and universal suffrage was still ignored. Furthermore, a new clause set penalties for anyone making "defamatory" statements on the conduct of the elections.[23] The amendment spurred much criticism among the opposition parties; their determination to bring about free and direct elections was one of the causes of the 1952 uprising (intifada). To suppress the intifada, martial law was announced, all political parties were banned, and political leaders arrested. However, at the same time, a committee was appointed to draft a new elections law; in December 1952, an electoral decree was promulgated that provided for direct elections.[24] The idea of women's rights was again raised in Parliament in the early 1950s, but the electoral decree, or the provision later added to it, did not enfranchise women as some claimed.

On the contrary, it emphasized that the right to vote was reserved, as before, for men alone.[25]

As noted in the introduction, the first direct elections, conducted in January 1953 under martial law, were once again rigidly controlled by the government. Less than half of the seats were actually contested. According to historian ʿAbd al-Razzaq al-Hasani, even Jamil Midfaʿi, who became prime minister following these elections, noted that some of the indirect elections had been conducted better than the direct ones.[26]

The next elections, however, held in June 1954, were considered the freest elections in the monarchy period. The election resulted in the loss of the controlling majority by the party of the powerful Nuri al-Saʿid. But within two months al-Saʿid returned as prime minister, immediately repressing all political activities. In elections that September, most deputies retained their seats because no opposition was present.[27]

From September 1954 through March 1958, there were no elections at all in Iraq. Yet the end of the period saw some developments with regard to women's suffrage. The formation of the United Arab Republic in February 1958, uniting Syria and Egypt, prompted the formation, as a defensive measure, of the Arab Union composed of monarchial Iraq and Jordan. This union required that certain amendments to the Iraqi Constitution be introduced. An opportunity was thus created for amending those articles on which the elections laws had been based, which had ruled out the possibility of women's suffrage. In March 1958, the Parliament approved an amendment to the Constitution; it stated that the Iraqi Constitution may be revised within a year and would include the granting of political rights to educated women.[28] But the promise to enfranchise women never materialized under the monarchy, which was overthrown in July.

THE "NATURE OF WOMEN" AND THE "NATURE OF POLITICS": OPPOSITION TO WOMEN'S SUFFRAGE

The Iraqi government had good reason for procrastinating before giving women political rights: the prospect of rocking the political boat was a serious source of trepidation. Opposition parties, in their quest to change the composition of the Iraqi Parliament and to undermine the socioeconomic and political order, sought to mobilize women for their cause, but on the other side an even more immediate threat was the antagonistic reaction to women's suffrage among conservative factions and religious circles, which the government had no interest in alienating.

Many members of the pro-government Parliament opposed the idea of women's suffrage. The most vocal among them presented women's participation in formal politics as incompatible both with their "nature" and with the "proper" social order and gender hierarchies. Parliaments repeatedly refused to give serious consideration to women's enfranchisement. During the parliamentary debates at the end of March and the beginning of April 1951 over changes to the elections law, for example, several deputies, among them members of al-Istiqlal Party and Sami Shawkat, who was then the head of al-Islah (Reform) Party, raised the idea of enfranchising women; the majority of the MPs roundly ignored the suggestion.[29] Yet the parliamentarians' antagonism found its expression in the press of the period. More often than not, this antagonism took the form of remarks quoted in the less "serious" sections of the newspapers. In the latter half of the 1940s, angry responses to the idea of enfranchisement were cited by the pro-government *al-Hawadith* in its gossip column "Talk, Comments, and Rumors." An example is the response by Khawwam Al ʿAbd al-ʿAbbas, an MP representing Diwaniyya, when women's rights were mentioned in Parliament during the discussion of the new elections law in 1946. Shiʿi shaikh of Bani Zurayyij who would later become a member of al-Saʿid's CUP, ʿAbd al-ʿAbbas dismissed out of hand the notion that men and women should sit together in the Chamber of Deputies, asking: "Is this not forbidden? Are we not all of Islam?"[30] Another example is the comment by Farhan al-ʿIrs, a Shiʿi landed merchant and the MP representing al-ʿAmara who would also later join al-Saʿid's party. In 1949, when educated women in Syria received the right to vote, al-ʿIrs declared that if he were a member of the Syrian Parliament, he would not agree to sit there with women. "Women are shameful. How could they possibly sit with men?" he said.[31] Another unnamed MP was quoted by *al-Hawadith* as stating that he would not run against a female candidate—if he were to win, he said, people would say he had defeated a woman, whereas if he were to lose, they would say he had been defeated by a woman. When told that this position meant he would essentially be forfeiting the race before it had even begun, he replied that he was not alone in his stance. The voters, too, he said, would not allow a woman to rule them because they would regard it as a great dishonor.[32] Reports by the press reflecting similar sentiment on the part of parliamentarians continued well into the 1950s. As late as March 1958, when the government seemed poised to approve an amendment to the Constitution so that educated women could be granted political rights, MPs were quoted as opposing the idea. *Al-Zaman*, for example, reported that during a parliamentary session on the subject, Sadiq al-Bassam, a Shiʻi MP representing Baghdad, jokingly demanded that the Constitution ensure not only the rights of women, but also the rights of men. The MPs burst into laughter, and, according to the newspaper report of that day, the most conspicuous among those laughing was Tawfiq al-Mukhtar, another MP representing Baghdad. Asked later by the reporter why he had laughed, al-Mukhtar replied: "Friends, women's rights bother me a lot, and anybody who condemns or criticizes them gives me great pleasure."[33] When then asked what he would do if a female candidate were to run against him, he stated that he would withdraw. Al-Mukhtar went even further: he and four other MPs, both Sunnis and Shiʻis, attempted to revoke the clause in the proposed amendment that gave educated women political rights.[34]

Opposition to women's suffrage also came from the clergy. Sunni and Shiʻi religious figures were in tandem on their views on the "nature of women" and women's "natural roles." Yet whereas some presented the notion of women's suffrage as a threat to the proper social order prescribed by Islam, others also pointed to the corrupt nature of the political system that made granting political rights to women futile. In 1946, after the idea of enfranchising women had been raised in Parliament, *al-Sijill*, a newspaper whose opinions reflected those of Sunni religious scholars and that defined itself as "defending the virtues of Islam," declared its strong opposition to the notion. In a front-page article titled "The Crime of Equality Between Men and Women," equality of the sexes was dismissed as the "joke of the day" and as a direct attack on the laws of nature and proper way of life. Women, it asserted, had always been and would always be both weaker than men and dependent on them. Recent events, the article continued, had proven this. Even while demanding their so-called stolen rights, women did not accept the burden and the sacrifices that needed to be made to obtain them. They called upon men to fight for them, while they stayed at home and looked at themselves in the mirror. Their pride, the article continued, pushed them to aspire to become lawyers, judges, MPs, ministers, and presidents. However, women lacked the necessary qualities for these tasks: sound judgment, a sharp intellect, and calm nerves; as Schopenhauer had said, women are lesser persons, like children, incapable of ascending beyond the mundane. Equality between men and women, the article concluded, was thus a fantasy that could not be accepted under any circumstances. It would lead to anarchy and disorder.[35]

Such opinions were reflected, too, in letters to the editor in the press of the time. For example, on 28 October 1952 one reader, a graduate of the prestigious al-Azhar University who served as imam and *khatib* in several mosques of Baghdad, sent an angry letter in response to an article in *al-Ahali* newspaper discussing "the development of the modern Iraqi woman." He assailed the effort to "push women forcefully" into politics as a plot against Islam and its traditions. He based his opposition on Qur'anic verses that, by his interpretation, delineated specific gender hierarchies and roles that were incompatible with granting women political rights.[36]

The strength of the opposition on the part of the Sunni 'ulama' can be inferred also from their reaction to the Week of Women's Rights in October 1953, organized by the Iraqi Women's Union in support of women's political rights. Activities included lectures and a symposium at the union's clubhouse, radio programs, and articles in the newspapers, all dedicated to this cause. To counteract their efforts, clerics demanded a "Week of Virtue." Their demand was accompanied by the threat of a general strike.[37] Women's rights activists complained that the government gave clerics twice the broadcasting time and reported that this Week of Virtue was used to call upon women "to stay at home." Reverberations from the Week of Virtue could be felt in an article by Sunni Nihal al-Zahawi, daughter of Amjad al-Zahawi and head of the Muslim Sisters' Society (Jam'iyyat al-Aukht al-Muslima), established in 1951. Al-Zahawi began her article by emphasizing the ways in which Islam had promoted the status of women. It made men and women equal in their creation, humanity, and value, as evident from the following Qur'anic verse: "O mankind! Reverence your Guardian-Lord, who created you from a single Person, created, of like nature, his mate, and from them twain scattered (like seeds) countless men and women; Reverence God, through Whom ye demand your mutual (rights), and (reverence) the wombs (that bore you): for God ever watches over you."[38]

Because both sexes, al-Zahawi explained, were created in a similar fashion and from one soul, they are equal in their worth and in their
humanity. Islam gave women rights that they had not dreamt of prior to
Islam—the right to inherit, the right to agree or object to marriage, and
the right to *mahr* and maintenance. Islam encouraged women to seek
knowledge and education and gave them the right to own property; draw
up business contracts; enter into business partnerships; and buy, sell, and
serve as the administrators of inheritances on behalf of minor heirs. Western women, whom Muslim women had rushed to emulate, she stressed,
had only recently received the rights Muslim women had enjoyed for cen-
turies. "Are all these rights not enough for women?" she asked, directing
her words against those women who, so she claimed, had revolted against
the religion that had protected them and raised their status. She then explained that she was referring to those Iraqi women who were demanding political rights in blind imitation of Western women. Their aspiration
to occupy high positions and hold parliamentary seats was lamentable
because it would lead to a forbidden commingling between the sexes and
the type of unrestrained liberty that Islam loathes and condemns. Politics
demands special qualifications that not even every man possesses, she argued, so how could women, who were less qualified and informed, man-
age? "Do women believe that they have greater abilities than men that
would allow them to fulfill two difficult tasks simultaneously—the task
they are interested in, and the natural task for which they were created?
Do they intend to fulfill this new task at the cost of breaking up the family and society and spreading anarchy?" Al-Zahawi did not demand that
women confine their activities to being good wives and mothers, which
she saw as "fundamental and natural roles." She also assigned to women
a role in spreading the principles of religion and strengthening religious
spirit through performing charitable acts as well as by raising donations
and providing services in times of war. She encouraged women to endeavor to implement the rights Islam had granted to women, especially
in rural areas. There was nothing to prevent women from participating
in every field of activity, she said, as long as it was compatible with their
nature and circumstances and was not in conflict with Islam and its precepts. That being the case, why should women focus their efforts on the
narrow, crowded, and problematic field of politics?[39] It is interesting to
note the similarities between al-Zahawi's position and Gertrude Bell's,

the span of years between them notwithstanding, concerning women's nature and roles.

Shiʻi religious scholars expressed their opposition to granting women political rights in similar terms. Yet for them it was not the complexity of politics that made this arena unsuitable for women, but rather the collaborative and corrupt nature of politics. At the end of 1953, at a time when the Iraqi press was preoccupied with the issue, following activists' efforts to further women's political rights, a disciple of the prominent Shiʻi *mujtahid* Muhammad Husain Kashif al-Ghita' asked him to comment on the idea. Kashif al-Ghita' responded at length. He began by saying that the Islamic shariʻa devoted a great deal of attention to women, giving them liberties that no other religion had given them as well as the highest status in society. The Qur'an devoted a sura to them and strove to ensure their well-being and to protect their rights. Similar attention had been given by Prophet Muhammad, whose first follower was a woman; he said that God created humans as social creatures who needed each other, and he distributed roles among people, giving each one of the sexes its own special tasks. Women were allotted pregnancy, birth and breastfeeding, and the most honorable task of education: if the task was successful, humanity would thrive; if corrupted, it would be marred. Mothers provide children with their first schooling. Beyond the household responsibilities, he argued, God had assigned women the role of teaching their children honesty, introducing them to the principles and pillars of Islam, and educating them to maintain cleanliness and order. What task could be greater, what occupation could be more exalted than this? he asked and proceeded to criticize those women who nonetheless sought to take up different roles. Some women, he said, wanted to receive political rights and become governors and administrative officials themselves, whereas God wanted them to rear good and proper governors and officials. Women wished to be MPs, and we want them to repair the damage the Chamber of Deputies caused. If politics, he said, had corrupted men who are strong and endowed with sound judgment, how could it not corrupt women, who were delicate, fragile, and easy to influence? To drive his point home, Kashif al-Ghita' referred to the interference in politics by ʻA'isha, the third and favorite wife of Prophet Muhammad and daughter of Abu Bakr, the first caliph (the Prophet's political successor). ʻA'isha's involvement in the conflict over the political control of the Islamic community, he stressed, when she and a couple of male allies opposed the fourth caliph, 'Ali Ibn Abi Talib, brought about the first battle in the history of Islam—the Battle of the Camel, in which Muslim armies fought each other. The battle opened the floodgates for civil wars, which brought great losses in terms of lives and property. If all the force and energy invested in these wars had been directed outside the borders of Islam, he argued, Muslims would have gained control over the entire world. He then declared that if the involvement in politics of the perfect woman, the wife of the great Prophet and the daughter of a caliph, had brought such terrible destruction to the Muslims, imagine what would happen if ordinary women were to enter politics![40]

Kashif al-Ghita' believed that women should shy away from Parliament for another reason as well. Running for Parliament was futile due to the nature of formal politics. Women wanted to enter the turmoil of politics, "but what is politics today if not deception, craftiness, lies, betrayal of the nation, haggling over the homeland and serving the imperialists?"[41] He criticized the corruption and moral decay that was spreading in society, particularly among state officials. He argued that the government—meaning the secular-oriented Sunni-dominated government—was not fighting social evils which aided imperialism in subjugating the Islamic nations. Therefore, he called upon women to fight oppression, to establish societies to aid the weak and downtrodden, and to concern themselves with finding jobs for the unemployed and caring for the sick and disabled. He also urged women to combat prostitution, alcohol consumption, and gambling. Kashif al-Ghita' thus described the role women should play in creating a politically, socially, and morally upstanding society; in society as he envisioned it, however, there was no suggestion that women's nature could enable them to play a role in formal politics.

CITIZENSHIP ON MALE TERMS:
THE SUPPORTERS OF WOMEN'S SUFFRAGE

The Iraqi government had no interest in alienating conservative supporters and religious circles on the issue of women's suffrage especially when opposition parties sought to mobilize women for their cause. At the same time, it could not ignore the growing calls to change women's status; these calls came from several directions, some quite close to home. In the early 1950s, many wives and relatives of members of the ruling elite, by way of the Iraqi Women's Union, intensified their efforts to carve out a space for women in formal politics.

Among the most vocal supporters of women's suffrage were the opposition parties. Their demand to enfranchise women was part of a general critique of the Iraqi social and political order. Some presented the granting of political rights to women as a necessary step for the creation of a true democracy in Iraq, an essential precondition for comprehensive social reform, and a prerequisite for the formation of a modern state that harnesses all of its human resources. Others, rather than presenting women's suffrage as a means of creating a liberal state, saw it as an integral part of women's liberation and the outcome of their country's liberation from imperialism and local reactionary forces. All called on women to support their cause. At first glance, the opposition's backing of women's suffrage seemed to support equal citizenship for both men and women as free individuals. A closer look, however, reveals that the opposition's rhetoric in fact laid additional stumbling blocks in women's path. The arguments they deployed to promote a change in women's status and political participation often constructed women once again as members of a collective—the family or the nation or both. More important, according to their own assertions, women's admission into full citizenship, unlike men's, would not be automatic but would depend on the fulfillment of certain terms. Implicit in their rhetoric was the assumption that women were not yet ready for the task, an assumption that played into the government's hands. Three of the main opposition parties—the Independence (al-Istiqlal) Party, the NDP, and the ICP—may be looked at as examples of such presentations.

AL-ISTIQLAL PARTY

The Istiqlal Party platform, published in April 1946, indicated the need to encourage childbirth and create "a strong generation both physically and morally," promising to care for women throughout pregnancy and help them care for the health, good nutrition, and upbringing of their children. Furthermore, it stated that the party pledged to focus on the family, "the most basic unit of the nation." Because it considered women to be "one of the pillars of the family," it promised to strive to provide for women's education, raise their social status, and "prepare them" to be good house-wives, proper mothers, and useful members of society "capable of per-forming other tasks to the extent that their talents and character allow them."[42] Women, in other words, were perceived less as individuals than as members of collectives: the family and the nation. The call to improve their status was based on the important roles they were destined to play in each. Training and education were designated as the key to women's advancement and proper performance of their familial and national ob-ligations. Women's education was implicitly set as a precondition for the fulfillment of their duties. From here, the road to determining that their education was also a prerequisite to receiving full rights was short.

What was implied in the party's platform of April 1946 became clear two months later, when al-Istiqlal published a comprehensive statement outlining its goals. The statement referred to women only in one context: their right to vote. It charged that elections in Iraq had become a farce, leading voters to shun them; this shunning made it easy for the govern-ment itself to pick the members of the Chamber of Deputies. Proper rep-resentation of the people, it said, could be secured only by general elec-tions, participation in which should be limited only by the principle of "political maturity." Educated women possessed such maturity and were thus qualified to vote.[43] Hence, education, which was not a requirement for men, was set as a prerequisite for granting women political rights.

In the late 1940s and early 1950s, women in general and educated women in particular greatly impressed the party's leaders with their po-litical savvy. During the January 1948 *wathba*, women, the most conspic-uous of whom were students, took part in the demonstrations and strikes. One of the party leaders, Muhammad Siddiq Shanshal, stated in a special interview afterward that women's involvement in the *wathba* had proven that they fully understood their patriotic obligations. Thus, it was neces-sary to consider the participation of women with special qualifications in the elections of the nation's representatives.[44] Gaining full political rights according to al-Istiqlal, however, required educated women to make an additional effort. In November 1950, another comprehensive party state-ment reiterated its support on this matter. A few days later Shanshal set out to clarify the party's position on women's suffrage in the party's mouthpiece, *Liwa' al-Istiqlal*. He quoted the party's June 1946 statement on educated women's eligibility to vote and said that since then women had demonstrated their qualification to enjoy political rights. Women not only had increased their representation in higher education and entered professional occupations but also had proved their political awareness by participating in internal and external struggles. He commended women's efforts in supporting Palestine: their participation in demonstrations, fund-raising, and the sending of clothes and aid for Palestinian refugees. Nevertheless, to him, educated, professional, and politically active women did not yet fulfill all the conditions necessary to entitle them to full political participation. He rebuked them for not doing enough for the party's cause, saying that Iraqi women, among them staunch supporters of the party, were concerned only with the larger patriotic and pan-Arab problems. Neither in organization, research, or writing, however, did they support the party's struggle for reforms in general and those affecting women in particular. The party's proposed social reforms, such as those in the fields of health and the elimination of illiteracy, he argued, would come closer to fruition if educated women would add in their support and efforts. "Our educated women should demonstrate their ability to practice these rights," he concluded, referring to their organizing and writing in support of the party, "as preparation for progressing toward exercising wider rights."[45]

It should be noted how supporters of women's political rights such as al-Istiqlal actually facilitated their exclusion from politics by setting these conditions. For the minority of educated women, the requirement to support the party's cause meant that fulfilling the hope of gaining full political rights would be postponed, though not interminably. For the illiterate—that is, most women—however, setting education as a precondition for enfranchisement spelled a likely end to their hopes for a change in status; if they thought they could see the day when they would have a say politically, that day was now buried under a pile of other issues, to be unearthed at an undetermined time in the future.

THE NATIONAL DEMOCRATIC PARTY

The NDP platform, published in 1946, saw the individual rather than the family as the basic unit of society, and women were promised emancipation and rights. The party favored state legislation that would ensure "the regulation of personal status matters, the happiness of the family and the

liberation of women." The roles it assigned to women were not the biological and ideological reproduction of the national collective, but rather
participation in national, social, economic, and political struggles.[46] At
the same time, however, the NDP, like al-Istiqlal, saw women as a "backward" sector of society in need of "advancement." The party platform
stated that women's "level" needed to be raised so that they might prop-
erly fulfill their social, political, and economic roles.[47]

Support of women's political rights was incorporated into the party's
platform in 1950, when it openly committed itself to democratic social-
ism. The new platform clearly stated that the party was seeking to liberate women and grant them citizens' political rights.[48] It did not make any
distinction between educated and illiterate women or between the right
to vote and the right to be elected. However, in other party publications
such distinctions were implicit. In the early 1950s, when the pressure to
change the election system intensified, the party's paper, *Sada al-Ahali*,
devoted several articles to the issue of women's rights in general and to
their political rights in particular. One editorial entitled "The Rights of
the Iraqi Woman" declared that women's political rights must be supported as a part of the call to liberate women from the shackles of ignorance
and backwardness and as a means to pave the way for them to work for
the benefit of society. The article pointed to two worldwide simultaneous
processes in modern times: the change in women's roles and the adoption
of democratic principles by free nations. It stated that as women began
contributing to the social and economic construction of modern societies, receiving and promoting education as well as entering the workforce
and occupying all types of occupations similarly to men, they gained the
right to participate in determining the rules and the laws regulating individual–state relations. Legislating these issues without hearing the opinion of half of the society's members, it stated, could not be considered a
response to society's true needs. Women in Iraq, too, had shown achievements in education, in the workforce, and in social welfare activities.
Thus, they were entitled to demand participation in determining policies
in these and other fields.[49] Another editorial, written in response to an
Iraqi Women's Union memorandum demanding political rights, opposed
denying women's political rights because doing so thwarted any chance
for successful social reform in the country. It is essential, the article declared, to benefit from all forces available, but the efforts of many women

in the public realm were marginalized and impeded, among them educated women who were capable of participating in "intellectually directing the country." The simplest path for educated women's participation, it stated, was through the vote in general elections.[50]

Some suggested that this stand was part of a piecemeal approach. Educated women's entitlement to the vote was brought to the fore only as a first step toward granting all women full political rights.[51] However, by taking up the cause only of the privileged minority, the NDP undermined the eligibility of the majority of Iraqi women to enjoy political rights.

THE IRAQI COMMUNIST PARTY

The ICP failed to escape similar pitfalls. Founded in 1934, it became a significant factor in Iraqi politics by the early 1940s. As noted in the introduction, the party favored independence, democracy, constitutionality, economic independence from foreign companies, distribution of land to peasants, labor unions and labor laws, as well as education and health for everyone. The party's platform—or, more accurately, the party's National Charter, published in 1944—stated that the party would struggle on women's behalf "as citizens" to grant them equal political, social, and economic rights.[52] It was nowhere stated that their education level should be raised in order to transform them into productive members of the family or society, and "advancement" was not set as a prerequisite for obtaining full rights. The party believed that the achievement of real citizenship rights in Iraq, for both men and women, entailed an intense joint struggle to change the existing political, economic, and social order. However, in this context, women's ability to act as free and equal political agents was called into question, and differentiations among women were again made.

In his famous article published on the occasion of International Women's Day on 8 March 1944, Yusuf Salman Yusuf ("Fahd") argued that a common enemy prevented both women and the country from being liberated. Iraq had lost its sovereignty to imperialism, which fortified its position by allying with reactionary forces and reinforcing backward customs. He thus urged women to join the struggle for liberation. Their struggle was two pronged: nationalist and feminist. Women should pursue their "own particular issues" as well as the nationalist cause. Fahd's

instructions for the leaders of the women's movement—or, as he called
them, "women of awareness"—were extremely thorough. They were to
organize, to form cells in high schools and higher education institutions
in order to recruit young women, to encourage young educated women
to extend education to illiterate women in order to mobilize them for the
struggle for liberation, and to infiltrate existing women's societies and
turn them into mass organizations serving thousands of women and children. He also encouraged them to publish a newspaper and establish a
clubhouse where all women could receive an education and attend lectures in order to make the largest possible number of women aware of
women's issues. At the same time, he called upon them to participate in
national struggles by organizing women's demonstrations and petitions
and to support any nationalist group promising the defense of women's
rights.[53] Nowhere in Fahd's speech were "women of awareness" given
an opportunity to define their own goals or means of participation in the
struggle for their and their country's liberation. According to a Communist activist who worked with Fahd, this International Women's Day was
not the only occasion female party members were instructed—rather than
consulted—on how they should perform the main role assigned to them:
the mobilization of the masses of women to the party cause. Fahd supervised and directed the first Communist women's cell, set up in 1946.[54] He
not only accorded himself the role of guiding women but at the end of his
1944 speech also instructed "men of awareness" and loyal male citizens
to assume a similar guiding role with regard to their female relatives. His
instructions and actions reflected again a perception of women as backward. Male guidance was set as a precondition for the proper participation of "women of awareness" in the struggle that eventually would lead
them to liberation, equal rights, and full citizenship.

Supporters of women's political rights, as these three examples demonstrate, shared with opponents doubts concerning women's competence
for the task. The naysayers believed that women were unfit for politics,
and advocates agreed on the need to educate women, "raise their level,"
or guide them as a precondition for political participation. This shared
assumption concerning women's incompetence left the door wide open

for the deferral of women's suffrage, and the government eagerly used this opening to serve its purposes.

WOMEN'S RIGHTS AND THE TACTIC OF "GRADUAL MODERNIZATION"

Granting women political rights was a potential liability for the Iraqi government because it might alienate pro-government MPs, while drawing opposition from the *'ulama'*. Allowing women to vote en masse also had the potential to destabilize the political status quo as opposition parties endeavored to mobilize them for their cause of changing the composition of Parliament and undermining the existing socioeconomic and political order. Faced with a growing demand to enfranchise women, however, the government saw an advantage in responding or at least in giving the impression it was responding to demands. To this end, it invoked the notion of "gradual modernization."

"Gradual modernization" was an important part of post–World War II governments' platform in Iraq, most notably those governments headed by Nuri al-Sa'id. This theme merged well with the general aspiration to transform Iraq into a modern state. Indeed, a discourse of modernity, promising a better social, economic, and political future for all, was a salient aspect of Hashemite Iraq. Successive governments highlighted their interest in Iraq's becoming "modern" and promised "progress" through reforms in all aspects of life. Al-Sa'id's CUP championed a fundamental and comprehensive "awakening" through a series of far-reaching social, economic, and political reforms.[55]

The prime minister and his associates made it clear, however, that rapid changes would be impossible—that reforms would be introduced only gradually, taking into consideration the country's "reality and its possibilities." A balanced reform movement, they contended, required stability and should aim at adopting what is good in Western civilization while preserving what is best in Iraq's own heritage.[56] The linkage between the country's "reality and its possibilities" and "reform" opened many possibilities for staving off reform. It enabled the government to decide which developments should occur or what change one particular section of society ought to exhibit before reforms affecting it could be introduced. This linkage, as shown in chapter 1, provided justification for preserving the TCCDR and for refraining from touching detrimental practices affecting women. It was now used to perpetuate an exclusive political system and to hinder women from gaining political rights. Spurred by objections raised in religious circles, the government could argue that Iraq was not ready for such a change; and buttressed by the consensus among many intellectuals, according to which women were unfit or at least still unfit to take part in politics, it could easily claim that most women were not ready for such a reform.

Al-Saʿid, the "arch-politician" of the monarchy period, was the most conspicuous in making this linkage to subvert the struggle for women's political rights. Generally speaking, the roles he assigned to women over the years corresponded to a large extent to what Nira Yuval-Davis and Floya Anthias call the biological and ideological reproduction of the national collective.[57] At the end of the 1930s, for example, al-Saʿid's third government pledged to encourage marriage, promote childbirth, and provide care for mothers and children. It also promised to take care of the education of young women in a way that would allow them to fulfill their obligations toward both their families and society.[58] In 1943, on a visit to Egypt during al-Saʿid's eighth term as Iraq's prime minister, his wife, Naʿima, spelled out these obligations. The primary duty of women in contemporary Iraq, she asserted, was to produce a proper, educated next generation.[59] The CUP's 1949 platform reiterated this notion, reaffirming the party's aspiration of increasing the Iraqi birthrate and promising to establish maternity centers, provide care for mothers and children, and attend to their health and proper nutrition. Another platform article stated that the party would devote its attention to the family, which it viewed as the foundation of the nation and its most basic unit. "The woman," the article stated, "is one of two pillars of the family; therefore, the party will strive to provide her with the training and education that will prepare her to be a good and proper housewife and useful member of society, to the extent that her 'talents and character' allow."[60] It is important to note that this aspect of the platform was almost identical to al-Istiqlal's platform and yet was not incompatible with the attitudes of both Nihal al-Zahawi and Muhammad Husain Kashif al-Ghitaʾ. It placed women, as Cromer and Bell had done long before, in the realm of "backwardness," which manifested itself not only in the public, but also in the private realm, and it singled out education as a means of transferring them from the realm of "backwardness" to that of "progress."

These views on women neatly figured in the tactic of "gradual modernization." They allowed for the argument that a change in women's status was indeed required and that women's suffrage, although a just demand, required women to "develop". Education would then appear a logical prerequisite for political rights. But while the government was demanding women to exhibit "progress" as a prerequisite for gaining rights, it was far from doing its utmost to enable women this kind of "progress." Ruth Woodsmall, who visited Iraq at the end of the 1920s and again in the mid-1950s for her research on Middle Eastern women, commented, "There is unusual awareness of the necessity for universal education, government policy being based on the belief that the primary education of the people is the key to the progress of Iraq as a modern state." However, she also indicated that demand far exceeded government response. The press openly criticized the government for the delay in providing education, and parents of all economic and religious circles, villagers, and shaikhs were pressing the government for more girls' schools; compulsory education was impossible owing to the shortage of schools and teachers.[61] Indeed, the government's lack of effort was clearly reflected in the 1957 census, which indicated that under the monarchy the literacy rate even among the urban, more privileged women did not exceed 10 percent.[62] Al-Saʿid's government, in other words, could both support the demand to enfranchise women and claim that a delay was an unfortunate necessity.

Al-Saʿid repeatedly deployed the tactic of "gradual modernization" when women activists approached him with their demands. In the early 1950s, the Iraqi Women's Union redoubled its struggle for political rights and began to disseminate memorandums to this effect. The first memorandum presented was dated April 1951. The second followed in June 1952, when a revised draft of the Electoral Law was in the making.[63] Al-Saʿid responded much later, indirectly, and only after resigning as prime minister. In the midst of the riots of November 1952, which in part resulted from popular dissatisfaction with the electoral system, he issued a statement to the press in which he delineated the areas in which change was most needed. Among these areas were "women's issues." Under this heading, al-Saʿid stated that "the status of women should be raised so that they can play their part in the life of the community."[64] Rather than acknowledging women's rights as citizens, al-Saʿid referred to them as a "backward sector" that needed to attain "progress" before it could be fully admitted into society. In other words, his response to the union's demands was that women had yet to exhibit the "development" that would entitle them to the reform they had been demanding. That this was al-Saʿid's stance became apparent in 1956, when an amendment to the Electoral Law was again up for consideration. A delegation of women met with al-Saʿid, now prime minister for the seventh time, and again demanded women's suffrage. They left the meeting saying he was sympathetic and that he had expressed his support for granting women full rights and promised to study how the relevant clauses in the Constitution could be amended to enable women to participate in the political process. However, he then declared that his government "would make efforts to grant the vote only to women who had completed an elementary education, as a first step on the way towards achieving their rights."[65] While presenting women's demand as just and worthy, al-Saʿid suggested a piecemeal approach, a reform that would occur in step with development. Women would indeed be granted full political rights, but only gradually, in keeping with their "progress" and qualifications as they appeared. Only women who had completed an elementary education would be allowed to participate in the formal political process, and even they would receive, as a first step, only the right to vote. In other words, al-Saʿid was laying out a long and winding road for women to travel before they could become players in the political arena.

In early 1958, however, newly elected as prime minister yet again, al-Saʿid was compelled to respond to activists' demands because of some new developments. As noted earlier, the formation of the United Arab Republic in February 1958 prompted the establishment of the Arab Union, composed of Iraq and Jordan. This change required certain amendments to the Iraqi Constitution. It was an opportunity for women to demand the amendment of those articles in the Constitution on which the electoral regulations were based that had ruled out the possibility of women's suffrage. Activists seized the opportunity and intensified their pressure. On 6 March 1958, al-Saʿid announced that the forthcoming amendment to the Constitution "will aim at correcting the shortcomings existing in the Iraqi Constitution and at introducing new principles made necessary by Iraq's political and social development during recent years, including the granting of political rights to the women of Iraq in accordance with certain rules and qualifications suitable to the social and cultural conditions of the country."[66]

On 26 and 27 March, the Chamber of Deputies and Senate voted unanimously in favor of an amendment to the Constitution that among other things specified the qualifications to which al-Saʿid had referred in detail. The amendment stated that "the Iraqi Constitution may be amended within a year from the enforcement of this law, and this shall include the granting of political rights to educated women." It added that "if the [future] two chambers approve this [second] amendment, it shall be forwarded for Royal assent without dissolving the Chamber of Deputies [in contrast to the usual procedure]."[67]

Though presented as a reform, this amendment did not represent a departure from the tactic of "gradual modernization." On the contrary, al-Saʿid's announcement preceding the passage of the amendment was clearly couched in such terms: Iraq's social and political development made introducing new principles into the Constitution possible and necessary. And some women's progress made them eligible for political rights. The amendment itself reiterated that the bridge between "backwardness" and "progress"—the development needed as a prerequisite for citizenship—was education. Under the guise of recognizing and supporting women's political rights, al-Saʿid actually deferred their citizenship rights to some later point in time. For the educated, this future seemed near; for the illiterate masses, it was more distant. The former had to wait a year before gaining their rights, but the latter would have to attain an education or wage a new campaign to amend the Constitution yet again. A closer look at the wording of the amendment, however, reveals that even the educated were not given any solid assurances that they would enjoy full rights within a specified period of time. Rather than guaranteeing a future change in the Constitution, the amendment stated only that the Constitution "may be changed." It did not clearly state that women would receive both the right to vote and the right to be elected, nor did it specify the level of education required for gaining rights. It ensured a swift passage of any future amendment if a future Parliament approved it. Thus, it in fact left it up to a future Parliament to decide whether educated women should receive political rights, the minimum level of education required for political participation, and the nature of the rights women would be granted. In other words, had the coup d'état of July 1958 not occurred, the amendment would have been just another way of deferring the granting of political rights to women.

It is important to emphasize that the planned amendment not only deferred the granting of rights to a future time but also assured that, even if it were implemented, only a negligible number of women would enjoy political rights. The census conducted in Iraq in 1957 showed that the number of women age twenty (the legal voting age) and older who had at least an elementary-school education was less than twenty thousand. At the time, the total number of women age twenty and older in Iraq was one and a half million. Even a broader definition of "educated," one that included women who, according to the census data, could "read and write" or "read only," would thus have resulted in political rights for only five percent of all women of voting age.[68]

Women in Iraq did not receive the basic civic rights given to men until the end of the monarchy period; their construction as "backward" by successive governments had facilitated this denial. By tying education—which was insufficiently provided—to "progress" and "progress" to rights, the government made women's disenfranchisement a logical element of its gender discourse.

4

GENDER DISCOURSE AND DISCONTENT

ACTIVISM UNRAVELED

Iraqi women did not remain silent in the face of government gender discourse, as we have seen. And yet their efforts, especially their early efforts, have not been recognized as a challenge to this discourse, mainly because the restrictive nature of Iraq's political system reined in the women's movement. Like a host of other organizations, women's groups required the Ministry of the Interior's approval for their establishment. Because only associations that curbed their feminist and political goals were sanctioned, challenge to government gender discourse was not readily apparent. However, there is another reason why the full scale of women's response was difficult to trace, even for the period after World War II, when more diverse organizations appeared and women's activism became increasingly apparent. This reason is rooted in the nature of the accounts portraying the history of the women's movement that Iraqi women's activists provided and that contemporary scholarly literature later reproduced in English.

Contemporary scholarly literature published in English about the history of the women's movement in Iraq has largely overlooked the Hashemite period. Researchers have tended to treat the period in a cursory fashion as a prologue to more elaborate discussions of the condition of women and their organized activities under Ba'th rule. Moreover, available accounts, in addition to their brevity, are inconsistent. Closer examination of this literature, however, reveals two historiographical approaches. One primarily follows the development of women's activities sanctioned by the regime, focusing on the organizations and activists associated with the Iraqi Women's Union. The most representative example of this approach is Doreen Ingrams's *The Awakened: Women in Iraq*, published in 1983.[1] The second approach follows developments and organizations linked with the one-time underground League for the Defense of Women's Rights. This approach finds its most coherent expression in Deborah Cobbett's 1989 article "Women in Iraq."[2] These two competing narratives evolved in presenting the history of the women's movement of pre-1958 Iraq, and scholars have tended to base their accounts on one or the other narrative. The narratives were originally articulated by members of the Iraqi Women's Union, established in 1945, and by its rival, the underground League for the Defense of Women's Rights, founded in 1952, and scholars reproduced them, so that both activists and researchers became active participants in a "war of narratives" that would eventually leave women's history the unfortunate casualty.[3] My main aim here is to piece together the two narratives to offer a more elaborate portrayal of the evolution of the women's movement in Iraq, from its beginnings in the early twentieth century until the end of the Hashemite period.

THE ORIGINS OF THE COMPETING NARRATIVES

To trace the origins of the competing narratives and better understand their conflicting nature, however, one must return to 1945. In that year, women's societies first joined hands and formed a coalition designed to support and coordinate their activities: the Iraqi Women's Union. The union sought to increase cooperation among different women's associations in Iraq and thus to strengthen women's efforts toward improving their social, civil, and economic position as well as their health and legal status. It demanded that its constituent societies rise above sectarian, ethnic, and religious differences.[4]

The union initially demonstrated a considerable degree of tolerance for political differences. It consisted of five societies; within them were three women's branches of mixed-gender philanthropic groups: the Red Crescent Society (Jam'iyyat al-Hilal al-Ahmar), the Child Protection Society (Jam'iyyat Himayat al-Atfal), and the Houses of the People Society (Jam'iyyat Buyut al-Umma). It also encompassed the Women's Temperance and Social Welfare Society (Jam'iyyat Mukafahat al-'Ilal al-Ijtima'iyya). Many members of these groups were wives and relatives of politicians aligned with the government, but the Iraqi Women's Union also included the left-leaning Women's League Society (Jam'iyyat al-Rabita al-Nisa'iyya).

The members of these bodies, regardless of their political convictions, had many reasons to become active and work together. As the first to benefit from new opportunities in education, the labor market, and public life, these socially and politically conscious women were eager to participate in the process of state building. At the same time, all encountered many gender-based obstacles that hindered them from doing so despite their ability and skills. Many felt the discrimination with acuity because all men, the illiterate included, were allowed to participate in the elections process, whereas they, despite their education and contributions, were not.

Middle-class urban women were prompted to action also by increasingly harsh realities. From the late 1920s and continuing throughout the monarchy period, Baghdad was the prime destination of a large-scale rural-to-urban migration. The land-tenure system, which, as noted earlier, enabled registration of tribal land as the property of shaikhs, city merchants, and former tax farmers, left cultivators with small reward for their labor or, worse, forced them into debt. Hunger, sickness, natural disasters, and almost total subjugation to landlords combined to spur this migration. Migrants crowded along the outskirts of the big cities, living in small and crammed mud or reed huts that lacked even basic facilities. Poverty, disease, and illiteracy were rampant. Activists saw it as their patriotic, not to mention human, duty to alleviate these conditions. Some presented this plight as proof that their country needed women's contributions. Others, on the left, saw it as confirmation of a much further-reaching need to radically change the socioeconomic and political order.[5]

Amid the 1947 government crackdown against left-wing organizations, however, the Iraqi Women's Union yielded and removed the representatives of the leftist Women's League Society from its directorate. This dismissal split the women's movement and heralded the development of the two competing women's organizations, the Iraqi Women's Union and the eventually named League for the Defense of Women's Rights.

After 1947, the union continued working within the boundaries of the socioeconomic and political order, enjoying support from the government and the royal family. The government allocated a clubhouse and grounds, and Faisal II's mother, 'Aliya, served as the union's royal patroness.[6] The union's leaders, who hailed mostly from families of the ruling elite,[7] believed that improving women's situation could be achieved through political, social, and economic reforms, and they pledged to conduct their struggle by legal and constitutional means. The union remained throughout the period a relatively small, elitist organization loyal to the regime. Although its members saw themselves as part of a larger movement of "women's awakening" and concentrated their efforts against illiteracy, poverty, and disease—issues that affected the vast majority of Iraqi women—they did not attempt to mobilize women en masse, cautiously avoiding action that could have been perceived as critical of the regime. Although allowing criticism against imperialist aggression in other Arab countries, they refrained from explicitly protesting British influence and involvement in Iraq.

After failed attempts to revive the suppressed Women's League Society and to obtain government permission to replace it, both Communist women and others decided in 1952 to work underground and set up the League for the Defense of Women's Rights. League leaders, who came mainly from the lower middle class,[8] believed that the liberation of women required a comprehensive economic and political change. They were inspired by the influential ICP head, Yusuf Salman Yusuf, who insisted that the problems faced by urban and rural women had to be resolved within the context of the country's fundamental dilemma: Iraq had lost its sovereignty to imperialist forces, who had fortified their position by allying with local reactionaries.

League leaders argued that the genuine liberation of women could occur only with Iraq's liberation. To affect such a radical change, its members sought to mobilize "the masses of women." They tried to win over lower-class women by addressing their daily problems and by linking their hardships to the political and socioeconomic order.[9]

The union and the league were at odds ideologically and had very different relationships with the center of power. Their goals and modes of operation in promoting women's causes diverged, as did the historical accounts offered by their respective members. The union's narrative is most clearly articulated by attorney Sabiha al-Shaikh Da'ud (1912–1975), author of one of the most comprehensive books about the women's movement during the Hashemite period, *Awwal al-Tariq Ila al-Nahda al-Niswiyya fi al-'Iraq* (The Beginning of the Road Toward Women's Awakening in Iraq). A member of the directorate of two of the Iraqi Women's Union's constituent organizations since the 1940s, Da'ud became union vice president in the early 1950s.[10] The league narrative finds its most coherent expression in writings by Naziha al-Dulaimi (1923–2007), a physician and Communist and the organization's leader from its inception in 1952. In 1959, under Prime Minister 'Abd al-Karim Qasim, al-Dulaimi was appointed minister of municipalities and became the first woman cabinet member in the Arab world. From the beginning of the 1950s, she provided a wealth of accounts and analyses of the conditions of women in Iraq, keeping track of their organized activities both before and after 1958.[11]

Understanding al-Dulaimi and Da'ud's accounts as the unfolding of two competing narratives is the key to explaining contemporary scholars' different historiographical approaches. Presenting them as such enriches our perspective on the evolution of the women's movement in Iraq and begins to unveil some of the earliest scenes of activists' challenging government's gender discourse.

BEGINNINGS: 1910-1932

Both al-Dulaimi and Da'ud attributed the inspiration for the birth of an Iraqi women's movement to male intellectuals. They concurred on two figures of special importance: the poets Jamil Sidqi al-Zahawi (1863–1936) and Ma'ruf al-Rusafi (1875–1945), whose writings on behalf of women preceded the establishment of the Iraqi state.[12] Jamil Sidqi al-Zahawi's writings on women were inspired by the work of his contemporary, Qasim Amin (1865–1908), regarded until recently as the father of Egyptian and Arab feminism.[13] According to some, al-Zahawi was personally acquainted with Amin. Al-Zahawi called for the education of women and argued against veiling and seclusion, polygamy and male privileges in divorce, forced marriage, marriage without previous acquaintance, and large differences in age between spouses. Like his contemporaries in neighboring countries, he linked national development to the status of women, arguing that a nation could not expect progress when half of its population was stymied and uneducated.[14] With this in mind, al-Zahawi urged the Ottoman governor of Baghdad to open a school for girls, and, indeed, such an institution was inaugurated in 1899 with almost one hundred pupils.

In 1910, al-Zahawi published in an Egyptian newspaper an article entitled "The Woman and Her Defense," in which he chastised men's oppressive treatment of women, the use of the veil, and Muslim male privileges in marriage, divorce, and inheritance. He claimed that women's seclusion and ignorance explained the "backwardness" of Muslims in comparison to "Westerners." His article raised an outcry in Baghdad and led to his dismissal from the faculty of the Baghdad Law School (later the Iraq Law School).[15] This dismissal did not deter him. He continued to send poems supporting women's issues to Arab and Eastern women's conferences outside the country as well as to women's magazines, and he participated in the Arab women's conference held in Baghdad in 1932.[16] Those who sought to discredit him emphasized al-Zahawi's connections with the British authorities and the public support he lent to their occupation.[17] However, Da'ud, whose parents actively opposed the British occupation in 1920, managed to isolate these facts from his efforts on behalf of women. In a memorial service for al-Zahawi in March 1937, Da'ud gave a speech in which she praised him as "a supporter of Arab women." Al-Dulaimi associated al-Zahawi with what she termed the "nationalist bourgeoisie," but she avoided discussion of his political inclinations.[18]

Both activists also depicted Ma'ruf al-Rusafi as a source of inspiration.[19] He not only opposed veiling, seclusion, and forced marriages but also advocated marriage based on mutual affection. His support for the education of women was already evident in his first collection of poems, published in 1910. Linking the status of women to the woes of his "Eastern society," he argued that progress hinged on their education and advancement.[20] Although critical of the "backward" East, al-Rusafi looked to the Islamic past rather than to the Western present as a model. He argued that in Islam the pursuit of knowledge was a duty for both boys and girls, noting that 'A'isha, the Prophet's wife, was taught by Muhammad himself and became a great scholar. He challenged underlying fears of destabilizing the social status quo, declaring that Muslims should follow their ancestors and stop looking at women's ignorance as a virtue and a safeguard.[21] Al-Rusafi's opinions, like al-Zahawi's, caused a flurry in Baghdad. In response to a poem published in the newspaper al-Istiqlal in

March 1922, a fatwa was issued against him, and on one occasion he only narrowly escaped a physical attack by critics.[22]

Al-Dulaimi and Da'ud were not in agreement, however, in assessing other male figures' impact. In keeping with the nationalist government line, Da'ud emphasized supporters of women's issues from Iraq's diverse factions, listing the Shi'i *mujtahid* Husain al-Na'ini (1857–1936) and the Christian but secular-minded journalist Rufa'il Butti (1900–1956), along with al-Zahawi and al-Rusafi, who were of Kurdish or mixed origin. According to Da'ud, al-Na'ini had supported the education of women in the early years of the twentieth century and had stressed that seeking knowledge was the religious duty of every Muslim man and woman. She claimed that his opinions, unusual in Najaf and its religious surroundings, aroused a controversy that threatened to undermine his religious authority and that did silence his voice. Rufa'il Butti, Christian founder of the newspaper *al-Bilad* was, according to Da'ud, the first publisher to devote an entire newspaper page to women. Articles in his paper followed women's activities in Iraq and around the world and encouraged women to play an important role in the life of the nation and its progress.[23]

Da'ud also stressed the work of a prominent government official Sati' al-Husri (1880–1968). A former Ottoman official from Aleppo, al-Husri joined King Faisal's staff in Syria after the collapse of the Ottoman Empire and came to Iraq after the fall of the Sharifian administration in Damascus. As director-general of education between 1923 and 1927, he laid the foundations for an ordered, centralized, and elitist education system in Iraq and formulated a curriculum based on a secular understanding of Arab nationalism. Da'ud praised his promotion of education for girls "in spite of all the obstacles standing in his way." It should be noted, however, that the table of statistics included at the end of her book indicates that during the 1925–1926 school year, in the midst of al-Husri's career, only 4,053 female students attended government elementary and primary schools. British statistics corroborate Da'ud's figures but also reveal that the number of boys at these schools that year was four times as great. They also show approximately the same number of girls in the previous year and only a slight increase in the year that followed.[24] Da'ud clearly had access to the British statistics. Her praise for al-Husri was probably a subjective expression of appreciation for the education that she herself had enjoyed and for an education system that had been established in response to demands by the first Iraqi women activists, which included her mother.

Al-Dulaimi and other left-leaning league activists emphasized a different cast of characters among the early promoters of women's causes. Heading the list were the first Iraqi Marxists, led by Husain al-Rahhal (1900–1971). The Marxists' mouthpiece was the periodical *al-Sahifa*, which began publication at the end of 1924, after other newspapers refused to publish their articles. It advocated not only unveiling and education, but also women's social and economic liberation through entrance into the labor force.[25] Historian Hanna Batatu sees al-Rahhal's article "Determinism in Society" as the embodiment of the "feminist argument" put forth by al-Rahhal and his circle. It posits that there is no "natural" or "immutable" social order; rather, all social institutions are transitory in nature because they are "the product of a changing economic environment." The position of women was dictated by this "general law." According to the article, the Arab family was a vestige of feudalism, and the harem and the veil bore the imprint of a feudal system of values. The aristocracy was "able to build harems and keep so many women in them only by exploiting the labor of the people." Among the "people's class" of laboring peasants, argued al-Rahhal, the harem and the veil were unknown. When the people's class establishes its supremacy, the harem and the veil will disappear altogether, he predicted. Al-Rahhal's circle further questioned the relevance of the shari'a and its implications for the position of women in contemporary Iraqi society. This assertion and declarations such as "It is not religion that propels social life, but social life that propels religion" roused the fury of conservatives and clerics, and *al-Sahifa* was shut down.[26]

Although it is true that neither Da'ud nor al-Dulaimi saw women as the first to advocate their own cause, Da'ud brought enough evidence to suggest that women in Iraq, like their sisters in neighboring countries, were not merely passive objects of the debate.[27] She cited, for example, the teacher Zahra Khidir, who in 1918 opened a private school for girls in Baghdad.[28] In a letter to the periodical *al-Lisan* in 1919, Khidir, like al-Zahawi and al-Rusafi, linked the cause of educating women to the nation's progress. She stressed the contribution of educated mothers to the rearing of healthy, virtuous, and patriotic children—the future members of the modern nation. She rejected the proposition that female illiteracy in Iraq was rooted in Islam or Eastern culture, noting that Islam called for the education of girls and that the East had produced remarkable women throughout history. Instead, she looked for the cause in the absence of government girls' schools in Baghdad, thereby implicitly criticizing British education policy and registering one of the earliest expressions of women's challenge to the gender discourse of the rulers of Iraq.[29] When the British authorities finally opened a school for girls in Baghdad in 1920, Khidir closed her school and joined the teaching staff of the new institution. According to one source, it was her pupils, in fact, who filled the new classrooms.[30]

Yet another expression of women's challenge at this early stage can be found in Da'ud's work. When Gertrude Bell invited prominent women from Baghdad to a tea party on May 1919 and asked for their opinion regarding planned British reforms in Iraq, Da'ud's mother, Na'ima Sultan Hamuda, declared in the name of all the women present that any reforms not giving due consideration to women would be deficient, and this included education for girls.[31]

Both Da'ud and al-Dulaimi present the 1920 revolt against the British occupation as a defining moment for the women's movement.[32] Catalyzed by the announcement that the San Remo Conference had awarded Great Britain the mandate for Iraq, the uprising was instigated by a coalition of nationalists in Baghdad, Shi'i religious leaders of the Holy Cities, and mid-Euphrates tribal leaders. Although their motivations differed, these groups were united in their desire to shed British rule. Women participated in both urban and rural areas. In Baghdad, a women's committee was organized, headed by Na'ima Sultan Hamuda, wife of Ahmad al-Shaikh Da'ud, who was among the Iraqi leaders arrested during the revolt and thereafter exiled. The committee explained the revolt's goals to women, encouraged their support, and collected donations of cash and jewelry. Their activities were acknowledged in a letter from the leaders of the uprising.

Baghdadi women appealed to Bell regarding the fate of nationalist detainees and participated in mass funeral processions, thereby transforming the funerals into nationalist demonstrations. Dressed in black and veiled, they shouted nationalist slogans against British imperialism. In the countryside, rural women accompanied fighting men to battle and urged them on. They also carried equipment and provided supplies. There have been claims that women actually participated in combat, but details of when and where they did so were not provided. The 1920 revolt, according to both al-Dulaimi and Da'ud, spurred the awakening of women in Iraq—rousing their hopes, uniting their voices with those demanding freedom and sovereignty for their country, and prompting them to act. The revolt, they claimed, not only manifested women's nationalist awareness but also demonstrated their willingness to make sacrifices for their country. It broke down barriers that had prevented them from realizing their talents and capabilities. Their participation encouraged more positive attitudes toward women and prompted "progressive" elements to call for the acknowledging of women's roles in the development of society and for giving them the rights that were their due.[33]

The period following the revolt saw the establishment in 1923 of the first Iraqi women's organization, the Women's Awakening Club, but the two activists treated its formation differently in their narratives. Da'ud saw its appearance as an important step in the development of the women's movement, but al-Dulaimi mentioned it as a product of "nationalist bourgeoisie" efforts, dedicated to educated women, incapable of withstanding social and political pressures, and unable to bring about a real "women's awakening."[34] The members of the Women's Awakening Club were, indeed, mostly wives and relatives of the political and intellectual elite. Its president was Asma' al-Zahawi, sister of the poet Jamil Sidqi al-Zahawi; the vice president was Na'ima al-Sa'id, sister of the then–prime minister Ja'far al-'Askari and wife of Nuri al-Sa'id, minister of defense and later prime minister; the secretary was Mari, wife of the Christian author and translator 'Abd al-Masih Wazir; and the treasurer was Fakhriyya al-'Askari, wife of Ja'far al-'Askari and sister of Nuri al-Sa'id. Others included Rafiqa al-Hashimi, the wife of Yasin al-Hashimi, prime minister in 1924; Fatima Jawdat, wife of the interior minister 'Ali Jawdat; Jamila al-Husri, the wife of Sati' al-Husri, director-general of the Education Ministry, and his niece, Badi'a Afnan, wife of Husain Afnan; Na'ima Sultan Hamuda, Da'ud's mother; and publisher Paulina Hassun. The club also numbered British women among its honorary members: British Oriental secretary Gertrude Bell, author E. S. (Ethel Stefana) Stevens, wife of Edwin Drower, who was adviser to the Ministry of Justice; and Agnes Esme Dobbs, wife of High Commissioner Henry Dobbs. In all, there were about sixty members.[35]

The Women's Awakening Club's objectives were to guide women and girls toward recognizing "their true identity," to encourage "their enlightenment" in order to improve their social and cultural circumstances, and to prepare them to perform the duties "their nation expected of them" to help themselves, their families, and their homeland. It sought to expand and improve the education of girls and young women and offered special classes in economics, hygiene, childcare, and housework. The club concentrated its practical efforts in three fields: opening literacy classes for women, sewing clothes for the poor, and educating orphan girls. Members met every other week and listened to lectures and speeches. Symposiums were held once or twice a year. Free sewing classes were also offered.[36] At first, meetings were held in the members' residences; a house was later rented for the club's activities. Early in 1924, members of the club were invited to a meeting with King Faisal and Queen Huzaima, at which time the king expressed his support as well as his intent to allot them a permanent facility. Activities were financed by membership dues and donations, but whether the royal family ultimately made good on its promises is unknown.[37]

Da'ud marked the 1923 appearance of the Women's Awakening Club as a significant first step in the development of the women's movement. As a daughter of one of the club's founding members and heir to its legacy, she was concerned with how its establishment and later demise were portrayed. She took issue with E. S. Stevens, an honorary member of the club, regarding her description in 1929 of Asma' al-Zahawi as the moving spirit behind the movement.[38] Probably speaking for her mother as well, Da'ud saw the excessive credit Stevens attributed to al-Zahawi as a distortion of history. She argued that the idea for the club had ripened simultaneously in the minds of a number of Iraqi women and noted that the club founders had met several times before al-Zahawi joined them.[39] Da'ud also countered versions of the club's history that overemphasized external intervention as a major factor leading to its foundation.[40] She acknowledged that in the early 1920s women had been greatly affected by the news about women's struggles that emanated from Turkey, Egypt, and Syria and that Egyptian women's participation in the 1919 nationalist struggle had had a profound impact.[41] She stressed however, that the club was the initiative of Iraqi women alone.

Da'ud was also annoyed that Stevens refused to see the connection between opposition aroused by the club and the decline in its activities. Stevens had written that the establishment of the club had produced an immediate outcry. "Reactionaries fulminated against it in the newspapers, die-hards appealed to the government to scotch the movement in its infancy." Iraqi society was on the verge of *sufur* (unveiling), they said, "and Muslim homes were threatened by Western abomination."[42] Stevens, however, saw no correlation between this response and the decline of the organization, which she blamed on a lack of enthusiasm and an incompetent steering committee. These claims Da'ud rejected. She pointed out that according to the club president, Asma' al-Zahawi, a group of clerics had objected to the name "Women's Awakening Club"; they registered official complaints with the government and demanded that the word *awakening* be removed. Al-Zahawi refused, arguing that "awakening" was one of the club's manifest aims. A prominent club member, whose name was not mentioned, explained that the club's adversaries had misinterpreted the word *awakening*, assuming that it called for discarding the veil rather than working for the advancement of the nation, caring for orphans, and helping the needy. Despite this explanation, the authorities, al-Zahawi recounted, nonetheless supported the club's opponents, which led to its disbandment.[43]

The importance of Da'ud's remarks goes beyond using members' own voices to set the record straight concerning the club's demise. In describing members' insistence on having their own interpretation of the term *women's awakening* and their reluctance to succumb to government and conservative pressure, she appears to have documented one of the earliest organized efforts made by women's activists in Iraq to challenge their government's gender discourse.

The inauguration of the Awakening Club's activities in October 1923 was accompanied by the appearance of the first women's journal in Iraq, *Laila*, issued over a period of two years. Although the club did not own the magazine, its publisher, Paulina Hassun, was a member, and it expressed many of the club's ideas. Da'ud presented *Laila* as the first modern women's magazine in Iraq that succeeded, within a short period of time, in becoming a true mouthpiece for women's demands. The magazine urged members of the Iraqi Constituent Assembly to improve women's status and to recognize their democratic rights. It also advocated education for girls and concerned itself with the upbringing of children and women's health, especially during pregnancy.[44] Al-Dulaimi, in contrast, acknowledged the existence of the publication only in passing, presenting it as the magazine of the ineffective Awakening Club,[45] thus underscoring the difference between her view and Da'ud's.

Finally, both women depicted advancements in the education of Iraqi women during these early days as a victory for those advocating change in women's status and as an impetus for the establishment of the women's movement. Making progress in this area, however, demanded an intense struggle. Families who sent their daughters to the government school in Baghdad received anonymous threatening letters, and in the early stages students were pelted with stones.[46] Nevertheless, the obstacles notwithstanding, al-Dulaimi and Da'ud noted similar milestones and indicators of progress in the development of women's education: the establishment in 1920 of a government school for girls by British authorities; a rise in the number of government elementary and primary schools for girls to twenty-seven schools in 1926 and forty-five in 1930; an increase in the number of Iraqi women teachers who were graduates of the Iraqi teaching-training institutions; the opening of a secondary school for girls during the 1929–1930 school year; and the entrance in the 1930s of the first women to the medical college and law school in Baghdad.

Da'ud credited these achievements to King Faisal, who held women's education "close to his heart," and to Sati' al-Husri. In contrast, league members emphasized the backing of women's causes by "nationalist and progressive elements."[47]

FROM THE END OF THE MANDATE TO THE END OF WORLD WAR II

The end of the mandate marks a further divergence in the two activists' historiographical trajectories, yet it is noteworthy that neither acknowledged receipt of formal independence as a turning point. Al-Dulaimi placed developments affecting working-class women and the role played by the ICP and leftist women in the foreground of her narrative. She argued that the 1930s marked the awakening of the Iraqi working class, which started defending its rights and participating in the nationalist and democratic struggle. Working-class women were influenced by this struggle, and their awareness grew. During this time, the ICP included women's liberation in its platform and inculcated the idea that women's social and democratic rights would be realized only through the struggle of the female masses. It was the ICP, together with women "communists and democrats," who set out to organize the masses of women and rally them to the nationalist and democratic cause. As noted earlier, a group of "communist and democratic" women subsequently approached the government in 1935 with a formal request for permission to establish a women's organization; their request was denied. Al-Dulaimi contended that until the early 1940s the only open, serious discussion of the liberation of women in Iraq "based on proletarian ideology" was to be found in the Marxist and Communist press.[48]

It is surprising that al-Dulaimi did not elaborate on the early Communist platform regarding women and referred only to women's affiliation with Communist activity in the mid-1930s. Other sources, however, give more details. In 1929, Communists from Nasiriyya and Basra established the Association of Liberals (Jam'iyyat al-Ahrar), or, as it soon became known, the Irreligious Liberal Party (al-Hizb al-Hurr al-Ladini). In its program, which, according to Batatu, was the earliest Iraqi statement of Communist intent on record, the association included among its aims "liberating the Arab woman from the fetters of degradation and ignorance" and working "for the separation of religion from all temporal affairs" such as politics, education, and "family life."[49] Batatu depicts the Youth Club (Nadi al-Shabiba), where the Association of Liberals was first introduced in 1929, as a center for activities of the earliest Communist circle in Basra, "a club in which the young men of the town foregathered to discuss the varied new-fashioned theories that were beginning to percolate into Iraqi social life."[50] British accounts, however, noted the involvement of women in the club's activities as well. A report from Basra stated that up to eighty people had gathered in January 1930 in an apparent attempt to reorganize the club as a Communist organization, among them twelve women teachers. Two of the meeting's initiators were 'Abd al-Hamid al-Khatib and Zakariyya Elias Duka, members of the earliest Communist circle in Basra. During the meeting, Duka spoke about the status of women in the East, saying that they had always been oppressed by men and insisting that only in those countries in which women were granted their rights had progress been made. He advised the women of Iraq to "follow their sisters and obtain their rights."[51]

Da'ud did not see the 1930s as a particularly important or decisive historical period for Iraqi women. She therefore did not discuss major achievements of the time in a chronological context. For example, she mentioned the appearance of women's magazines, such as *al-Mar'a al-Haditha* (The Modern Woman, 1936), *Fatat al-'Iraq* (The Young Iraqi Woman, 1936), and *Fatat al-'Arab* (The Young Arab Woman, 1937), together with both the earlier *Laila* (1923) and later magazines affiliated with the Iraqi Women's Union: the Child Protection Society's *al-Umm wa-l-Tifl* (The Mother and Child, 1946); *al-Hilal al-Ahmar* (The Red Crescent, 1951) affiliated with the Red Crescent Society; and *al-Ittihad al-Nisa'i*, the mouthpiece of the Iraqi Women's Union since 1949.[52]

Da'ud likewise referred to women's organizations appearing in the 1930s as part of her discussion of later organizations. Two such organizations were the Temperance Society (Jam'iyyat Mukafahat al-Muskirat) and the women's branch of the Red Crescent Society, both eventually encompassed in the Iraqi Women's Union. The Temperance Society was established in 1937 by Sara Fadil al-Jamali[53] and was affiliated with the World's Women's Christian Temperance Union. Its initial primary aim was to combat alcoholism. However, its goals were soon expanded to include three major social ills: poverty, illiteracy, and disease. As a result, the organization eventually changed its name to Women's Temperance and Social Welfare Society. More specifically, the organization focused on antialcohol education, aid to disabled children and women prisoners, the education of young women, and occupational training. It founded a school for disabled children and opened sewing and home economics workshops for destitute women.[54] The second organization, the women's branch of the Red Crescent Society, was established in 1933 under Queen Huzaima's auspices. Until 1945, this branch was dependent administratively and monetarily on the general Red Crescent Society.[55]

Da'ud neglected to mention organizational efforts of the 1930s mentioned by al-Dulaimi, whereas al-Dulaimi played down the significance of the two women's organizations mentioned by Da'ud. For example, al-Dulaimi dismissed the women's branch of the Red Crescent Society as an association set up by "nationalist–bourgeois" circles, with limited charitable goals and membership.[56] Indeed, some scholars agreed with al-Dulaimi and depicted the women's branch, at this stage, as not much more than a sewing circle, entirely dependent on male members of the society and with no separate programs for women.[57] A survey of the available Iraqi press from the 1930s, however, contradicts this representation. In 1936, for example, the women's branch organized a series of lectures for women on first aid and childcare, given by a nurse sent to Iraq by the Red Cross. The branch operated a clinic that provided medical care and guidance for mothers and trained women to work in additional clinics the branch intended to open. The primary target of these efforts was combating infant mortality. Branch members also prepared for emergencies and disasters, and with that goal in mind they organized the collection and sewing of items of clothing.[58]

Al-Dulaimi and Da'ud concurred on the contribution of one particular prominent activist during the 1930s. They give Amina al-Rahhal, sister of Marxist Husain al-Rahhal, a place of prominence as one of the first women to represent Iraq in women's regional conferences; she took part in the first conference of Eastern Arab women held in Damascus. According to al-Dulaimi, this conference took place in 1938, but Da'ud rightly put the date at 1930. It is surprising that it is Da'ud who presents us with a detailed account of al-Rahhal's speech on that occasion. In that speech, al-Rahhal called upon Arab women to stand by men in their struggle for liberation, stressed the importance of women's domestic roles, but at the same time underscored the need for their economic independence.[59] Al-Dulaimi pointed out that in 1938 al-Rahhal was a prominent member of the ICP, but she surprisingly failed to mention that between 1941 and 1943 al-Rahhal was one of its highest-ranking members, serving on the ICP Central Committee.

Both al-Dulaimi and Da'ud discussed the establishment of the (Women's) League Against Nazism and Fascism (LANF, Jam'iyyat Mukafahat al-Naziyya wa-l-Fashiyya), which became the Women's League Society in the early 1940s,[60] but again they did not always agree on the dating of milestones in these leagues' development and viewed them from completely different perspectives. Deemphasizing their "political character," Da'ud saw their appearance as part of a natural progression; as in other organizations of that time, she claimed, a primary aspect of their mission was to raise women's "cultural level" and to combat illiteracy.[61] Al-Dulaimi, in contrast, saw the formation of the LANF as a watershed— "an indicator of the birth of a democratic women's movement in Iraq." Merely hinting at the anti-British Rashid 'Ali coup and disregarding the consequent British reoccupation of the country in 1941, she nevertheless noted that before Iraq had entered the war on the side of the Allies, the German embassy had taken advantage of nationalist anti-British feelings to promote National Socialist ideology. She pointed out that even after the embassy had been closed, sympathy for Hitler persisted, explaining this phenomenon as a conviction among some that "the enemy of your enemy is your friend." She perceived the founding of the LANF as part of an overall effort to combat Nazi and fascist ideas. At the end of the war, with the Allies' victory, the LANF changed its name and adopted a broader set of goals. Al-Dulaimi saw the primary significance of the establishment of these organizations as a reflection of the seriousness with which "the proletariat and its party" regarded the liberation of women and the creation of a nationalist democratic women's organization that would mobilize the mass of women toward the struggle for their rights, for their people, and for their homeland. At a time when the nationalist–bourgeois parties contented themselves with working through existing charitable societies and concerned themselves only with the issues of providing education, combating illiteracy, and extending help to some poor families, this approach marked, according to al-Dulaimi, a leap forward in the development of women's organizations.[62]

THE POSTWAR YEARS

The end of World War II, according to activists of the Iraqi Women's Union and the League for the Defense of Women's Rights, marked a turning point in the development of the women's movement in Iraq. Scholar Ruth Woodsmall, who in the mid-1950s interviewed women affiliated with the Iraqi Women's Union, quotes one leader as saying in reference to the postwar period: "It seemed that a flood of activities and ideals had been dammed-up, waiting for the final breakthrough."[63] Da'ud noted the increase in the number of women's organizations. She focused in particular on the establishment of the Iraqi Women's Union in 1945 and its constituent organizations, which were either created or gained momentum that year; the women's branch of the Red Crescent Society, founded in the 1930s but becoming financially and administratively independent in 1945; the women's branch of the Child Protection Society, set up in March 1945, and Sara Fadil al-Jamali's Temperance Society, which changed its name to the Women's Temperance and Social Welfare Society and noticeably expanded its activities the same year. Da'ud also gave attention to the Houses of the People Society, which opened a women's branch in

1944.[64] Al-Dulaimi saw these developments as a direct outcome of the relatively liberal political atmosphere characterizing the postwar period. She focused her attention on the left-oriented Women's League Society, the successor of the war era's LANF.[65]

In 1945, the women's branches of the Red Crescent Society, the Child Protection Society, and the Houses of the People Society as well as the Women's Temperance and Social Welfare Society and the left-oriented Women's League Society all joined to form the Iraqi Women's Union. Both al-Dulaimi and Da'ud credited the Cairo Women's Conference of December 1944 as a catalyst for this union. The Iraqi delegation to the conference included, among others, Ma'ida Najib Mahmud, who represented the Child Protection Society and was also a member of the Red Crescent Society; Rose Khadduri, who represented the Houses of the People Society; and 'Afifa Ra'uf, who spoke for the Women's League Society. Responding to the conference's call to establish unions for women's societies in all Arab states, participants returned home determined to organize themselves. The Ministry of the Interior was duly approached, meetings took place, and plans were made. Finally, in mid-1945 the Iraqi Women's Union was founded.[66]

Encouraged by regional support and the relatively tolerant political climate, women's rights activists strove to organize and to rise above differences among them, political and otherwise, to confront women's subordination and exclusion. Each of the five societies composing the union had three representatives in the executive committee, and the union required its members to rise above sectarian, racial, and religious considerations.[67]

Until 1947, not only did the Women's League Society have three representatives in the union's directorate, but 'Afifa Ra'uf, head of the society, had served since June 1946 as the union's secretary.[68] However, in 1947, with the repression of left-wing organizations, the society's gatherings, illiteracy schools, and publications were banned, and its representation in the union's directorate was cancelled. Al-Dulaimi, as a leftist, depicted this event as a defining moment in the history of the women's movement because at that point groups associated with the government took over the union, and the Women's League Society activities ceased. Da'ud, in line with her pro-government sympathies, completely ignored this moment.[69] Henceforward, Da'ud and al-Dulaimi's accounts of the women's movement increasingly diverge and exclude developments and events not directly associated with their respective organizations.

It is evident from Da'ud's account that after 1947 the Iraqi Women's Union continued as before to pursue its stated goals. It encouraged women's education; organized special lectures, films, and plays for women; and supported and coordinated the various charitable activities of its constituent organizations. Through these organizations and on its own, it aided casualties of natural disasters and supported Iraqi troops fighting in Palestine in 1948. Through protest letters sent to the United Nations and foreign representatives in Iraq, fund-raising, organization of first-aid courses, and so on, the union expressed its support of the Palestinian, Algerian, and Egyptian national struggles. In addition, as the union sought to strengthen ties with Arab and international women's organizations, it represented Iraq in Arab and international women's conferences. The union was affiliated with the International Alliance of Women,[70] a global sisterhood promoting universal suffrage and other women's rights without confronting colonialism and imperialism.

During the 1950s, union activities for women's causes gained momentum. It submitted a request to Parliament to discuss divorce and demanded a law that "would restrict divorce as much as possible."[71] It demanded that in divorce cases child custody be granted to the most competent parent. The union was responsible for inserting a clause into the law regulating juvenile courts that required judicial panels to include a woman. It strove to improve working conditions for women, notably nurses. Finally, during the 1950s the union led the struggle for women's political rights.[72]

Members of the Iraqi Women's Union and its constituent organizations saw their work as benefiting the nation in general and women in particular. Al-Dulaimi, however, like other critics of upper-class, state-supported organizations in the Middle East, depicted union activities as government controlled, elitist, and ineffectual in bringing about change for women and to the country.[73] Yet the union societies' work in combating the country's ills was not insignificant, and their contribution to the development of the country's social services should be noted. The government in fact later imitated or took over and expanded many welfare and social projects that these societies had initiated.[74] Available data regarding projects begun by the women's branch of the Child Protection Society, for example, serve to counter al-Dulaimi's criticism. The society opened several clinics in Baghdad, including one in 1946 in Shaikh Omar, a migrant slum adjoining the sewage dumps. Observers reported that disease was rampant among its poor and neglected inhabitants, with infant mortality reaching 250 per 1,000; children had only a 50 percent chance of reaching the age of ten.[75] The clinic provided fresh milk, fish oil, and clothing for babies and inoculated children against typhoid and smallpox. The number of people assisted by this clinic grew steadily, reaching about 30,000 in 1948.[76]

The women's branch of the Child Protection Society operated several other projects for urban mothers and children. In 1953, it was caring for almost 100,000 people, its representatives visiting about 4,500 homes to instruct mothers on how to breastfeed and raise their children. Almost 18,000 women attended lectures on these subjects, and more than 2,000 pregnant women received attention. The society claimed that from its inception and due to its efforts child mortality rates dropped from 33 percent in the mid-1940s to 3 percent in the mid-1950s.[77] Even if these numbers cannot be confirmed,[78] the society's contribution to decreasing urban child mortality cannot be ignored. Moreover, when a maternal and childcare section was created in the Health Ministry, officials approached the women's branch of the Child Protection Society to work through one of its centers.[79] Through such actions, Iraqi Women's Union activists not only improved the lives of many women but also asserted women's competency.

When elaborating on developments that occurred after World War II and the 1947 split, activists in the League for the Defense of Women's Rights emphasized events leading to the establishment of the league in 1952 and its underground activities. Although al-Dulaimi and other league members acknowledged the Communist Party connection, they denied persistent claims that the league was merely a front organization for the ICP.[80] The first Communist women's cell, the Women's Committee, was set up in 1946 and was supervised and directed by the party's secretary-general, Yusuf Salman Yusuf. Women active in this and similar cells were arrested and sentenced with up to life imprisonment.[81] Yet al-Dulaimi refrained from mentioning these cells among the developments leading up to the league's establishment. She pointed to the January 1948 *wathba* and the participation of peasant and working-class women as well as female students in its demonstrations and strikes as the impetus that propelled the resumption of efforts to organize women. She believed that the sheer number of women who were involved in this event and who became active afterward heralded a democratic women's organization that would combine the struggle for women's rights with the struggle for nationalist and popular demands.

After several years of government persecutions of left-leaning activists, an attempt was made in 1950 to revive the Women's League Society on the grounds that it had never officially been dissolved even though its membership in the Iraqi Women's Union had been cancelled. Its former head, 'Afifa Ra'uf, was asked to reassume her old role, but she declined. About thirty women—students, university graduates, and housewives, both Communist and non-Communist—convened to draft a program and to tackle the bureaucratic requirements for the establishment of a new society. An application to form an organization, Women's Liberation (Tahrir al-Mar'a), was finally submitted in 1951.[82] Taking advantage of the grace period afforded until the ministry made a final decision on the application, the group published articles outlining the new organization's goals in an effort to rally support. According to al-Dulaimi, the press published letters from all parts of Iraq with hundreds of signatures in support of the organization. A month later, however, the government denied the application.[83]

Iraqi Communist activists wrote conflicting accounts of what happened next. This confusion reflects the debate about the role of women in founding the League for the Defense of Women's Rights and the degree of ICP involvement. According to al-Dulaimi, after the government denied the application to form a new organization, women petitioners and others who joined them, both Communist and non-Communist women, met to discuss their future actions. After a heated debate, they decided to continue their work underground, changing their organization's name from Women's Liberation to the League for the Defense of Women's Rights.

However, Baha' al-Din Nuri, then secretary-general of the ICP, rejected al-Dulaimi's contention that it was women primarily who had initiated either the legal organization or the underground organization. He maintained that the idea for both came from the party, which had encouraged women to appeal to the Ministry of the Interior. When their appeal was rejected, the women Communists turned to the party and were instructed to resume activities as an underground organization.[84] Bushra Perto,

Communist league member, gave a third version of the league's history. She asserted in an interview in 1997 that the league was not a Communist organization, although Communists were among its leaders. According to her version, Communist members did receive instructions, which they endeavored to promote, but the party did not dictate decisions and actions.[85]

The League for the Defense of Women's Rights fought for national liberation and democracy and opposed "imperialist schemes" such as the Baghdad Pact. It campaigned for world peace, education, health and welfare, and women's rights. Many among the league's leaders believed that women's liberation would follow Iraq's liberation from imperialism; the marginalization of women would be resolved once the socioeconomic and political order it supported was changed. The league sought to include women from all social classes, religious and political beliefs, and ethnic communities. To win over "the masses of women," members addressed women's daily problems, drawing connections to the socioeconomic and political order in Iraq and to the need to fight "imperialism and reactionism." They helped women from poor neighborhoods to organize and demand schools, health clinics, running water, electricity, and women doctors. They also provided free legal and childcare advice.

In 1953, the league joined the Women's International Democratic Federation, an organization in which gender and class struggle were fused with a strong anti-imperialist campaign. The league's delegate to the federation's 1953 Copenhagen conference described the harsh conditions in which Iraqi women lived and brought to light their struggle against "the Iraqi reactionary government propped up by imperialism."[86] Empowered by international support and experience, league members returned home to pursue actions proposed at the conference. By March 1955, when the league's first national conference took place, it had branches in most of the country's districts, and its membership, they claimed, had swelled to around one thousand.

League members often mention women's participation in the 1952 intifada and the 1956 demonstrations, but the league's actual role in the organization of women in these events remains unclear. On 14 July 1958, the day of the military coup d'état that overthrew the monarchy, members of the League for the Defense of Women's Rights, successor of the Women's League Society, which had been ousted from the Iraqi Women's Union in 1947, overtook the union offices.[87] The union was no longer.

COMPLETING NARRATIVES

Sabiha al-Shaikh Da'ud and Naziha al-Dulaimi constructed two very different and competing narratives, as we have seen, that to an extent parallel the historical depictions of the development of the women's movements in countries neighboring Iraq. Both address such issues as the emergence of intellectual debate on the position of women, which paved the way for the appearance of the women's movement; education and participation in the national struggle as catalysts to "women's awakening"; as well as the empowerment of women by organizing and by fostering bonds of national and international sisterhood.[88]

The critical point in the divergence of their narratives is the year 1947, when conflicting ideologies and loyalties overrode solidarity among women: the pro-government Iraqi Women's Union forced the left-leaning Women's League Society out of its executive committee, barred leftist activists from its legally organized women's activities, and helped push them underground. Al-Dulaimi and Da'ud each gave a voice to the histories of the two rival women's organizations that subsequently emerged: the Iraqi Women's Union and the League for the Defense of Women's Rights.

Allowing these narratives to complete each other rather than to compete against each other enables us to piece together a layered and highly textured portrait of past events. It more accurately indicates the breadth of the intellectual debate about women's issues, the immense impact that participation in the 1920 revolt had on women's awareness, as well as the scope of their struggle for education. It also highlights the wide range of organizations active during the Hashemite period and the transregional and international relationships forged among women. It better reveals the true scope of women's contributions and the hardships they endured. If the Iraqi Women's Union narrative is ignored, the pioneering role women activists played in the development of state welfare, health, and education systems cannot be fully appreciated. Without the League for the Defense of Women's Rights narrative, the degree of repression that many women activists suffered may be overlooked. If underground work goes unnoticed, it is also impossible to understand the broad support women lent to the overthrow of the monarchy and the immediate appearance of a massive women's movement led by the league after 1958. No less important, allowing these narratives to complete each other unveils

some of the earliest scenes in which women posed a challenge to government gender discourse. From the days of the British occupation, women
had protested their marginalization. In the 1920s, members of the first
Iraqi women's club, in the very act of insisting that their own interpretation of the term *women's awakening* be heard, challenged their government. Then and in the years to follow, in the light of government reluctance to license groups openly supporting women's rights, any mustering
for women's causes was an act of defiance; from the 1930s through the
1950s, when government education and health services for women were
almost nonexistent, and the government had no qualms in refusing rights
for women because they were "backward," promoting girls schools and
offering education for illiterate women were, to say the least, a challenge.

THE WAR OF NARRATIVES

Western researchers, as noted earlier, have tended to adopt either one
narrative or the other in their own work, and this tendency deserves
comment. Doreen Ingrams and Deborah Cobbett present the clearest examples of following only one narrative. Whereas Ingrams favors the Iraqi
Women's Union narrative, Cobbett bases her work on the League for the
Defense of Women's Rights narrative. Their contrasting historical probes
were probably influenced mainly by their conflicting attitudes toward the
Ba'th regime as well as by their personal connections with different Iraqi
women. Ingrams, at least at the beginning of the 1980s, sided with regime
supporters, whereas Cobbett sided with its opponents.

A founder in 1967 of the Council for the Advancement of Arab–British
Understanding (CAABU), Ingrams maintained a long connection to the
Arab world and took a keen interest in Arab women's situation.[89] One of
the CAABU's aims was to counter negative images of Arabs and misconceptions about the Arab world. Indeed, what prompted Ingrams to visit
Iraq and write about Iraqi women in the early 1980s, as she notes in the
introduction to her book *The Awakened: Women in Iraq*, was an effort to
remove Western misconceptions about Arab women. She was warmly received by the Iraqi Ministry of Information and especially by the Ba'thi
General Federation of Iraqi Women. She was so impressed with these
women's hard work and devotion to women's causes that she dedicated
her book to the federation.

Throughout her book, Ingrams hails the Ba'th regime for its "policy of equality for women," which could not have been achieved without the work of its women's organization and the support of a courageous president. She accepts the Ba'th portrayal of women's reality and adopts its version of the history of the early women's movement. The brutal nature of Saddam Husain's regime had not fully surfaced when Ingrams visited Iraq, but the state-sponsored effort to reconstruct the country's history was already in full force. The history of the women's movement received its due, and it was the Iraqi Women's Union narrative that was adopted.[90] In embracing Da'ud's account, the Ba'th Party obliterated almost all reference to the League for the Defense of Women's Rights, which in its eyes posed an enormous threat. Under 'Abd al-Karim Qasim from 1958 to 1963, the league had received government sanction and enjoyed considerable power. It had 42,000 members, 53 branches, 87 literacy centers, and 111 housework-training centers. Naziha al-Dulaimi was appointed a cabinet minister, and the league played a role in formulating legislation. When Qasim clashed with the ICP, though, league activities were severely curtailed. Then the league was banned in 1963, when the Ba'th regime first seized power.[91] After 1968, when the Ba'th regime again rose to power, league members, although not the league itself, were allowed for several years to engage in the women's movement. Over time, however, the league came to be depicted as a tool in the hands of the dangerous ICP, and league leaders and activists were persecuted, detained, tortured, and even murdered.[92] When Ingrams remarks that during the days of the monarchy "there was an Iraqi Women's Federation . . . and after the revolution of 1958 there was the Women of the Republic Association [an organization competing with the league],"[93] she is uncritically following the official line of the Ba'th regime, which had completely erased the league from the pages of the history books.

Deborah Cobbett, meanwhile, was a researcher and editor for the Committee Against Repression and for Democratic Rights in Iraq (CARDRI), formed in 1979 with the stated aim of "exposing the brutality of the Ba'th regime and developing solidarity with those in Iraq struggling for human and democratic rights." In her article "Women in Iraq," which appeared in a book published by CARDRI, she attempts to trace the changes that had taken place over the previous decades in the lives of women in Iraq "and, in particular, to study the impact of the Ba'thist dictatorship."[94]

She severely criticizes Ba'th policies toward women and exposes the fate of women who opposed the regime. Women in Iraq, she contends, were granted equal rights with men only in detention and torture.

Cobbett interviewed league activists who had managed to escape persecution. In the 1980s, she edited for CARDRI the writings of dissident Iraqi women living in London.[95] At that time, the league was preparing its own version of events, no doubt in an effort to counter the Ba'th rewriting of history. Indeed, an unpublished league manuscript entitled "A Brief History of Iraqi Women" was Cobbett's main source of information about the early history of the women's movement. When Cobbett plays down the activities of all other women's organizations besides the league in the 1950s and fails to even mention the Iraqi Women's Union, however, she is perpetuating the league's narrative in her work.

Ingrams and Cobbett, like Da'ud and al-Dulaimi, were active participants in a "war of narratives" that obscured the full scope of activists' challenge to government discourse. That war left women's history an unfortunate casualty.

5

CHALLENGING THE GOVERNMENT'S GENDER DISCOURSE

By the mid-1940s, women's organization had broadened, strengthened, and, to an extent, institutionalized. But the relatively liberal political atmosphere that infused the postwar period was not to stay; before the decade closed, the government's reigning in of the women's movement was acutely felt once again. As noted in chapter 4, with the repression of left-wing organizations in 1947, the Women's League Society's gatherings, illiteracy schools, and publications were banned, and its representation in the Iraqi Women's Union's directorate was cancelled. In 1951, the government denied a request to form the Women's Liberation organization, thus pushing activists to establish the underground League for the Defense of Women's Rights. Neither did the union remain intact. In 1954, after the government had dismantled 465 societies and clubs and banned the existence of unions, the Iraqi Women's Union had to be reestablished as a single society rather than as a federation; it would be called the Women's Union Society (Jam'iyyat al-Ittihad al-Nisa'i).[1] Although contemporary observers report that the new entity maintained the same contacts, more research is needed to determine the significance of this step. Nevertheless, in the 1950s activists' criticism became increasingly palpable. Members of the union and the league now explicitly challenged the different elements of their government's gender discourse that constructed women as noncitizens: the TCCDR, the absence of state intervention in matters of personal status, and women's disenfranchisement.

THE WOMEN'S UNION'S QUEST FOR REFORMS

The Iraqi Women's Union, whose leaders came mostly from families of the ruling elite, pledged to conduct its struggle in an "orderly manner," acting only through legal and constitutional channels.[2] Union members reiterated regime rhetoric that the government and the people, both men and women, must join hands to create a better future for all. Thus, its members pressed the government to expand women's education, extend health services and health care for mothers and children, support women's entrance to new professions, and improve female government employees' conditions. Developments, especially in the field of education, were hailed.[3] Outspoken union leader Sabiha al-Shaikh Da'ud, in her book describing women's "awakening" in Iraq, *Awwal al-Tariq Ila al-Nahda al-Niswiyya fi al-'Iraq*, voiced their belief that bettering women's position in Iraq and achieving full citizenship for women could be realized through political, social, and economic reforms.[4]

Da'ud devoted an entire chapter to exposing the appalling situation of women in the Iraqi countryside. She was strongly influenced by attitudes expressed by both Ma'ruf al-Rusafi and Naziha al-Dulaimi on the subject and borrowed al-Dulaimi's assertion that rural women were subjected to "double servitude"—enslaved like rural men to the landlords and enslaved by their husbands as well. She agreed with al-Dulaimi that rural women, overworked and abused, had lost any personal freedom as human beings. Da'ud criticized the TCCDR for its part in degrading rural women. She buttressed this criticism with al-Rusafi's description of the proceedings of cases brought before Iraqi officials that were to be tried under the TCCDR, which required the officials to impose tribal customary law that was abusive to women (see chapter 1). Da'ud, however, treated the TCCDR more as a contributing factor to rural women's overall misery rather than as the main cause. She noted efforts to amend or cancel the regulation but declared that she did not see the solution in legislation. Rural women's predicament, she said, was part of the broader problem of Iraq's rural society, a society suffering not only from a "historical enslavement" inherited from the past, but also from poverty, disease, and ignorance. She did not expect to see any improvement in women's conditions as long as the economic situation of rural men, who were much to blame for rural women's deplorable situation, was not resolved. So Da'ud

advocated a "comprehensive fundamental solution": land and social reforms that would eventually secure for both rural men and women improvement in their socioeconomic conditions. Turkey, she said, offered
a good example of such reforms because it made landowners responsible
for their cultivators' future.[5]

In spite of Da'ud's grim description and her call upon the government
not to neglect women in countryside reforms, her suggestions were not
incompatible with government policies and with Nuri al-Sa'id's views,
as expressed in the CUP's platform and in the 1951 parliamentary debates
about an amendment to the regulation. Although clearly demanding an
improvement to the socioeconomic situation of the toilers of the soil,
Da'ud was careful not to support openly the undermining of govern-
ment-backed landlords' position, and despite the role she attributed to
the TCCDR in degrading rural women, she did not call for the abolition
of this tool that the government still relied on to control the countryside.

One of the Iraqi Women's Union's declared aims was to elevate women
in the realm of personal status.[6] Customary law affecting this realm was
a serious concern. Da'ud lamented that marriage in the countryside was
a transaction in which a tool was sold by the father and bought by the
husband. Rural men often weighed getting married against buying an
ox. Moreover, polygamy served as a means to increase their workforce,
she pointed out. That was not hard to achieve: women could be coerced
into marriages; with no other concern than financial gain guardians of
rural women could force them into early marriage or a second marriage
without divorce. Brides could also serve as recompense for murder or humiliation. Da'ud's suggested countryside reform, however, encompassed
merely setting a minimum age for marriage and restricting the sums used
for *mahr*. Unlike al-Rusafi, she did not argue that government-sanctioned
customary law, adversely affecting women in marriage and divorce, was
incompatible with Islamic law.

Union members were also concerned with issues determined by the
shari'a. The union's president, Asiya Tawfiq Wahbi, was greatly troubled
by the matter of women's being trapped in polygamous marriages. She
suggested at an Arab women's conference in Beirut in 1954 that women
be given a choice with regard to polygamous marriage by way of a clause
in their marriage contracts. Inspired by the Hanbali rather than the
Hanafi view concerning the inclusion of conditions in the marriage con-

tract, she advised women to stipulate that their husbands were not to wed other wives and argued that women should retain the right to end the marriage should their husbands take additional wives "without justification."[7] Renowned poet Nazik al-Mala'ika had expressed concern about maternal child custody in a speech delivered during the Iraqi Women's Union's Week of Women's Rights in October 1953. She lamented that fathers' ability to tear children away from their mothers was the harshest, most unreasonable type of deprivation. Union members argued that in divorce, custody of the children should be granted to the most competent parent. The ease with which a man could irrevocably divorce his wife incited union members to approach Parliament. The union submitted a request to discuss this issue in Parliament and demanded the enactment of a law that "would restrict divorce as much as possible." In addition, the union sought a special law requiring a medical examination that would attest to future groom's health.[8]

Union members were extremely cautious in their efforts to effect change in the realm of women's personal status. This might explain why it is difficult now to find references in the contemporaneous press to government–union negotiations on the matter. However, the draft Code of Personal Status, considered in the 1940s and 1950s, paralleled to a large extent issues raised by the union. A juxtaposition of union demands with the government-proposed law suggests that such negotiations did in fact take place. More specifically, the proposal's treatment of *mahr*, child custody, the registration of the marriage contract and men's privileges in divorce suggests not only that the government kept up to date on activists' concerns, but also that it wanted to be seen as responding to those concerns. The proposed law's emphasis on the wife's right to *mahr*, its detailed discussion of the matter, and a declaration that *mahr* was a woman's sole property paralleled activists' criticism that women were treated as objects for sale when their *muhur* were confiscated by their guardians. The emphasis seen in the proposal that mothers have preferential rights with regard to custody over their children both in marriage and after divorce also corresponded with activists' protests; permitting judges to extend the period of maternal custody in cases where doing so was in the interest of the child can be compared with the union demand that in divorce custody of children should be granted to the most competent parent.[9] Registration of the marriage contract, as stipulated in the draft Code of Personal Status, addressed union members' concerns. It offered some protection from child and forced marriage and enabled women to determine their husbands' true marital status (e.g., by ensuring that preexisting marriages be revealed before the contract is signed). It also allowed women the right to clarify the state of their intended husbands' health and helped them secure such matrimonial rights as *mahr* and maintenance.[10] Finally, the Iraqi Women's Union was concerned over the ease with which a man could irrevocably divorce his wife and demanded that arbitrary divorce be restricted as much as possible. The proposal prescribed that divorce formulae accompanied by a number would effect only a single and therefore revocable divorce. It determined that the formula of repudiation uttered by a husband not fully aware of his actions due to drunkenness, sleep, or insanity would have no legal effect; that suspended or conditional divorce (i.e., a pronouncement that makes the divorce contingent on the occurrence of some future event or sets it to take effect at some future time) would have no effect if intended only as a threat or an attempt at coercion; and that metaphorical expressions that may be construed as alluding to divorce would not have that effect unless divorce was indeed the desired outcome.[11] The government's conservative proposal, however, stopped far short of offering resolution of the personal status issues that concerned Da'ud, Wahbi, and their union colleagues.

THE STRUGGLE FOR WOMEN'S ENFRANCHISEMENT AND THE PITFALLS OF "GRADUAL MODERNIZATION"

Iraqi Women's Union members were dissatisfied with the TCCDR and the lack of state intervention in personal-status matters, but what prompted their most open protest was the issue of women's political rights. They viewed their exclusion from formal politics as a blunt infringement of women's status as citizens of a modern state, and they vociferously fought for Iraqi women's enfranchisement. To this end, the union stepped up its efforts in the early 1950s by a variety of means. Members sent missives to successive prime ministers, heads of Parliament, and party leaders. They met with senior state figures and initiated special activities and events devoted to women's enfranchisement. In 1953, during the premiership of Muhammad Fadil al-Jamali, for example, the union succeeded in organizing a special week in support of women's political rights. The events during that week included lectures, a symposium, radio programs, and a meeting with the prime minister, all dedicated to women's suffrage. Union members mobilized the press by giving interviews, providing information to the media, and making sure daily newspapers regularly covered union actions.

It is essential here, however, to remember the backdrop of government's modernizing discourse which so profoundly affected those who worked within the social, economic, and political order. As described in chapter 3, government rhetoric and policies affecting women in the 1950s dovetailed nicely with the regime's platform of how to transform Iraq into a modern state. Successive governments touted "modernity," promising progress through far-reaching reforms. Nuri al-Sa'id, prime minister during most of the 1950s, and his CUP called for a fundamental and comprehensive "awakening" through a series of social, economic, and political reforms. His party pledged to expand education, extend health services, and modernize agriculture. It would, it claimed, combat poverty and unemployment, encourage industry, promote distribution of government land and private land ownership, and create modern villages. It promised a sovereign, independent Iraq by altering the 1930 Anglo–Iraqi Treaty as well as by amending the Electoral Law "to guarantee freedom to the voters."[12] The prime minister cautioned, however, that reform must be gradual and take into account the country's "reality and its possibilities." Reforms must be balanced, he stressed, adopting what is good in Western civilization while preserving what is best in Iraq's own heritage.[13]

The idealistic view cultivated by the government trumpeted a better future for all citizens. It encouraged both men and women to join in efforts to create a modern state. Improving women's position was presented as an integral part of the processes of modernization. As "the pillar of society," women were entrusted with the responsibility for the "proper" upbringing of the next generation.[14] At the same time, however, al-Sa'id and his associates' concept of "a modernization that goes hand in hand with [the] development"[15] of the country as a whole or of specific sections of society opened many possibilities for delaying reforms in general and those concerning women in particular.

The government's notion of modernity seems to have empowered Iraqi Women's Union members who negotiated within its confines. It strengthened their resolve even in the face of strong opposition and a repressive political climate; it gave them hope that in spite of the enormity of the task of altering the Constitution and election laws, their mission of achieving equal political rights and bringing about a better future was indeed possible. More important, the government's rhetoric gave them the ammunition they needed to promote their demands because it allowed them to manipulate the concepts of "backwardness" and "progress" to their own benefit. However, they had to confront not only the government's notion that change in the position of women must be closely tied to the country's "progress," but also its demand that women as a group exhibit "progress" as a prerequisite to attaining rights.

Scholars of the Middle East have already pointed out that modernizing discourses may be simultaneously emancipatory and repressive for women.[16] Nowhere is this more evident than in union members' entanglement with their government's modernizing discourse in their struggle for political rights. Tracing the ways they negotiated their rights through an analysis of union pronouncements and writings from 1950 to 1958 clearly illustrates this point.

WOMEN'S SUFFRAGE AND IRAQ'S PATH TO BECOMING MODERN

Union rhetoric during the 1950s, as articulated in memoranda sent to the prime minister, cabinet members, and heads of Parliament, reveals that members did indeed endeavor to promote political rights for women by linking women's enfranchisement with the yearning to turn Iraq into a modern state. Acceptance of their demands, they claimed, would further the realization of the ideals of modernization such as economic prosperity, social and technological progress, democracy, and justice. By allowing women to enter public life and giving them political rights, all hands would be mobilized for the common good, which in turn would bring Iraq numerous scientific, economic, and cultural advantages. Unionists pointed to countries that had already recognized women's political rights and that were deriving great benefit from the successful activities of women ministers, ambassadors, and MPs in the political, social, and economic arenas.[17] The democratic and free nations of the world recognized women's political rights, and if Iraq wanted to be part of that world, it ought to conform to these same standards. Iraqi women, the unionists declared, were ready and able to help build Iraqi society "according to constitutional and democratic principles."[18]

Union members also pointed to the United Nations charter, which affirms equal rights for men and women, and emphasized that every person has the right to take part in the governing of his or her country and should have equal access to public service. When Iraq joined the United Nations, they said, it accepted all the commitments this membership entailed, so Iraq could not now ignore these commitments. The right to vote and to be elected was predictably championed as every human being's or citizen's natural right. No less important, their demand for political rights was a just demand, and the government was obliged to consider it fairly; it was unjust that the opinion of half the population should be ignored and that they be banned from taking part in legislation.[19]

Just as women's enfranchisement was a means whereby Iraq could transform itself into a modern state, denying women their rights meant steering away from modernization while the rest of the world advanced. In a lengthy memorandum to the senior state figures and heads of political parties in April 1951, for example, the union made clear that any delay in carrying out their wishes would hold back Iraq's "civilization" and hamper the country's progress.[20] In part, the members' tactic was indeed to play on the wish in government circles not to be seen as "backward" in the world's opinion, and they frequently depicted Iraq as lagging behind the "civilized" European, Arab, and Islamic states that had already extended political rights to their female citizens. As late as February 1958, members of the union stated openly that "many countries, Israel among them, stigmatize us as being backward and their most powerful argument for this is [the Iraqi] women's non-participation in public life and especially in the field of political activity."[21] In light of the worldwide recognition of these rights, it was inevitable that women in Iraq should also be given political rights. The only valid question was why a vital nation interested in progress, such as Iraq, should come at the end of this procession, they asked.

Support of women's political rights was also proffered as a sign of an individual's status vis-à-vis modernization and progress. The union's own members and supporters were of course modern and progressive, and others would soon adopt the same outlook as well, they believed. In April

1951, they struck a confident note: "The progressive spirit we note in the present government and Parliament indicates an understanding that the present time requires swift action. This prompts us to be confident that the day of equality and the day of freedom for men as well as women is within reach."[22] Furthermore, their opponents' ideas, they claimed, were simply incompatible with Iraq's current development and reality. They had been inspired by an old and obsolete reactionary point of view having little to do with modern life.[23]

Union members thus reiterated government rhetoric linking women's rights to their country's progress in an empowering way. Inverting the main argument used by Nuri al-Saʿid and his associates against them, they argued that it was not the granting of women's rights that was predicated upon how far Iraq had traveled on the road toward modernity, but the advancement of modernization that depended on women enjoying full rights.

"PROGRESS"—A DISCRIMINATORY CONCEPT

The Iraqi Women's Union continued navigating within the boundaries of the government's modernity rhetoric as it sought to counter the notion that women first needed to progress before they could be granted full citizenship rights. Iraqi women, they claimed, had already made much progress and their contribution to society was well attested to, certainly to a sufficient degree to make them eligible for full rights and full participation in the building of a modern Iraq. At all levels of education and in such important professions as medicine, advocacy, pharmacy, and teaching, Iraqi women had proved themselves equal to men. They were certainly on a par with men in their understanding of their civic duties and public responsibilities. Especially women active in or associated with the union were "a useful element to the country" in fields benefiting men and women.

First raised in the April 1951 memorandum, these arguments were brought up again in March 1956. Iraqi women have come a long way in the fields of education and national consciousness, the latter communiqué said. It went on: they have successfully entered different fields of life and side by side with men have faced the country's many problems. They still remain deprived, however, of the fundamental political rights that are an integral part of any individual's life in the "civilized world." There is no reason why the degree of national consciousness and the extent of social progress they have acquired should not qualify them to be given their full rights and allow them to participate in the building of the Iraqi society.[24]

It is here, however, in their argument that women had progressed sufficiently and thus deserved equal political rights that the entanglement with the government's notion of "gradual modernity" surfaces. In countering the perception of women as backward, unionists were assuming the position of a backward sector eager to prove itself. Moreover, arguing that women were no longer backward and adducing proof to that effect essentially opened the way for debate on what the criteria were for judging development and on whether these criteria had been met or not. Equally problematic was the way the argument inherently differentiated and discriminated between women themselves. The intention may well have been to point out the "progress" of some women for the benefit of all women. In practice, however, the picture presented was one in which only middle- and upper-class women who could afford education, who had entered professions, and who had enough leisure time to devote to community service had sufficiently "progressed" to be deserving of political rights. This point was further accentuated when they argued that it was unacceptable that illiterate men be allowed to vote whereas educated women could not.[25] Here educated women are presented as the most discriminated against and thus the most entitled to these rights: the link between rights and education as an indicator of progress is stressed, as is the still greater entitlement of upper-class women, who could afford education.

THE IMAGE OF THE MODERN WOMAN

Throughout their campaign for political rights, union members spoke out against the portrayal of Iraqi women as passive and backward. They instead portrayed women, especially the "new women" such as themselves, as active and assertive. The "modern woman" was an educated, professional, patriotic, and capable citizen. She was ready and willing to fulfill her duties and offer her talents to help build the modern state. In return, however, she expected her full rights.

This image of Iraqi women as "modern"—that is, socially assertive and politically astute—was threatening to the government, however. It evoked opposition from conservative circles that supported al-Saʿid's government and that the government had no desire to alienate. In these circles, as we saw in chapter 3, this image of the modern woman was not considered compatible with Islam and was seen as posing a threat to the existing social order and family structure. Individuals and groups in these circles accused union members of uncritically emulating Western women, of turning their backs on their duties at home, and of jeopardizing their own and society's morality. Union leaders realized that this perception was deleterious to their chances of winning their rights and looked for ways to ameliorate antagonism, which involved creating a more subdued image of the modern Iraqi woman; in this process of ameliorization, though, they at the same time deepened their entanglement in the government's modernizing rhetoric.

To dampen concerns that modern women posed a threat to the political order and men's position therein, the union adopted a tactic that differentiated between two spheres of politics. The first sphere involved the struggle for power and domination; the second concentrated on solving the country's deep-rooted problems. They associated the first sphere with men only but proposed the second as a public arena where men and women could join efforts. They then emphasized that they were interested only in the latter. For example, in their opening words at the Week of Women's Rights in October 1953, union members claimed that they did not relate to politics in its narrow sense—that is, as nothing but a struggle for power. They were not seeking to capture the seat of power, to obtain influence, or to enjoy fame. Instead, they understood politics in its "modern and wide meaning": "There are national problems that are in need of a prompt solution that we feel men and women can cooperate in managing and solving."[26] They singled out such problems as illiteracy, poverty, and disease. In light of frequent changes in government and growing public dissatisfaction with the socioeconomic and political situation, the expression of disinterest in power struggles and of interest only in attending to the country's most entrenched problems might be read as criticism of contemporary politics. It clearly reveals, however, how union members were voluntarily imposing restrictions on themselves in an effort to enhance their chances to enter politics.

In countering the claim that their actions worked to disrupt social order and family structure, union leaders drew parallels between the sphere of modern politics and modern motherhood, stating in 1953,

> Our concern, ladies and gentlemen, is the concern of a mother seeking to allot justice among her children: strong and weak, sick and healthy, boy and girl, big and small. This is not the concern of a woman blinded by the light of a new civilization, rushing to imitate it, as they say, abandoning her motherly duties and her familial responsibilities. Rather, it is the concern of a woman who holds her motherly duties sacred. . . . This is a broad motherhood that seeks to contain all the children of humanity, to guarantee their rights and to defend the oppressed from their oppressors. This is the woman who is now demanding her right to participate in the legislation of laws for her sons and daughters.[27]

Solving the country's most pressing problems was the essence of modern politics, the "second sphere." Women's entry into this sphere was only a natural extension of their maternal duties and could not therefore threaten the family structure, let alone the political and social order.

More significant, perhaps, union members rejected not only accusations that they blindly emulated Western women and turned their backs on their duties at home, but also the notion that their demands and activities were incompatible with Islam. Nothing in their religion, they argued, prevented their demands from being realized. On the contrary, Islamic law for the most part guarantees equal rights and duties for both women and men. It secures women's personal freedom as it does their property rights and aims at turning women into an "active element" in all aspects of life. In early Islam, women played an important role in politics, war, legislation, trade, the transmission of hadith, and so on. Examples of the high status women enjoyed in the Golden Age of Islam are innumerable, and Arab and Islamic history abounds with the names of women who stood out in their society. Far from jeopardizing their own or their society's morality in their work for the benefit of men and women, they added, Iraqi women had proved not only their deep devotion to work, but also their loyal dedication to preserving their own respectability and the honor of their traditions and customs.[28]

The image of the modern Iraqi woman the union was now crafting not only was nonthreatening but also conformed to Nuri al-Saʿid's concept of gradual and balanced modernization. The modern Iraqi woman who clamors for her political rights may be assertive and determined as well as visible and active in the public sphere, but she is not interested in competing with men for power or domination. She is committed to her motherly responsibilities and domestic duties. She is indeed inspired by Western women, but she does not imitate their ways blindly. She respects her society's customs and traditions and is far from turning her back on Islam. The modern Iraqi woman seeks to adopt "what is best in Western civilization" while endeavoring to preserve "the best in her country's own heritage," to respect her society's traditions and customs. She will not rush reform and will take into consideration her country's realities and possibilities. This description notably signaled that union members were willing to compromise even with respect to the specific reform they were now struggling for.

WOMEN'S "OCCUPATION" OF THE CHAMBER OF DEPUTIES

The union's deployment of the government discourse of modernity thus revealed both the empowering and the repressive aspects of that discourse. That the repressive aspects were of greater weight becomes inescapable when we reach 1958 and negotiations intensify. The union's struggle for political rights had repeatedly stumbled over the obstacle of the Iraqi Constitution, on which the election laws that prescribed women's disenfranchisement were based. But changing the Constitution was a long and complicated process. Any amendment had to be approved by a two-thirds majority of the members of both the Chamber of Deputies and the Senate. After approval, the Chamber of Deputies had to be dissolved, and a new Chamber elected. The amendment then had to be resubmitted. Again, after approval by a two-thirds majority of both houses, the amendment had to be submitted to the king for assent and publication.[29] In February 1958, however, Iraq's union with Jordan made changes in the Constitution inevitable. Now that the complicated process of changing the Constitution was set in motion, women activists mobilized with yet greater vigor to win their rights.

When in the second half of February 1958 the government set up a legal committee to prepare the amendment to the Constitution required by the union with Jordan, women activists were ready to make sure the recognition of women's political rights would be included. On 23 February, a union memorandum to the prime minister and heads of Parliament reiterated that the way to becoming modern lay in granting women their political rights and argued again that women, far from being backward, had made enough progress to entitle them to these rights. In a concluding paragraph in the memo, however, the authors reflected on the ongoing debate about conditions under which women were to be granted political rights. They suggested that even if, "as some argue," certain conditions were required for women to enjoy full political rights, this should not prevent inclusion of their entitlement to these rights within the body of the amended Constitution. The conditions could be spelled out later in a special law and could even be reconsidered from time to time.[30]

This paragraph can again be read as part of a piecemeal approach intended to gain recognition of women's political rights in the Constitution at the temporary price of postponing the actual implementations of these rights in practice. Once the Constitution recognized women's political rights, any restricting law could be fought against as contradicting the Constitution. Nevertheless, the very acceptance of the notion that there could be conditions for women to receive rights actually contributed to the perception of women as backward because they, unlike men, needed to meet certain criteria before being considered full citizens. Also, allowing for periodical debates of these criteria opened the gate for continued deferral of political rights for all women, and recognizing only those women who had shown enough progress as deserving of rights discriminated according to class.

On 6 March 1958, al-Saʿid announced that the forthcoming amendment to the Constitution would aim at correcting the shortcomings existing in the Iraqi Constitution and at introducing new principles made necessary by Iraq's political and social development during recent years, including the granting of political rights to the women of Iraq "in accordance with certain rules and qualifications suitable to the social and cultural conditions of the country."[31] His announcement, as indicated earlier, signaled that his ideas about reforms in general and changes in women's position in particular had not changed. Reforms should be gradual, taking into consideration "reality and its possibilities," and changes in women's position were dependent both on the country's "progress" and on women's "development." Al-Saʿid's announcement was thus ambiguous. The precise rights and qualifications mentioned were left undetermined at this point in time, as the newspaper *al-Zaman* was quick to point out.[32]

Thus, the struggle continued, as activists insisted on full rights for all women. Two delegations headed by the union's chairperson, Asiya Tawfiq Wahbi, were sent to meet with Prime Minister al-Sa'id. The first went to thank him for his recognition of women's political rights and to demand that he not stop at the vote but grant women the right to be elected as well.[33] When union members learned that on 25 March al-Sa'id would be meeting with jurists, members of the Chamber of Deputies, to discuss the planned amendment to the Constitution, they sent a second delegation to reiterate the demand for full political rights for women. The delegation extracted a promise to that effect from the prime minister, his deputy, the minister of justice, and every MP they encountered. Wahbi was quoted as saying: "We occupied the Chamber of Deputies before entering it as members."[34]

A newspaper interview given by Wahbi following this encounter reveals that the union's delegation was apprehensive not only vis-à-vis the nature of the rights granted to women, but also with regard to the qualifications that had been set as a precondition. They had learned that only women holding "school diplomas" would be given political rights, which they thought was an offense to Iraqi women. Thus, they had insisted that both educated and illiterate women be granted full political rights—just as men enjoyed. The prime minister, his deputy, and all MPs they met expressed their support for women's rights and their appreciation of women's efforts in serving the country. However, again deploying the notion of "gradual progress" and insisting that women's rights were dependent on their "development," the decision makers responded that it was impossible at the present time to equalize illiterate women with educated women.

At this point, according to the newspaper report, the delegation did not further protest the discrimination between men and women or even among women but rather entered into a negotiation regarding the level of education that should be a prerequisite for receiving political rights. In other words, how many women had "developed" to the point that they could be considered full citizens? This negotiation may well have been the only sensible thing to do after the leading politicians had made it clear that only educated women would be enfranchised. However, in doing so the delegation once again donned the mantle of a backward sector of society that needed to prove its progress, and it accepted discrimination between women according to such "progress." This shift in approach became clearer later in the delegation's response when it received a promise from the deputy prime minister and several parliamentarians that educated women would receive full political rights even if their learning had been done at home and they did not hold school diplomas. Wahbi considered this promise a victory. She expressed her satisfaction that Iraqi women would finally become citizens, thus disregarding the fact that only a small number of women, not more than 5 percent of all women of voting age, would enjoy this achievement. At the end of her interview, Wahbi thanked those who had supported women "in this crucial stage of their political lives," apparently in acknowledgment of the end of the campaign.[35]

On 26 and 27 March 1958, the Chamber of Deputies and Senate unanimously passed the amendment to the Constitution stating that the "Iraqi constitution may be amended within a year" and that this amendment "shall include the granting of political rights to educated women."[36] This wording, as noted in chapter 3, in fact deferred the granting of political rights to all women to some point in the future. Educated women would have to wait for the approval of the amendment by the Senate, the dispersal of the Chamber of Deputies, the election of a new Chamber, and the reapproval of the amendment by both the Senate and the new Chamber. The illiterate would have to attain an education or wage a new campaign to amend the Constitution yet again in order to gain political rights for themselves. Thus, even what appeared to be at least a partial success, an achievement for the union, was an illusion. The amendment, as noted earlier, actually left a future Parliament to decide whether educated women would receive political rights or not, the level of education that would allow women's political participation, as well as the nature of the rights women would be granted. In other words, after a long struggle, the union and women throughout Iraq were left with no more than the same old promise of a better future.

In seeking to carve out a space for women in formal politics, union members sought to refute al-Saʿid's constructs only within the boundaries of his discourse, and in articulating their demands, they had inadvertently reinforced ideas that worked against them. Arguing against women's backwardness, they in actuality contributed to their construction as such; the claim that women had progressed and therefore deserved rights opened the gate for denying rights to women who had not "progressed." Accepting the promise that a better future was near helped rationalize the deferral of women's rights. Although the "victory" activists prided themselves on winning their campaign, they in fact buttressed the existing system instead of bringing about a change in the political arena. The "victory" was ultimately Nuri al-Sa'id's. By postponing the granting of women's rights to an unknown time in the future and ensuring that even then only a small number of women would enjoy those rights, he and others in power circumvented both any threat the entrance of women en masse into politics could present to the political order and any opposition this entrance could have raised.

Government gender discourse abandoned women outside state protection from coercive customs and unfavorable interpretation of Islamic law and excluded them from formal politics. Union members, careful not to undermine the base upon which the government's power was balanced, however, targeted the manifestations of this discourse rather than the strategies that generated it. True, acting openly against abandonment and exclusion was in itself a challenge, and the union's "modern Iraqi woman" was very distinct from the government construction of women as subordinate, economically dependent, and backward; likewise, the women activists' struggle for political rights resulted in the government's relating to women as political actors, often within the actual corridors of power. But because the union members were all too entangled in the notion of gradual modernization, which was really intended to secure the status quo, it is no wonder that none of the reforms they were seeking ever materialized.

THE LEAGUE FOR THE DEFENSE OF WOMEN'S RIGHTS AND ITS QUEST FOR A NEW ORDER

In stark contrast to Iraqi Women's Union members, who subscribed to the notion that full citizenship could be gained only through gradual political, social, and economic reforms within the confines of the existing order, members of the League for the Defense of Women's Rights flatly rejected the idea. Working within the framework of a competing modernizing discourse prevalent among opposition circles in Iraq, the latter believed that Iraq's road to becoming modern—achieving economic prosperity, technological progress, social justice, rights for women, and political freedom—required radical change. League leaders held that problems facing urban and rural women were the result of Iraq's losing its sovereignty to imperialist forces, which had fortified their position by allying with local reactionaries and in this way controlled and exploited the masses. It was not the country's backwardness that stifled progress, but government policy that was keeping the country in general and women in particular subjugated and "backward." Women's liberation would thus only follow Iraq's liberation from imperialism, and the subordination of women would similarly be resolved once the socioeconomic and political order imperialism had propped up was overthrown.[37]

League positions were most clearly articulated by their leader Naziha al-Dulaimi in her book *Al-Mar'a al-'Iraqiyya* (The Iraqi Woman). Al-Dulaimi, after graduating medical school in 1948, worked for a year in a Baghdad hospital. But the government, seeking to put an end to her political activity, transferred her from Baghdad to al-Sulaimaniyya, Karbala, and Kufa. Her work as a physician in these various places ironically provided her with a golden opportunity to study the condition of Iraqi women of different classes, sects, and settings. Her findings were made public in this book in 1950. The book was probably the first comprehensive critique of women's condition to be published by a woman in contemporary Iraq.[38]

For al-Dulaimi, women in Iraq were divided along class lines and were profoundly affected by this division. Yet despite their different circumstances all were in one way or another victims of the socioeconomic and political circumstances of their country. As a physician, al-Dulaimi was greatly concerned with women's health, and she set out to expose the emptiness of government promises to expand and modernize health services. She claimed that the health of peasant women, like that of the working class, was deplorable, mainly due to their poor nutrition and exhausting work. The number of calories burned by women was greater than their intake and resulted in emaciation; a grave deficiency of vitamins and proteins led to severe anemia and weakening of the immune system, leaving the malnourished peasants exposed to all kinds of diseases. Flies, mosquitoes, fleas, and lice spread trachoma, typhoid, tuber-

culosis, dysentery, malaria, and the plague. Lack of sanitary facilities and
sewage systems meant that raw sewage mixed freely with freshwater, facilitating the spread of all sorts of parasitic worms. Crowded one-room
homes further helped propagate infectious diseases among family members. Inadequate clothing in the cold season exacerbated the situation.

According to al-Dulaimi, in 1948 official reports indicated that there
were 603,698 new cases of malaria, 24,272 of bilharzias, 6,752 of tuberculosis, and 25,114 of dysentery. But these figures, she insisted, represented
only treated cases, estimating the numbers of those stricken to be three
times higher. Government and health facilities in urban areas, she said,
were scarce and ill equipped, and some rural areas were never visited by a
physician or any other health official; mother-and-child health care, too,
was almost nonexistent. She exposed the enormous gap between the government's modernization rhetoric and the reality of mothers and infants
dying from a lack of proper treatment. People in Iraq, she lamented, were
dying from malaria, anemia, and hunger "in the twentieth century, a century when [even] the most severe diseases can be easily cured."[39]

Al-Dulaimi preceded Da'ud in exposing the predicament of rural
women and the role the TCCDR played in subjugating women of "the
peasant class." The oppressive land-tenure system in the countryside created for the *fallahat*, peasant women, what she called "double servitude,"
as discussed in chapter 1. Al-Dulaimi was the first to show how the government's TCCDR, in acknowledging customary law, was at the heart of
peasant women's coercion. Condoning the murder of women without re-
prisal put women at men's mercy.

Al-Dulaimi also detailed the grave ramifications of leaving all women
outside state protection in the realm of family matters. Women of the
"peasant class," who were treated as work tools first by their fathers and
later by their husbands, suffered from child and forced marriages, con-
fiscation of their *mahr*, and polygamy. In addition, they could easily be
divorced, and their children could be taken away from them. At an early
age, peasant girls start working for their fathers, who hoped to profit further from their daughters' *muhur* as soon as they reached puberty. Child
marriages, more prevalent in years of drought and grave economic need,
saw fathers offering their daughters at a very young age for paltry sums or
even without *mahr* so as to be absolved of the burden of supporting them.
Like animals, women were bought and sold in marriage. They were trad-

ed for livestock or other women, their prices influenced by market conditions. Perceived as the property of their kin, they could also be married off as recompense for murder or humiliation. Polygamy was perceived as a means of expanding the labor force. Divorce was the inevitable lot of the peasant woman who became weak, handicapped, or unable to work for any other reason or even if her "owner" simply got tired of her. The threat of divorce compelled women to be obedient and endure hard work, beatings, and humiliations; otherwise, they could find themselves homeless, hungry, poor, and devoid of any rights, even concerning their own children.

Women among "the feudal class," despite their higher standard of living, according to al-Dulaimi, also suffered from forced marriages. Their economic dependency on their fathers or husbands prescribed their complete subservience. The situation of urban working-class women, many recent migrants from the countryside, was no better. They often found themselves unemployed and dependent on fathers or husbands who subsequently had complete control over their lives. Work outside the home required the husband's permission. Like women of the "peasant class," they had the threat of divorce hanging over their heads constantly and forcing them to be submissive and to tolerate hard and tedious work, battering, and verbal abuse; otherwise, they, too, could find themselves destitute and their children taken away.

Finally, al-Dulaimi noted, even upper-class women, those who belonged to the bourgeoisie, could not totally escape the lot of their less-privileged sisters. Their marriages, too, had the characteristics of a financial transaction between their fathers and future husbands, which did not allow them any real say regarding their marriage. In such a transaction, a woman's worth was measured according to her family's financial and social position as well as according to her beauty.[40]

Al-Dulaimi, however, did not seek the solution for women's hardships in legislation by the existing government. Although pointing a finger at customary law as being responsible for Iraqi women's predicament, she did not call for protective legislation or for the annulment of existing law. Like other league members, she believed that any legislation that reinforced "backward customs" and worked for the benefit of the current "reactionary government" on which imperialism relied would naturally be done away with in a liberated Iraq.

The same logic applied to personal status matters. A marriage contract, al-Dulaimi said, should be a contract between equals, and the only way to achieve that would be by securing economic independence for women. *Fallahat*, for example, should be able to support themselves and provide for their own needs. Only then would they become an equal party in the marriage contract, with the ability to form and support a happy and strong family and base their relationship with their husbands on mutual respect and understanding. "But could the Iraqi *fallaha* be economically liberated within the existing feudal system?" al-Dulaimi asked, stating that there was no freedom in a system in which feudal lords exploited both men and women *fallahin*. This feudal system, she held, stood between the *fallahin* and their social and economic liberation and must be done away with. Its elimination, however, would be difficult because it was supported by imperialism. Imperialism favors a backward society in which the masses of *fallahin* are controlled and exploited by a few landlords. Imperialism tempts these few to cooperate by powerful means so that it may in turn exploit and control millions of people to the benefit of its own interests.[41]

Introducing change through legislation in the prevalent socioeconomic and political conditions in Iraq, then, seemed implausible to league members; a struggle for women's enfranchisement was therefore futile. They depicted the lack of political rights as one of many factors contributing to the sad situation facing women in Iraq and criticized the Iraqi Women's Union campaign for creating division between men and women and for discriminating among women based on their level of education.[42] League activists believed that political rights would follow inevitably once a fundamental change in the socioeconomic and political order was achieved. Mubejel Baban, a member of the league's executive committee from 1952, commented later in this regard: "We thought these things would come later. We could not open [too] many channels in our [underground] work. So we did not put that as our priority. We put it in our manifesto, *haqq al-intikhab* [the right to vote], but we did not put it in our practice."[43]

In the conclusion to her book *The Iraqi Woman*, al-Dulaimi stated that Iraqi women's "backwardness" in all aspects of life was obvious. She then delineated women's road to salvation. In order to be free, gain human dignity, and secure for themselves life's basic needs, women needed to walk down one road together with all those who are exploited in their society. The road is long and winding, but one that "any soul aspiring to freedom" would desire. Women could not emancipate themselves unless they achieved economic independence. This independence, in turn, was impossible without solving the problem of joblessness among the entire population. However, in order to reduce unemployment significantly, national industries would have to be established in urban centers and private land owned and worked by *fallahin* of both sexes in the countryside. But local industry and agriculture could not succeed as long as foreign monopolies were draining raw materials and flooding the local market with foreign goods. Hence, these foreign monopolies had to be driven out of Iraq. Because foreign military forces protected the monopolies' interests, and their presence was mandated by the Anglo–Iraqi Treaty of 1930, it was obvious that the treaty had to be annulled. The genuine liberation of women, al-Dulaimi concluded, could be attained only following Iraq's liberation.[44]

After the country's liberation, al-Dulaimi implied, state treatment of women would totally change. Harmful customs would no longer be acknowledged; Iraqi citizens, urban and rural, men and women, would be subjected to one law. Legal, social, and economic measures taken by the state would contribute to the change in women's position in the family, making men and women equal partners in marriage; all would enjoy state health and education services as well as full democratic rights. According to al-Dulaimi's vision, with their country's liberation women would be saved from their own backwardness; rather than be constructed as a possession, devoid of rights and state protection, they would become equal and protected individuals: full citizens of a modern state.

To effect such a radical change, members of the League for the Defense of Women's Rights, unlike members of the Iraqi Women's Union, set out to occupy the streets, not the Parliament. They sought to mobilize "the masses of women" to the struggle against "Iraqi reactionist government propped up by imperialism."[45] Unlike elite women, who had a patronizing attitude toward their more common sisters, league members set out to shatter boundaries. They made a point of reaching women everywhere. They tried to win over lower-class women by visiting their homes and instructing them on health and legal issues. They formulated poor neighborhood women's grievances regarding a host of issues—the supply of water, electricity, housing, and so forth—into petitions. They also helped these women to register their children for school or to organize and demand the opening of new schools. As they addressed women's daily problems, they made and then highlighted the link between women's hardships and the political and socioeconomic order, emphasizing the need to join the fight against "imperialism and reactionary forces."[46]

By the mid-1950s, within three years of its inception, the underground league had, according to its leaders, branches in most of the country's provinces and about one thousand members.[47] Although the league's actual role in the organization of women in the antigovernment 1952 intifada and 1956 demonstrations remains unclear, many women participated in opposition activities, and league members were conspicuous among them. Some members later recounted how poor neighborhood women who benefited from league activities sheltered activists in their time of need, taking them into their homes while antigovernment demonstrations were under way.[48] The league's influence before 1958 can also be inferred from its swift appearance as a massive women's organization after 1958. In March 1959, the league claimed to have twenty thousand members, and a year later it claimed to have doubled that number to forty-two thousand.[49]

The League for the Defense of Women's Rights posed a direct challenge to the status quo, to the facade of gradual modernization that perpetuated it, and hence to government gender discourse. It clearly addressed the underlying roots of women's construction as second-class citizens. It is noteworthy that in their mobilization to the overall struggle, league members stopped short of insisting on the immediate abolition of the TCCDR and state intervention in family matters or of insisting on the vote for women. They concentrated solely on securing a better future, and this decision in essence facilitated the perpetuation of women's harsh present. Yet the league's rejection of all solutions that could serve "gradual modernization" and its choices in the struggle for women's rights can be seen as a productive course of action. A mere six years passed from the time the league was established in 1952, with the intention to combine the struggle for women's rights with the struggle for nationalist and popular demands, until the monarchy was overthrown in 1958 and profound changes occurred in the three major factors responsible for the unfavorable construction of women in Iraq.

CONTORTING A NEW GENDER DISCOURSE

For the duration of the monarchy period and especially in the 1950s, Iraqi women's rights activists confronted their government's construction of women as second-class citizens. They exposed women's lot in the countryside and the TCCDR's contribution to their oppression. They bemoaned the government's nonintervention in the field of personal status. They pushed for women's full participation in their country's economic, political, and social life and drew attention to the marginalization of female citizens. Their struggle constituted a competing construction of Iraqi women citizens. This construction comes into relief, however, only after the July 1958 coup.

Following that coup, the new republican government initiated measures largely portrayed as influenced by the efforts of the League for the Defense of Women's Rights, which now worked legally under the name of the Iraqi Women's League. However, these measures clearly reflect to no less an extent a response to the Iraqi Women's Union's efforts before 1958. The TCCDR was swiftly annulled, and Article 41 of the penal code, which permitted referring offenders to "tribal adjudication," was later deleted.[50] Women's formal tribalization was thus erased. In addition, an agrarian reform, demanded by both organizations, was introduced. It was presented as intending to tackle the deplorable situation in the Iraqi countryside and to open the way for rural men and women to possess land.[51]

The new republican regime also promised women political rights once political life renewed and gave a clear signal that it intended to end women's exclusion from formal politics. Naziha al-Dulaimi was appointed as a minister, setting a precedent not only in Iraq, but in the entire Arab world. Women now became part of the administration and took part in formulating laws. Al-Dulaimi, appointed minister of municipalities, was among the specialists, jurists, 'ulama', and politicians who prepared the new Personal Status Law, and the league prepared and presented a draft of this law to the Ministry of the Interior.

On 30 December 1959, Iraq's Personal Status Law was introduced with the declared intent "to ensure women their legal rights and family independence."[52] Personal status issues came under state control, and by borrowing lenient provisions from the various schools of Islamic law, it was attuned to criticism regarding family matters and gender relations raised by activists prior to 1958. The law moved toward securing women's personal rights, such as the right to consent to marriage, the right to choose a spouse, and the right to decide when to marry. It made an effort to address the problem of child brides by setting a legal minimum age for marriage and, by emphasizing their entitlement to *mahr*, made women a party to the marriage contract rather than objects of transaction. Women were thus to a much greater degree able to make free and rational decisions.

The law also severely curtailed polygamy, sanctioning it only with the express permission of a judge. In addition, it restricted a man's ability to divorce his wife. Repudiation became void if uttered by a man whose mental capacities were in doubt—due to intoxication or extreme anger, for instance. A triple declaration of divorce could now result in a single divorce only, and men were required to commence divorce proceedings in court. The law also allowed women to seek the dissolution of their marriages through judicial proceedings on various grounds, including injury and domestic discord. The threat of divorce—with the resulting loss of a woman's financial support, home, and children that cemented dominant–submissive gender relations—was eased; the law gave mothers preferential rights regarding the custody of their children. Maternal custody following divorce was granted for children up to the age of seven, and the court was allowed to extend this upper age limit if the child's welfare so required. The new legislation also contained a particularly far-reaching reform: Islamic inheritance laws were abandoned in favor of equal inheritance status for men and women.[53] It is noteworthy that when religious leaders protested to Prime Minister 'Abd al-Karim Qasim over this clause, he replied that the public welfare of the Iraqi people demanded equality between men and women in every respect out of consideration for the rights of half of the Iraqi people.[54] But the significance of this clause lay not only in making men and women equal before the law, but also in strengthening women's economic base, thus undermining a major coercive element cementing men's dominance over women. Although in later years some critics pointed to the many loopholes contained within the 1959 law, it was in actuality a milestone when viewed against the draft Code of Personal Status and the TCCDR of the monarchy period. As the TCCDR was annulled, the law significantly offered the same treatment for rural and urban women in the personal status realm.

These measures may more closely resemble "first steps" than the comprehensive reform the Iraqi Women's Union had hoped for or the radical transformation the League for the Defense of Women's Rights had desired. There was no legislation tackling customary law (e.g., prohibiting the *nahwa* and *fasl* marriage or "honor" murders); the new Personal Status Law was far from perfect; Dulaimi's appointment was short lived; and because the new government failed to establish a Parliament, any provision in the new Constitution that could be interpreted as granting women political rights became a dead letter. Yet with these measures a new government gender discourse had clearly been born. The contour of that discourse, as we have seen, was shaped by the struggle of activists, both union and league, throughout the monarchy period. Although competing with other perceptions, entangled with the problematic notion of modernity, and often utilitarian and hypocritical, the new construction of women now gained dominance and prevailed well into the second half of the twentieth century.[55]

EPILOGUE

PAST MEETS PRESENT

The U.S.-led invasion of Iraq became a full-scale military occupation while I was in the midst of working on this book—a historical account of women under the British occupation and the British-installed monarchy in the first half of the twentieth century. I found myself more and more intrigued, as contemporary events cascaded, to find that the struggle of women's rights activists, especially between 2003 and 2005, to a large extent revolved around the same three issues that had concerned activists during the Hashemite period. Activists in fact warned that women were about to be dragged back to days of the monarchy. Few, however, appreciated the true weight of these warnings. Therefore, in this epilogue I place activists' post-2003 struggle to secure meaningful participation in politics, to prevent state tolerance of coercive practices pertaining to women, and to preserve Iraq's Personal Status Law against the backdrop of the Hashemite period. Similar threads running through past British and present American policies influenced the fate of two generations of Iraqi women separated by half a century.

MEANINGFUL POLITICAL PARTICIPATION?

In postinvasion Iraq, women's participation in the political process was quickly pushed to the top of women's rights activists' agenda. The coalition invasion had been accompanied by promises to enshrine women's rights. Yet although there was no movement to divest women of the franchise, women were almost totally absent in the leadership of the transi-

tion period. Of the twenty-five seats on the U.S.-appointed Iraqi Governing Council (IGC) installed in July 2003, women occupied only three; the
provisional government selected immediately thereafter had only one female minister. Activists concerned about marginalization in the political
process thus lobbied to secure no less than 30 percent representation for
women in the National Assembly and in all decision-making positions.
The Higher Women's Council was launched in October 2003 to increase
women's participation at all levels of government. A delegation of Iraqi
women professionals who met with U.S. president George W. Bush in November 2003 raised the idea of a quota for women in Parliament.[1] The
same demand was raised repeatedly in early 2004—at demonstrations,
in a communiqué sent to U.S. civil administrator Paul Bremer, and at a
meeting with the rotating chairman of the IGC, ʿAdnan Pachachi.[2] Under
pressure from activists, with the support of liberal Iraqi politicians and
Coalition Provisional Authority officials—who persuaded Bremer to drop
his resistance to the idea of a quota[3]—a provision was added to the Transitional Administrative Law (TAL) in this regard. It mandated that the
Electoral Law "aim to achieve the goal of having women constitute no
less than one-quarter of the members of the National Assembly."[4] By requiring each political party participating in the January 2005 elections to
present a list of candidates in which no fewer than one out of three candidates was to be a woman, the Electoral Law guaranteed to women an
unprecedented number of seats in the interim Parliament—almost one-
third of the total.[5]

In mid-2005, however, late drafts of the permanent constitution
emerged in which the 25 percent quota was removed or phased out.
Women's activists responded with protests and demonstrations. In the
beginning of August 2005, for example, ninety women's organizations
demonstrated, demanding that the permanent constitution maintain the
25 percent quota.[6] Their efforts were successful; the Constitution, as approved by public referendum in October 2005, affirmed that the Electoral
Law was to guarantee no less than a 25 percent representation to women
in Parliament.[7] True, many activists were disappointed with the result of
the 2005 elections—most of the women who entered Parliament were not
among those on whom women's rights activists had pinned their hopes.
Nevertheless, other activists emphasized the achievement of having a
constitutionally mandated quota for women and hailed the 25 percent al-
location as a "national milestone."[8]

The determination with which activists pursued the anchoring of their political rights in the Constitution and the Electoral Law must be seen not only against the background of post-2003 exclusion, but also in the broader historical perspective of women's marginalization in politics. Constitutions and election laws had been responsible for excluding women from formal politics from the inception of the state. The Constitution and Electoral Law during the mandate carved in stone women's disenfranchisement and set the stage for an uphill struggle that activists would engage in for decades. After the fall of the monarchy in 1958, the new constitution, which asserted that citizens were equal before the law with regard to their civic rights and duties, was interpreted as giving women full political rights.[9] Yet, as mentioned earlier, the new government failed to establish a Parliament, and the provision in the Constitution that had been interpreted as granting women political rights became a dead letter. When the Ba'th regime assumed power in 1968, its Interim Constitution of 1970 contained articles emphasizing the equal rights of women as citizens and prescribed the establishment of a National Assembly.[10] But only in 1980 was a National Assembly established, and only then did Iraqi women go to the ballot box for the first time. But the new Electoral Law, promulgated in March that year, required all candidates who wanted to run to obtain permission from an election commission; this meant that only women affiliated with the Ba'th Party could be elected.[11]

This "constitutional experience" spurred activists. Constitutions and election laws explicitly excluded women from formal politics in the country's first decades and severely restricted their political participation in the last few decades. The guarantee in the permanent constitution that women of all political beliefs would have representation in Parliament was thus an undeniable achievement, and securing 25 percent of parliamentary seats, a significant increase from a previous peak of only 13 percent,[12] was certainly a breakthrough.

Americans' rhetoric on the eve of their departure from a devastated Iraq credited the United States with securing the quota for women in Iraq's Constitution, which, they boasted, was drafted with "lots of American input." As the 2010 general election approached, American media proclaimed that political parties in Iraq for the first time ever had to take women's issues seriously and that political participation had empowered women in this male-dominated society.[13] But, as demonstrated earlier, the Iraqi activists' efforts were in no way insignificant. The claim that U.S.-led actions forced political parties for the first time to consider women's issues is similarly self-aggrandizing because since the 1930s parties opposing the socioeconomic and political order that evolved under the British Mandate had not only considered women's issues but openly supported women's rights. Furthermore, the claim that political participation gained during the American occupation truly empowered women comes into question as we turn to examine activists' struggle in the realms of personal status and customary law, which historically have been entwined with their struggle to gain political rights.

RETRIBALIZATION?

From the onset of the war in 2003, notwithstanding support for the idea that all groups with a stake in Iraq's future should be included in decision making, activists expressed concern regarding the incorporation of tribal leaders in positions of power. Turning tribal leaders into a political mainstay might result in acquiescence to values and customs detrimental to women.[14] Their concerns were no doubt influenced by the revival of tribalism under Saddam Husain. In the 1990s, Saddam recognized tribal shaikhs' authority in settling disputes among "their tribesmen," and as part of the restoration of tribal justice and values, his Revolutionary Command Council passed a decision in 1990 that exempted from punishment men who murdered their female relatives suspected of adultery.[15] The activists' fears, however, were rooted in the past, in the days of the British occupation and British-backed monarchy, when a special regulation allowed state-controlled sheikhs-turned-landlords to dispense justice among "their tribesmen" according to "tribal methods and customs." In 2005, Songul Chapuk, a member of the Iraqi IGC and a women's rights activist, cautioned that if the tribes were to take over matters of civil society, women would be deprived of their rights and be dragged back to "the days of the monarchy and the feudalist regime."[16] The tribal system, Chapuk noted, does not recognize women's rights; it does not view women as independent entities, but as possessions.

Fear that under the American-led coalition Iraq would revert to such policies was not unfounded. Following the 2003 invasion, British forces, faced with the urgent need to reestablish law and order across the southern part of the country, searched for precedents from their earlier experience in Iraq. Military lawyers, it was reported, were "dusting down the system of law used during the 38-year British Mandate in Iraq in an urgent effort to reach a workable interim criminal and civil code before a new constitution and legal system is agreed."[17] What they were in fact contemplating was a resurrection of the TCCDR.[18]

Moreover, irrespective of these deliberations, between 2003 and 2005 circumstances with worrisome historical parallels to the days of the British occupation and the British-backed monarchy were emerging. By 2005 and even before the Americans' massive use of the tribal "Awakening" fighters, coalition forces, increasingly desperate to impose order, were recruiting tribal elements to secure borders and protect oil facilities. Under the mounting disorder, tribal courts were convened, sanctioning coercive practices pertaining to women. At the same time, in debates regarding the permanent constitution, some negotiators were pressing for the recognition of tribal justice.[19]

Activists responded to this threat. From the very outset, they sought to write into the interim and permanent constitutions clauses that would afford legal protection to women against gender-based "tribal and cultural laws and practices."[20] Their protest apparently led to a modification of the article in the Constitution promising that the state shall seek the advancement of Iraqi tribes and uphold their noble human values to also guarantee that "the state shall prohibit tribal customs that are in contradiction of human rights."[21]

Since the end of 2006, however, the Americans began massively relying on tribal fighters to fight al-Qaʿida, even though they had initially opposed this approach. Prime Minister Nuri al-Maliki refused to integrate these militias into Iraq's security system but encouraged the establishment of tribal "support councils." He presented these efforts as contributing toward national reconciliation and security, but his opponents blamed him for the politicization of the tribes.[22] Time will tell how this round of dependence on tribal elements will affect the state, but for women a clear threat of tribalization is looming. In mid-2010, for example, it was reported that in Basra alone since the beginning of that year eight hundred women found themselves in *fasl* marriage—handed over in the settlement of disputes.[23] The rise in such practices has also been facilitated by the undermining of Iraq's Personal Status Law.

RESUBORDINATION?

Iraq's Personal Status Law was under threat almost immediately following the U.S. invasion. The 1959 law, as we saw, brought personal status issues under state control and, by borrowing lenient provisions from the various schools of Islamic law, was attuned to activists' demands concerning gender relations. In fact, the Iraqi Women's League (formerly the League for the Defense of Women's Rights) was involved in preparing it. The law applied to both rural and urban women because the TCCDR was annulled and made important steps in securing rights for women in marriage and divorce. Later amendments, especially the 1978 amendment, took additional steps in this direction. In 1978, the Ba'th regime introduced an extensive amendment to the 1959 law based on a selective integration of Sunni and Shi'i laws favorable to women. Limited pluralism in the early 1970s allowed women's activists to exert pressure on the regime to address unfavorable loopholes and provisions. This amendment eliminated the ambiguity in the law regarding the minimum age for marriage;[24] that age was set at fifteen. For the first time, severe restrictions were placed on customs that had still prevailed in the countryside. Punishments were set not only for forcing women into marriage, but also for preventing women from marrying, as had been made possible by such customs as *fasl* marriage and the *nahwa* (men's right to prevent the marriage of their female relatives). In other words, this amendment further undermined the control over female citizens wielded by their kin. The 1978 legislation also took steps to extend the conditions under which women were permitted to seek the dissolution of their marriages through judicial proceedings. It further weakened the threat of divorce and subsequent "loss of motherhood" by prolonging maternal custody until the child reached the age of ten and by extending custody until the age of fifteen if the child's welfare so dictated.[25]

During the 1980s and 1990s under Saddam Husain, some of these achievements were eroded; at the same time, several amendments favorable to women were introduced as a result of appeals on the part of the Ba'thi General Federation of Iraqi Women.[26] And the Personal Status Law remained in effect. On 29 December 2003, however, the U.S.-appointed IGC, chaired at the time by 'Abd al-'Aziz al-Hakim, a Shi'i cleric who also headed the Supreme Council for the Islamic Revolution in Iraq, passed Resolution 137 abolishing this law. Resolution 137 required that matters of personal status be handled in accordance with the various schools of Islamic jurisprudence to the exclusion of all previous legislation. In other words, the clerics of each and every community in Iraq were to take the state's place in administering matters of personal status for members of their respective sects or religious groups.[27]

Resolution 137 was immediately met with fierce resistance spearheaded by Iraqi women politicians and activists and was repealed two months later. However, this repeal did not prevent further moves to undermine the Personal Status Law on the part of both clerics and religious politicians who sat on the committee charged with the drafting of a permanent constitution. Throughout July and August 2005, the conflict continued between those advocating preservation of the existing Personal Status Law (the Kurds, liberal politicians, and women activists) and the Shi'i clerics and religious politicians seeking its abolition.[28] U.S. ambassador to Iraq Zalmay Khalilzad seemed initially to support the activists' view. In July 2005, when a draft constitution containing a provision stating that personal status matters would be regulated by law in accordance with the person's religion and sect (school of jurisprudence),[29] he left little doubt as to what he thought of proposals that turned family matters over to religious law: "A society cannot achieve all its potential if it does things that prevent—weaken [the] prospects of—half of its population to make the fullest contribution that it can."[30] However, the provision that was ultimately adopted—Article 41 in the official text of the Iraqi Constitution—stated that "Iraqis are free in their commitment to their personal status according to their religions, sects, beliefs or choices, and this shall be regulated by law."[31] Though clearly providing for recourse to religious jurisprudence, no specific provision was made to preserve the lenient, nonsectarian Personal Status Law as an option. The article allowed the law to remain à la carte, but because it still requires implementing legislation, it may be unfavorably amended or erased altogether.

In an interesting twist, Khalilzad described the final draft constitution as "the most progressive document of the Muslim world."[32] He interpreted Article 41 to mean that Iraqis would be able to choose between civil and shari'a law for their personal status needs. It is claimed that it was Khalilzad's intervention that produced a change in the wording of this article, allowing women to choose options other than forcing them to be subject to the law of their religious communities.[33] At the time, however, Kurdish and Sunni politicians involved in drafting the Constitution accused Khalilzad of pushing them, in his drive to complete the Constitution on time, to accept too great a role for Islamic law, which would thus facilitate clerical domination over personal status.[34]

Iraqi activists had dreaded this development. Throughout their struggle to preserve the Personal Status Law, they had predicted that its annulment would set Iraq back fifty years. They warned of the dire ramifications of wresting control over family affairs from the hands of the state and exposing women to unfavorable interpretations of Islamic law. Retired judge Zakiyya Isma'il Haqqi reflected most clearly the reason for women politicians and activists' protests. Since 1959, she said, Iraqi family law has developed and been amended under a series of secular governments, giving women a "half-share in society" and an opportunity to develop as individuals. Referring to Resolution 137, which was to a large extent accepted by Article 41, she said: "This new law will send Iraqi families back to the Middle Ages. It will allow men to have four or five or six wives. It will take children away from their mothers. It will allow anyone who calls himself a cleric to open an Islamic court in his house and decide who can marry and divorce and have rights."[35] Clearly referring to pre-1958 conditions and to practices not addressed until the 1978 amendment, activists chanted in their demonstration at the time the Constitution was being drafted: "No to the *nahwa*, no to *fasl* marriage, no to gift marriage, we want the Personal Status Law" ("la nahwa, la fasliyya, la hadiyya, nurid qanun al-ahwal al-shakhsiyya").[36]

Throughout their mobilization against the abolition of the Personal Status Law, activists were met by accusations from religious and conservative opponents. Endeavoring to delegitimize the activists' struggle, these opponents portrayed them as unauthentic and detached from Iraq's traditions and history, trying to impose foreign values or seeking to continue Saddam's secular policies.[37] As we saw, however, women's rights activists and the *'ulama'* had conflicting views concerning state law regulating personal status issues. From the first decades of the state's history, women's rights supporters had sought state intervention in this realm, whereas clerics had vehemently opposed it. The 1959 legislation, it should be remembered, marked the apex of a long struggle waged throughout the monarchy period over the authority to make laws governing personal status, the nature of the courts, and who should be entrusted with adjudication. From 1959 until 2003, the state maintained the upper hand. For activists, the state law not only had made significant steps toward constructing women as independent and protected citizens but also had created a framework that legitimized women's participation in the negotiations over their rights. In 2003, soon after the U.S.-led invasion, clerics the Americans had appointed to serve in the IGC seized the opportunity to regain lost power and prestige that the state had usurped with the introduction of the Personal Status Law.[38] It should be noted that it was under rotating chairman ʿAbd al-ʿAziz al-Hakim, son of long-time opponent of the Personal Status Law Grand Ayatulla Muhsin al-Hakim, that Resolution 137, abolishing the Personal Status Law, was passed.

In facilitating transformation of the Personal Status Law into the exception rather than the rule, Ambassador Khalilzad accepted the portrayal of activists and secular-oriented Sunni and Kurd politicians as being unrepresentative of the people in Iraq. He sided with clerics in a power struggle over who should control the personal-status realm. Iraqi activists, who historically have directed the political power they gained to improve women's rights and to protect women from harsh practices condoned by customary law and detrimental interpretations of Islamic law, now found that not only their hard-won advances were threatened, but also the very legal channel through which these achievements were made possible.

DÉJÀ VU

Under the Americans, who came to Iraq armed with a vision of creating a free and democratic state in which women's rights are enshrined, religious and tribal leaders were propped up, and the floodgates were opened to retribalize and resubordinate women. Scholars are increasingly turning attention to the rationale behind these American actions. Juan Cole noted the U.S. change of heart in August 2005. He suggested that after the invasion the Bush administration had an interest in "promoting a mild state feminism" in Iraq—both because it made for good U.S. domestic politics and because it might weaken the religious parties most closely associated to Iran. But in 2005 after the victory of the Shiʿi religious coalition in the January elections, Washington was increasingly tempted to cooperate with that coalition.[39] American involvement in the realm of personal status also drew attention from activists and scholars Nadje al-Ali and Nicola Pratt. They argued that the Bush administration had perceived Iraqi society in terms of a collection of distinct communities and that the coalition's policies thus encouraged sectarianism. They pointed out that Iraq's new constitution did not designate a personal status law as among the areas to be decided by the central government. Therefore, it allowed Kurd, Shi'i, and Sunni leaders to have separate laws while still being tied to one state. By devolving personal matters from the state to religion, sect, and region, they argued, communal leaders' loyalty was encouraged. But as the gates were opened to accommodate social and religious differences, they were also opened for washing out women's rights. Ali and Pratt's awareness of the Lebanese example led them to conclude that family law thus became "part of a 'social contract' trading communal autonomy for women's rights."[40]

Iraq's past is no less fertile soil for such insights. Indeed, Iraqi activists cautioned that under the American-led efforts to build a new Iraq, developments were pulling women back to pre-1958 conditions. As we saw, under British occupation and the British-backed monarchy the legal and political systems had harsh, long-lasting consequences for women. Such consequences were due not to a contrived gender policy, but to strategies aimed at ensuring efficient rule of the country. Specifically, they were the result of the British attempt to control Iraq through those individuals they perceived as or found useful to construct as Iraq's authentic leaders. State institutions, whether legal or political, were thus designed to tie tribal, religious, and secular leaders to the British-dominated state by giving them legal authority over "their communities" as well as political influence in the new Iraq. The end result for women, however, was not simply the marginalization of their interests, but rather the sacrifice of their well-being and rights. Women citizens in the nascent state of Iraq thus found themselves second-class citizens. A three-pronged government gender discourse had constructed them as tribal possessions, subordinate and disenfranchised.

Iraqi activists in postinvasion Iraq indeed faced the intrusion of a gender discourse all too similar to that of the monarchy period. But now disempowerment replaced disenfranchisement as women had to contend all over again for rights that they had already been granted. Today's activists' sense of déjà vu was informed by the generation of activists who had exposed and fought against this three-pronged gender discourse. Moreover, their struggle was not only against the return of the harsh discourse that in the past constructed women as second-class citizens, but in defense of the very discourse that the founding mothers of the Iraqi women's movement had helped set in place. Contrary to opponents' claims, then, activists' struggle today is far from unauthentic and is firmly rooted in Iraq's past.

NOTES

PREFACE

1. For a key work that meticulously portrays the situation Iraqi women found themselves in under American occupation, see Nadje al-Ali and Nicola Pratt, *What Kind of Liberation? Women and the Occupation of Iraq* (Berkeley and Los Angeles: University of California Press, 2009).

2. See more in the epilogue.

3. The exceptions are Doreen Ingrams, *The Awakened: Women in Iraq* (London: Third World Center, 1983); Martina Kamp, "Abschied von der Abaya? Eine historische Interpretation zur politischen und sozio-ökonomischen Situation irakischer Frauen während der Monarchie," master's thesis, Hamburg University, 1997; Deborah Cobbett, "Women in Iraq," in Committee Against Repression and for Democratic Rights in Iraq, *Saddam's Iraq: Revolution or Reaction?* 120–137 (London: Zed Books, 1989); Jacqueline S. Ismael and Shereen T. Ismael, "Gender and State in Iraq," in Suad Joseph, ed., *Gender and Citizenship in the Middle East*, 185–211 (Syracuse, N.Y.: Syracuse University Press, 2000); Jacqueline S. Ismael and Shereen T. Ismael, "Iraqi Women Under Occupation: From Tribalism to Neo-Feudalism," *International Journal of Contemporary Iraqi Studies* 1 (2007): 247–268; Nadje Sadig al-Ali, *Iraqi Women: Untold Stories from 1948 to the Present* (London: Zed Books, 2007); and Orit Bashkin, "Representations of Women in the Writings of the Intelligentsia in Hashemite Iraq, 1921–1958," *Journal of Middle East Women's Studies* 4, no. 1 (Winter 2008): 53–82. Most of these works, however, with the exception of Kamp's and Bashkin's, devote little attention to the Hashemite period. In their thought-provoking article "Iraqi Women Under Occupation," Ismael and Ismael relate some of the same seminal issues concerning women under the British Mandate that I elaborate on in my work. Their brevity and overall trajectory, however, lead them to different findings and conclusions.

4. See the epilogue.

5.   For more, see Beth Baron, "A Field Matures: Recent Literature on Women in the Middle East," *Middle Eastern Studies* 32 (1996): 172–186; Nikki R. Keddie, *Women in the Middle East: Past and Present* (Princeton, N.J.: Princeton University Press, 2007); Margaret L. Meriwether and Judith E. Tucker, "Introduction," in Margaret L. Meriwether and Judith E. Tucker, eds., *A Social History of Women and Gender in the Modern Middle East*, 1–24 (Boulder, Colo.: Westview, 1999).

6.   There are now numerous works published on the topic of women's movements in the Middle East. See, for example, Leila Ahmed, "Feminism and Feminist Movements in the Middle East, a Preliminary Exploration: Turkey, Egypt, Algeria, People's Democratic Republic of Yemen," *Women's Studies International Forum* 5 (1982): 153–168; Margot Badran, *Feminists, Islam, and Nation: Gender and the Making of Modern Egypt* (Princeton, N.J.: Princeton University Press, 1995); Beth Baron, *The Women's Awakening in Egypt: Culture, Society, and the Press* (New Haven, Conn.: Yale University Press, 1994); Ellen Fleischmann, *The Nation and Its "New" Women: The Palestinian Women's Movement, 1920–1948* (Berkeley and Los Angeles: University of California Press, 2003); Ingrams, *The Awakened*; Deniz Kandiyoti, "End of Empire: Islam, Nationalism, and Women in Turkey," in Deniz Kandiyoti, ed., *Women, Islam, and the State*, 22–47 (London: Macmillan, 1991); Cynthia Nelson, *Doria Shafik, Egyptian Feminist: A Woman Apart* (Gainesville: University Press of Florida, 1996); Eliz Sanasarian, *The Women's Rights Movement in Iran: Mutiny, Appeasement, and Repression, from 1900 to Khomeini* (New York: Praeger, 1982); Parvin Paidar, *Women and the Political Process in Twentieth-Century Iran* (Cambridge, U.K.: Cambridge University Press, 1995); Nükhet Sirman, "Feminism in Turkey: A Short History," *New Perspectives on Turkey* 3 (Fall 1989): 1–34; Elizabeth Thompson, *Colonial Citizens: Republican Rights, Paternal Privilege, and Gender in French Syria and Lebanon* (New York: Columbia University Press, 2000).

7.   Compare, for example, Lois Beck and Nikki Keddie, eds., *Women in the Muslim World* (Cambridge, Mass.: Harvard University Press, 1978), with Nikki R. Keddie and Beth Baron, eds., *Women in Middle Eastern History: Shifting Boundaries in Sex and Gender* (New Haven, Conn.: Yale University Press, 1991). See also Kandiyoti, *Women, Islam, and the State*; Judith E. Tucker, ed., *Arab Women: Old Boundaries, New Frontiers* (Bloomington: Indiana University Press, 1993); Fatma Müge Göçek and Shiva Balaghi, eds., *Reconstructing Gender in the Middle East: Tradition, Identity, and Power* (New York: Columbia University Press, 1994); Lila Abu-Lughod, ed., *Remaking Women: Feminism and Modernity in the Middle East* (Princeton, N.J.: Princeton University Press, 1998); and Joseph, *Gender and Citizenship in the Middle East*.

8.   The debate about the proper definition of the word *feminism* within the particular historical context of the Middle East is just one example. See Ellen Fleischmann, "The Other 'Awakening': The Emergence of Women's Movements in the Modern Middle East, 1900–1940," in Meriwether and Tucker, eds., *A Social History of Women and Gender in the Modern Middle East*, 90–93.

9. This criticism has followed the study of women in the Middle East since its early days. See, for example, Nikki R. Keddie, "Problems in the Study of Middle Eastern Women," *International Journal of Middle East Studies* 10 (1979): 225–240; Keddie, *Women in the Middle East*; Judith Tucker, "Problems in the Historiography of Women in the Middle East: The Case of Nineteenth-Century Egypt," *International Journal of Middle East Studies* 15 (1983): 321–336; Paidar, *Women and the Political Process in Twentieth-Century Iran*, 1–24; Mervat F. Hatem, "Modernization, the State, and the Family in Middle East Women's Studies," in Meriwether and Tucker, eds., *A Social History of Women and Gender in the Modern Middle East*, 63–87; Ruth Roded, *Women in Islam and the Middle East: A Reader*, 2d ed. (London: I. B. Tauris, 2008), 1–23.

10. See Meriwether and Tucker, "Introduction," 3–8.

11. This genre has a long indigenous history. For more, see Ruth Roded, *Women in Islamic Biographical Collections: From Ibn Sa'd to Who's Who* (Boulder, Colo.: Lynne Rienner, 1994).

12. Ahmed is retelling well-known historical events and emphasizes the part played by women, but the analysis of dominant and contesting discourses is her framework. In the second part of *Women and Gender in Islam: Historical Roots of a Modern Debate* (New Haven, Conn.: Yale University Press, 1992), "Founding Discourses," she argues that early Islam opened up possibilities for more egalitarian gender relations, but under succeeding Muslim rulers, in particular the Abbasids, the egalitarian voice was muted by a rigid and hierarchal "establishment Islam." Then, turning to discuss "new discourses," she points out the appearance from the nineteenth century on of the colonial discourse or an indigenous feminist discourse that did not derive its inspiration from the West. Paidar's work likewise deals with women and the political process, but she is also occupied with competing discourses. Her study focuses on the construction of women by three broad discourses that dominated Iranian political life in the twentieth century: the discourse of modernity (dominant between 1900 and 1977), the discourse of revolution (1977 to 1979), and the discourse of Islamization (prevalent since the establishment of the Islamic Republic in Iran).

13. For a useful introduction to the concept of discourse and a comprehensive overview of the different conceptions and methods of discourse analysis, see David Howarth, *Discourse* (Philadelphia: Open University Press, 2000).

14. Stuart Hall, "The Work of Representation," in Stuart Hall, ed., *Representation: Cultural Representations and Signifying Practices* (London: Sage, 1997), 44, emphasis in original; see also Stuart Hall, "The West and the Rest: Discourse and Power," in Stuart Hall and Bram Gieben, eds., *Formations of Modernity* (Cambridge, U.K.: Polity Press, 1992), 291–295.

15. I do not use the term *Efendiyya* in this work to refer to the Iraqi educated class because there is an inconsistency between the masculine connotation of the word and the historical realities of women's participation in the same sociopolitical movements and generational identifications that it is meant to evoke. See Noga

Efrati, "The *Effendiyya*: Where Have All the Women Gone?" *International Journal of Middle East Studies* 43, no. 1 (May 2011): 375–377.

INTRODUCTION: THE HISTORICAL SETTING

This chapter is based primarily on the following works: Charles Tripp, *A History of Iraq* (Cambridge, U.K.: Cambridge University Press, 2000), 30–147; Marion Farouk-Sluglett and Peter Sluglett, *Iraq Since 1958*, 3rd ed. (London: I. B. Tauris, 2001), 1–45; Phebe Marr, *The Modern History of Iraq*, 2d ed. (Boulder, Colo.: Westview, 2004), 3–79; and Thabit A. J. Abdullah, *A Short History of Iraq* (London: Pearson-Longman, 2003), 123–154.

1. Province: in Turkish *vilayet* and in Arabic *wilaya*.
2. See Marion Farouk-Sluglett and Peter Sluglett, "The Transformation of Land Tenure and Rural Social Structure in Central and Southern Iraq, c. 1870–1958," *International Journal of Middle East Studies* 15 (1983): 491–505.
3. Marr, *The Modern History of Iraq* (2004), 7.
4. "Ja'fari" is a reference to followers of Imam Ja'far al-Sadiq, one of the twelve recognized imams of the Shi'i tradition and regarded as the most competent of them in legal matters.
5. Yitzhak Nakash, *The Shi'is of Iraq* (Princeton, N.J.: Princeton University Press, 1994), 72.
6. Tripp, *A History of Iraq*, 44; Marr, *The Modern History of Iraq*, 24.
7. Marr, *The Modern History of Iraq* (2004), 24.
8. 'Abd al-Razzaq al-Hasani, *Ta'rikh al-Wizarat al-'Iraqiyya*, 10 vols., 7th ed. (Baghdad: Afaq 'Arabiyya, 1988), 3:315–316.
9. Tripp, *A History of Iraq*, 57.
10. C. A. Hooper, *The Constitutional Law of Iraq* (Baghdad: Mackenzie & Mackenzie, 1928), 15.
11. For the full text of the Iraqi Constitution in English and Arabic, see ibid.; and al-Hasani, *Ta'rikh al-Wizarat al-'Iraqiyya*, 1:339–354.
12. Iraq Ministry of Justice, *Compilation of Laws and Regulations Issued Between 1st January 1924 and 31st December 1925* (Baghdad: Government Press, 1926), 45–51.
13. It is important to note, as Marion Farouk-Sluglett and Peter Sluglett explain (*Iraq Since 1958*, 17), that with time the figures advancing Arab nationalism as well as the nationalistic doctrine itself changed significantly. The patriotic and nationalist attitudes of Iraqi officers such as Nuri al-Sa'id and Ja'far al-'Askari, who joined the Arab revolt and then supported Faisal and the Iraqi state, were initially not questioned. These individuals were involved in both the struggle for the Arab cause as well as the creation of an Arab state. By the end of the 1920s, however, they were seen as kowtowing to the British, and their Arab nationalist credentials were challenged. The banner of Arab or Iraqi nationalism then passed to more diverse groups, which appealed to the people by fusing the wish for Arab or Iraqi independence with other immediately pressing political and social desires.

14. For the program of the Popular Reform Association, see al-Hasani, *Ta'rikh al-Wizarat al-'Iraqiyya*, 4:287–289.

15. Hanna Batatu, *The Old Social Classes and the Revolutionary Movements of Iraq* (Princeton, N.J.: Princeton University Press, 1978), 471.

16. For the ICP platform, see "Al-Mithaq al-Watani li-l-Hizb al-Shuyu'i al-'Iraqi," in Fakhri Karim, ed., *Kitabat al-Rafiq Fahd,* 2d ed., 133–137 (Baghdad: al-Tariq al-Jadid, 1976); and Batatu, *The Old Social Classes*, 513–514.

17. For al-Istiqlal's program, see al-Hasani, *Ta'rikh al-Wizarat al-'Iraqiyya*, 7:25–33.

18. For the NDP program, see ibid., 37–41.

19. For more on the relationship between the Palestine issue and Iraq, see Michael Eppel, *The Palestine Conflict in the History of Modern Iraq: Dynamics of Involvement, 1928–1948* (London: Frank Cass, 1994).

20. Batatu, *The Old Social Classes*, 106–107.

21. Al-Hasani, *Ta'rikh al-Wizarat al-'Iraqiyya*, 8:118–123.

22. Marr, *The Modern History of Iraq* (2004), 69, 313, based on Batatu, *The Old Social Classes*, 54.

23. Marr, *The Modern History of Iraq* (2004), 70.

1. OCCUPATION, MONARCHY, AND CUSTOMARY LAW:
TRIBALIZING WOMEN

1. See, for example, Peter Sluglett, *Britain in Iraq, 1914–1932* (New York: Columbia University Press, 2007), 169–181; Toby Dodge, *Inventing Iraq: The Failure of Nation Building and a History Denied* (New York: Columbia University Press, 2003), 83–100.

2. Philip Willard Ireland, *Iraq: A Study in Political Development* (London: J. Cape, 1937), 89–95; Marion Farouk-Sluglett and Peter Sluglett, "The Transformation of Land Tenure and Rural Social Structure in Central and Southern Iraq, c. 1870–1958," *International Journal of Middle East Studies* 15 (1983): 491–505.

3. Major Pulley, Political Officer, Hilla, to Civil Commissioner, Baghdad, 6 August 1920, India Office (IO), Files of the Political and Secret Departments, L/P&S 10/4722/18/1920/8/6305, quoted in Farouk-Sluglett and Sluglett, "The Transformation of Land Tenure," 496.

4. "Administration Report of Sulaimaniyah Division for the Year 1919," in *Iraq Administration Reports: 1914–1932*, 10 vols., sources established by Robert L. Jarman (Slough, U.K.: Archive Editions, 1992), 4:719.

5. C. E. Bruce, "The Sandeman Policy as Applied to Tribal Problems of Today," *Journal of the Royal Central Asian Society* 19 (1932), 51.

6. *Tribal Criminal and Civil Disputes Regulations* (Bombay: The Times Press, 1916), IO, L/P&S 10/617; "Tribal Criminal and Civil Disputes Regulation (Revised)," in *Iraq Administration Reports*, 8:144–156.

7. "Mesopotamia: Tribal Disputes Regulation," *Arab Bureau Bulletin*, no. 86 (21 April 1918), in *The Arab Bulletin: Bulletin of the Arab Bureau in Cairo, 1916–1919*, 4 vols. (Buckinghamshire, U.K.: Archives Editions, 1986), 3:130.

8. "The Tribal and Civil Disputes Regulations Amendment Law of 1924," in Iraq Ministry of Justice, *Compilation of Laws and Regulations Issued Between 1st January 1924 and 31st December 1925* (Baghdad: Government Press, 1926), 63; Sluglett, *Britain in Iraq 1914–1932,* 169–172.

9. Great Britain, General Officer Commanding-in-Chief, Mesopotamia Expeditionary Force, *The Baghdad Penal Code* (Baghdad: n.p., 1918); "Report on the Administration of Civil Justice for the Year 1918," Public Record Office, London (PRO), Foreign Office (FO) 371/4150/24429, pp. 2–3.

10. I started developing my ideas concerning British perceptions and construction of Iraq in my article "Gender, Tribe, and the British Construction of Iraq," in Zach Levey and Elie Podeh, eds., *Britain and the Middle East,* 152–165 (Eastbourne, U.K.: Sussex Academic Press, 2008).

11. Arnold T. Wilson, *Loyalties, Mesopotamia, 1914–1917: A Personal and Historical Record,* 2 vols. (London: Oxford University Press, 1936), 1:69.

12. See, for example, "Administration Report of Suq al-Shuyukh and Hammar District for the Year 1918," in *Iraq Administration Reports,* 2:363; "Report on the Administration of Justice for the Year 1919," in *Iraq Administration Reports,* 3:380; "Monthly Report of Arbil District for the Month of October 1919," IO, L/P&S 11/168; "Monthly Report A.P.O. Basrah for the Month of December 1919, IO," L/P&S 10/621; "Review of the Civil Administration of Mesopotamia for 1920," in *Iraq Administration Reports,* 5:18; "Annual Administration Report of the Mosul Division for the Year 1921," PRO, FO 371/7801/E10742; E. S. Stevens, *By Tigris and Euphrates* (London: Hurst and Blackett, 1923), 275, 280–281; "Report by His Majesty's Government in the United Kingdom of Great Britain and Northern Ireland to the Council of the League of Nations on the Administration of ʿIraq for the Year 1929," in *Iraq Administration Reports,* 9:221.

13. See, for example, "Administration Report of the Amarah Division for the Year 1920–21," in *Iraq Administration Reports,* 5:175; "Review of the Civil Administration of Mesopotamia for 1920," 5:18; "The Court of Cassation, Annual Report for 1929," National Archives of India, New Delhi (NAI), Baghdad High Commission File (BHCF), Judicial Matters, 8/219; Stevens, *By Tigris and Euphrates,* 275.

14. See James Saumarez Mann, *An Administrator in the Making: James Saumarez Mann, 1893–1920,* edited by his father (London: Longmans, Green, 1921), 220–222; "Administration Report for the Qurnah Area for the Year 1919," in *Iraq Administration Reports,* 4:269, and compare "Review of the Civil Administration of the Occupied Territories of Al ʿIraq, 1914–1918," in *Iraq Administration Reports,* 1:57; "Review of the Civil Administration of Mesopotamia for 1920," 5:17–18.

15. Fulanain (pseudonym for S. E. Hedgcock and M. G. Hedgcock), *Haji Rikkan: Marsh Arab* (London: Chatto & Windus, 1927), 54–55, 245–246.

16. "The Court of Cassation, Annual Report for 1929"; see also Hanna Batatu, *The Old Social Classes and the Revolutionary Movements of Iraq* (Princeton, N.J.: Princeton University Press, 1978), 145–146.

17. According to Jaʿfar Hamandi, the Iraqi director of legal affairs in the Ministry of Interior at the time, he himself was responsible for convincing the ministry

to issue this decree. See Mohammed Fadhel Jamali, *The New Iraq: Its Problem of Bedouin Education* (New York: Bureau of Publication, Teachers College, Columbia University, 1934), 144. For the Arabic text of the decree, see Mustafa Muhammad Hasanain, *Nizam al-Mas'uliyya 'ind al-'Asha'ir al-'Iraqiyya al-'Arabiyya al-Mu'asira* (Cairo: Matba'at al-Istiqlal al-Kubra, 1967), 210–211.

18. "Report by His Majesty's Government in the United Kingdom of Great Britain and Northern Ireland to the Council of the League of Nations on the Administration of 'Iraq for the Year 1929," 9:221; *Lughat al-'Arab* 8 (1930), 187.

19. See, for example, "Administration Report of the Amarah Division for the Year 1920–21," 5:175; "Diary of the Political Officer, Nasiriyeh Division for the Fortnight Ending 15th July 1918," H. R. P. Dickson's Private Papers, Box 2A, File 1, Middle East Center Library, St. Antony's College, Oxford University.

20. "Review of the Civil Administration of the Occupied Territories of Al 'Iraq, 1914–1918," 1:57; "Review of the Civil Administration of Mesopotamia for 1920," 5:18.

21. TCCDR, section 34(1), in *Iraq Administration Reports*, 8:151.

22. Proposed Amendments to the Tribal Disputes Law, from H. Dobbs to E. M. Drower, 18 October 1923, PRO, Colonial Office (CO) 730/103; K. Cornwallis to Sir Henry Dobbs, 7 June 1926, PRO, CO 730/103; H. Dobbs to John Shuckburgh, 10 June 1926, PRO, CO 730/103.

23. Copy of Memorandum No. A.12/1571, Dated 12-4-21, from the Judicial Adviser to the Adviser to the Ministry of Interior, Baghdad, PRO, CO 730/6; "Report by His Britannic Majesty's Government to the Council of the League of Nations on the Administration of 'Iraq for the Year 1927," in *Iraq Administration Reports*, 8:466.

24. Dodge, *Inventing Iraq*, especially 1–2, 83–100, 175–176.

25. "Review of the Civil Administration of the Occupied Territories of Al 'Iraq, 1914–1918," 1:57; "Review of the Civil Administration of Mesopotamia for 1920," 5:18.

26. See "Review of the Civil Administration of Mesopotamia for 1920," 5:18.

27. See correspondence between Henry Dobbs and Kinahan Cornwallis, dated 7 and 8 June 1926, PRO, CO 730/103.

28. Proposed Amendments to the Tribal Disputes Law, from H. Dobbs to E. M. Drower, 18 October 1923, PRO, CO 730/103.

29. See "Administration Reports of the 'Amarah Division for the Years 1919 and 1920–21," in *Iraq Administration Reports*, 4:9 and 5:175.

30. "Report on the Administration of Justice for the Year 1919," 380.

31. Gayatry Chakravorty Spivak, "Can the Subaltern Speak?" in Cary Nelson and Laurence Grossberg, eds., *Marxism and the Interpretation of Culture* (Urbana: University of Illinois Press, 1988), 296.

32. "Administration Report of the 'Amarah Division for the Years 1919 and 1920–21," 4:9.

33. Copy of Confidential Memorandum No. S.679, Dated 30th July 1921, from the Judicial Adviser, Baghdad, to the High Commissioner, Baghdad, PRO, CO 730/6.

34. Great Britain, General Officer Commanding-in-Chief, *The Baghdad Penal Code*, 25; Iraq Ministry of Justice, *Draft: 'Iraq Penal Code, 1929* (Baghdad: Government Press, 1929), 15 and 36; Articles 55 and 283, NAI, BHCF, *Baghdad Penal Code* 8/50,

vol. II; Copy of Memorandum No. A.12/1571, Dated 12-4-21, from Judicial Adviser to the Adviser to the Ministry of Interior, Baghdad, PRO, CO 730/6; E. M. Drower to Sir Henry Dobbs, 21 October 1923, PRO, CO 730/103; "Report by His Britannic Majesty's Government to the Council of the League of Nations on the Administration of 'Iraq for the Year 1927," *Iraq Administration Reports*, 8:466.

35. As claimed by E. S. Stevens (Drower). See Stevens, *By Tigris and Euphrates*, 280.

36. Fulanain, *Haji Rikkan*, 55, 56–57.

37. Ibid., 46.

38. Ibid., 58.

39. Ibid., 55–56.

40. Dodge, *Inventing Iraq*, 97–98; Sir H. Dobbs to Mr. Amery, 4 December 1928, PRO, FO 406/63/E862/6/93; Jamali, *The New Iraq*, 73.

41. Jamali, *The New Iraq*, 144; *Lughat al-'Arab* 8 (1930), 187.

42. Jamali, *The New Iraq*, 73–74.

43. Ibid., 109–110 and 78.

44. Paul Monroe, *Report of the Educational Inquiry Commission* (Baghdad: Government Press, 1932), 132; Reeva S. Simon, *Iraq Between the Two World Wars: The Creation and Implementation of a Nationalist Ideology* (New York: Columbia University Press, 1986), 85, 89–90. For more about al-Jamali, see Yizhak Nakash, *The Shi'is of Iraq* (Princeton, N.J.: Princeton University Press, 1994), 109–138.

45. See Dobbs's comments following Bruce, "The Sandeman Policy," 66.

46. See Dobbs to Cornwallis, 9 June 1926, PRO, CO 730/103, as quoted in Dodge, *Inventing Iraq*, 98–99.

47. Makki Jamil, *Ta'liqat 'ala Nizam Da'awi al-'Asha'ir wa-Ta'dilatihi* (Baghdad: Matba'at al-Karah, 1935), 118–119.

48. C. A. Hooper, *The Constitutional Law of Iraq* (Baghdad: Mackenzie & Mackenzie, 1928), 145.

49. See "Iraq Police, Abstract of Intelligence," No. 13, 28 March 1933, PRO, Air Ministry, Royal Air Force, Overseas Commands, Air 23/589, vol. XV; "Tribal Code: Draft Law," February 1944, PRO, FO 624/38/493; and compare Fariq al-Muzhir al-Fir'awn, *Al-Qada' al-'Asha'iri* (Baghdad: Matba'at al-Najah, 1941), 205–206, with al-'Iraq, Majlis al-A'yan, *Mahdar al-Jalsa al-Hadiya 'Ashara min al-Ijtima' al-'Adi li-Sanat 1950–1951* (Baghdad: Matba'at al-Hukuma, 1951), 150.

50. "Tribal Code: Draft Law," February 1944, PRO, FO 624/38/493.

51. Ibid.

52. Al-Fir'awn, *Al-Qada' al-'Asha'iri*, 37–40, 75–88, 91–100, 110–114.

53. See the book review by H. S. B. Philby in *Journal of the Royal Central Asian Society* 29 (1942), 144–145.

54. Compare "Report by His Majesty's Government in the United Kingdom of Great Britain and Northern Ireland to the Council of the League of Nations on the Administration of Iraq for the Year 1929," 9:221, with Kazim Baji al-Khalidi's account, "'Ashirat al-Mushallab wa-l-Nahwa," *al-Turath al-Sha'bi* 2 (1978): 65–72.

55. Shakir Mustafa Salim, *Marsh Dwellers of the Euphrates Delta* (London: Athlone Press, 1962), 50.

56. "Report of Nasiriya District for the Month of October, 1919," IO, L/P&S 11/168; Hasanain, *Nizam al-Mas'uliyya*, 435 (Document No. 1); Muhammad al-Baqir al-Jalali, *Mujaz Ta'rikh 'Asha'ir al-'Amara* (Baghdad: al-Najah, 1947) 134–135.

57. Salim, *Marsh Dwellers*, 52; al-'Iraq, Majlis al-A'yan, *Mahdar al-Jalsa al-Hadiya 'Ashara, 1950–1951*, 150; Fulanain, *Haji Rikkan*, 55–56, 244–246.

58. See, for example, Hasanain, *Nizam al-Mas'uliyya*, 113–114; Fir'awn mentioned this example but also indicated that when the victim is an unmarried woman, the rapist would have to compensate the victim's family by handing over a woman. See al-Fir'awn, *Al-Qada' al-'Asha'iri*, 97–99.

59. "Tribal Code: Draft Law," February 1944, PRO, FO 624/38/493.

60. Dodge, *Inventing Iraq*, 63–100.

61. Such sentences were given to those convicted either for their part in the demonstration against Sir Alfred Mond in 1928 or in the general strike of 1931. See Sluglett, *Britain in Iraq 1914–1932*, 148, 172. See also the description of the expulsion of Rufa'il Butti and Fahmi al-Mudarris from Baghdad under the same section following the publication of an *al-Akhbar* article attacking the government, in "Intelligence Report for the Fortnight Ended 21st March, 1932," NAI, BHCF, Internal Intelligence Reports, 19/1, vol. XVI.

62. General Officer Commanding-in-Chief, *The Baghdad Penal Code*, 2, 5–6, 25; Hooper, *The Constitutional Law of Iraq*, 71, Article 26(10); 'Arif Rashid al-'Attar, *Al-Ijram fi al-Khalis* (Baghdad: al-Ma'arif, 1963), 85–86; M. Jamil, *Ta'liqat 'ala Nizam Da'awi al-'Asha'ir*, 93–96.

63. I thank Professor Peter Sluglett for suggesting I should study this case.

64. Extract from "Iraq Police, Abstract of Intelligence," No. 23, 14 November 1931, NAI, BHCF, Interior, "Murder of Abdullah al-Sani," File 7/17/168.

65. Batatu, *The Old Social Classes*, 95n.; Dodge, *Inventing Iraq*, 59–60; Sir H. Dobbs to Mr. Amery, December 4, 1928, PRO, FO 406/63/E862/6/93.

66. Sluglett, *Britain in Iraq*, 172; extract from "S.S.O. Nasiriyah Report, No. S/N/1 of the 10th November 1931," NAI, BHCF, Interior, "Murder of Abdullah al-Sani," File 7/17/168; "Iraq Police, Abstract of Intelligence," No. 21, 22 May 1933, PRO, Air 23/589, vol. XV; "Killing of Abdullah Beg Sana," Dispatch from A. K. Sloan to the Secretary of State, 9 November 1931, U.S. National Archives (USNA), Washington, D.C., 890G.405/1; Ernest Main, *Iraq: From Mandate to Independence* (London: Allen and Unwin, 1935), 253.

67. See, for example, "Translation of Confidential Memo No. 338 of 12th November 1931," from Mutasarrif Muntafiq Liwa, Nasiriyah, to the Ministry of Interior, NAI, BHCF, Interior, "Murder of Abdullah al-Sani," File 7/17/168; Main, *Iraq*, 253; "Killing of Abdullah Beg Sana," Dispatch from A. K. Sloan to the Secretary of State, 9 November 1931.

68. When the first Sa'duns came to Iraq from Najd, they brought with them a couple of slave families; the Sani' family, some of whose members were entrusted with the Sa'duns' business affairs, was one of them. See "The Tribal Viewpoint with Respect to the Murder of Abdullah Beg Sana," Dispatch from A. K. Sloan to the

Secretary of State, 31 May 1932, USNA, 890G.108/7, and Dispatch from A. K. Sloan to the Secretary of State, 31 May 1932, USNA, 890G.108/7.

69. From Special Service Officer, Baghdad, to Air Staff Intelligence, Air Headquarters, Hinaidi, 16 November 1931, NAI, BHCF, Interior, "Murder of Abdullah al-Sani," File 7/17/168; "The Sa'dun Trial," Dispatch from A. K. Sloan to the Secretary of State, 16 December 1931, USNA, 890G.00/169; "Trial of Falih Beg Sa'dun," Dispatch from A. K. Sloan, 30 December 1931, USNA, 890G.108/4; Dispatch from A. K. Sloan to the Secretary of State, 31 May 1932, USNA, 890G.108/7.

70. *Al-Waqa'i' al-'Iraqiyya* 1075 (11 January 1932), 1084 (4 February 1932), and 1191 (20 October 1932), in NAI, BHCF, Interior, "Murder of Abdullah al-Sani," File 7/17/168; "Iraq Police, Abstract of Intelligence," No. 20, 20 May 1933, PRO, Air 23/589, vol. XV.

71. Paul Knabenshue to the Secretary of State, 31 May 1933, USNA, 890G.108/8.

72. See, for example, al-'Attar, *Al-Ijram fi al-Khalis*, 86, and M. Jamil, *Ta'liqat 'ala Nizam Da'awi al-'Asha'ir*, 93–96.

73. "Tribal Code: Draft Law," February 1944, PRO, FO 624/38/493.

74. Stephen H. Longrigg, *Iraq, 1900 to 1950: A Political, Social, and Economic History* (London: Oxford University Press, 1953), 171.

75. Article 49 as quoted in Sluglett, *Britain in Iraq 1914–1932*, 180.

76. Paul Knabenshue to the Secretary of State, 21 April 1938, USNA, 890G.00, General Conditions/125; *al-Istiqlal*, 31 March 1938, 2. See 'Abd al-Karim al-Uzri's comments regarding the interior minister's defense of the TCCDR in 1945 in al-'Iraq, Majlis al-Nuwwab, *Mahdar al-Jalsa al-Thaniya wa-l-Thalathin min al-Ijtima' al-I'tiyadi li-Sanat 1950* (Baghdad: Matba'at al-Hukuma, 1951), 541; see also a quote from the interior minister from January 1956 in al-'Attar, *Al-Ijram fi al-Khalis*, 100.

77. See, for example, Mudhaffar Abdullah Amin, "Jama'at al-Ahali: Its Origin, Ideology, and Role in Iraqi Politics, 1932–1946," 2 vols., Ph.D. diss., University of Durham, 1980, 2:257; M. Jamil, *Ta'liqat 'ala Nizam Da'awi al-'Asha'ir*, passim; *Liwa' al-Istiqlal*, 25 September 1949, 1; *Sada al-Ahali*, 12 April 1951, 1. See also parliamentary debates from April through May 1951 in al-'Iraq, Majlis al-Nuwwab, *Mahdar al-Jalsa al-Thaniya wa-l-Thalathin min al-Ijtima' al-I'tiyadi li-Sanat 1950*; al-'Iraq, Majlis al-Nuwwab, *Mahdar al-Jalsa al-Thalitha wa-l-Thalathin min al-Ijtima' al-I'tiyadi li-Sanat 1950* (Baghdad: Matba'at al-Hukuma, 1951); al-'Iraq, Majlis al-Nuwwab, *Mahdar al-Jalsa al-Rabi'a wa-l-Thalathin min al-Ijtima' al-I'tiyadi li-Sanat 1950* (Baghdad: Matba'at al-Hukuma, 1951); al-'Iraq, Majlis al-A'yan, *Mahdar al-Jalsa al-Hadiya 'Ashara min al-Ijtima' al-'Adi li-Sanat 1950–1951*.

78. See the way women were incorporated in arguments against the TCCDR by members of the anti-British pan-Arab al-Istiqlal Party in al-'Iraq, Majlis al-Nuwwab, *Mahdar al-Jalsa al-Thaniya wa-l-Thalathin min al-Ijtima' al-I'tiyadi li-Sanat 1950*, 539–540, 542–543.

79. Ma'ruf al-Rusafi, "Al-Zu'ama fi al-'Iraq," in Sa'id al-Badri, ed., *Ara' al-Rusafi fi al-Siyasa wa-l-Din wa-l-Ijtima'*, 2d ed. (Baghdad: al-Ma'arif, 1951), 9–15.

80. Ma'ruf al-Rusafi, *Diwan al-Rusafi*, 2 vols., 2d ed. (Baghdad: Afaq 'Arabiyya, 1986), 2:332–369; Yousif Izzidein [Yusuf 'Izz al-Din], "The Emancipation of Iraqi Women: Women and Their Influence on Iraqi Life and Poetry," *Bulletin of the College of Arts, Baghdad University* 1 (1959), 35–38; Sabiha al-Shaikh Da'ud, *Awwal al-Tariq Ila al-Nahda al-Niswiyya fi al-'Iraq* (Baghdad: al-Rabita, 1958), 130–131, 205; Khairi al-'Umari, *Hikayat Siyasiyya min Ta'rikh al-'Iraq al-Hadith* (Baghdad: Dar al-Qadisiyya, 1980), 101–102; "Intelligence Report No. 7, 1 April 1922," NAI, BHCF, Internal Intelligence Reports 19/1, vol. III.

81. Khalid Kishtainy, "Women in Art and Literature," in Doreen Ingrams, *The Awakened: Women in Iraq* (London: Third World Center, 1983), 149–150.

82. Nazik al-Mala'ika, *Diwan Nazik al-Mala'ika*, 2 vols. (Beirut: Dar al-'Awda, 1986), 2:351–354. For an English translation, see Ingrams, *The Awakened*, 150–151.

83. Orit Bashkin, "Representations of Women in the Writings of the Intelligentsia in Hashemite Iraq, 1921–1958," *Journal of Middle East Journal Studies* 4, no. 1 (Winter 2008): 53–82.

84. See Yusuf Salman Yusuf, "Yawm al-Nisa' al-'Alami," in Fakhri Karim, ed., *Kitabat al-Rafiq Fahd*, 2d ed., 407–413 (Baghdad: al-Tariq al-Jadid, 1976).

85. Naziha al-Dulaimi, "Rabitat al-Mar'a al-'Iraqiyya," *al-Thaqafa al-Jadida* 5 (1982), 110.

86. Naziha al-Dulaimi, *Al-Mar'a al-'Iraqiyya* (Baghdad: al-Rabita, [1950?]), 8–10. According to al-Dulaimi, the book was first published in 1950 (see al-Dulaimi, "Rabitat al-Mar'a al-'Iraqiyya," 110). A 1958 reprint, however, dates the author's introduction to 1952.

87. M. S. Hassan, "Growth and Structure of Iraq's Population, 1867–1947," *Bulletin of Oxford University, Institute of Economics and Statistics* 20 (1958), 344.

88. Farouk-Sluglett and Sluglett, "The Transformation of Land Tenure," 493–495; Albertine Jwaideh, "Midhat Pasha and the Land System of Lower Iraq," *St. Antony's Papers: Middle East Affairs* 3 (1963): 106–136; Samira Haj, *The Making of Iraq 1900–1963: Capital, Power, and Ideology* (Albany: State University of New York Press, 1997), 18–27.

89. Haj, *The Making of Iraq 1900–1963*, 27–31; Dodge, *Inventing Iraq*, 101–129; Batatu, *The Old Social Classes*, 86–152.

90. David Pool, "From Elite to Class: The Transformation of Iraqi Leadership, 1920–1939," *International Journal of Middle East Studies* 12 (1980), 343–345; Charles Tripp, *A History of Iraq* (Cambridge, U.K.: Cambridge University Press, 2000), 69–70, 85.

91. Article 49, as quoted in Sluglett, *Britain in Iraq 1914–1932*, 180.

92. Farouk-Sluglett and Sluglett, "The Transformation of Land Tenure," 499–501; Batatu, *The Old Social Classes*, 139–147.

93. Ruth Frances Woodsmall and Charlotte Johnson, *Study of the Role of Women, Their Activities and Organizations in Lebanon, Egypt, Iraq, Jordan, and Syria, October 1954–August 1955* (New York: International Federation of Business and Professional Women, 1956), 43.

94. Hashim Al Witry, *Health Services in Iraq* (Jerusalem: A. Duncker, 1944), 16; Ja'far Khayyat, *Al-Qarya al-'Iraqiyya* (Beirut: Dar al-Kashshaf, 1950), 31.

95. Al-'Iraq, Wizarat al-Iqtisad, al-Da'ira al-Ra'isiyya li-l-Ihsa', *Al-Majmu'a al-Ihsa'iyya al-Sanawiyya al-'Amma, 1955* (Baghdad: Matba'at al-Zahra', 1956), 302.

96. For more information on maternal mortality, see al-Dulaimi, *Al-Mar'a al-'Iraqiyya*, 28–29; on infant mortality, see Sami Shawkat, *Hadhihi Ahdafuna* (Baghdad: n.p., 1939), 79 (Shawkat, who is best known as director-general of education, became director-general of public health in 1936). An estimate from 1956 suggests an infant mortality rate of 250–400 per 1,000 in rural areas and small towns. It also suggests that in areas where malaria was present, infant mortality was as high as 500 per 1,000. See Doris G. Adams, "Current Population Trends in Iraq," *Middle East Journal* 10 (1956), 159–160.

97. Monroe, *Report of the Educational Inquiry Commission*, 132; "Special Report by His Majesty's Government in the United Kingdom of Great Britain and Northern Ireland to the Council of the League of Nations on the Progress of Iraq During the Period 1920–1931," *Iraq Administration Reports*, 10:479–480; Iraq Ministry of Economics, Principal Bureau of Statistics, *Statistical Abstract, 1950* (Baghdad: Government Press, 1952), 75; Khayyat, *Al-Qarya al-'Iraqiyya*, 39.

98. Al-Jumhuriyya al-'Iraqiyya, Wizarat al-Dakhiliyya, Mudiriyyat al-Nufus al-'Amma, *Al-Majmu'a al-Ihsa'iyya li-Tasjil 'Am 1957*, 2 vols., 26 parts (Baghdad: Government Press, 1964), 2:16:24.

99. Ahmad Fahmi, *Taqrir Hawla al-'Iraq* (Baghdad: al-Maktaba al-'Asriyya, 1926), 32–33; Jamali, *The New Iraq*, 77–78; 'Abd al-Jabbar Faris, *'Aman fi al-Furat al-Awsat* (Najaf: Matba'at al-Ra'i, 1934), 118–119; Khayyat, *Al-Qarya al-'Iraqiyya*, 43; al-Dulaimi, *Al-Mar'a al-'Iraqiyya*, 8–9; Da'ud, *Awwal al-Tariq*, 223–225; 'Ali al-Wardi, *Dirasa fi Tabi'at al-Mujtama' al-'Iraqi* (Baghdad: Matba'at al-'Ani, 1965), 209–211.

100. See al-Dulaimi, *Al-Mar'a al-'Iraqiyya*, 10, and Da'ud, *Awwal al-Tariq*, 224–225.

101. Al-Dulaimi, *Al-Mar'a al-'Iraqiyya*, 8–11.

102. Batatu, *The Old Social Classes*, 101–110.

103. Al-'Iraq, Majlis al-A'yan, *Mahdar al-Jalsa al-Hadiya 'Asahra*, 157–159.

104. Al-'Iraq, Majlis al-Nuwwab, *Mahdar al-Jalsa al-Rabi'a wa-l-Thalathin*, 563.

105. The amendment for the TCCDR was discussed in Parliament in April and May 1951. For the government's and the supporters' positions, see, for example, al-'Iraq, Majlis al-Nuwwab, *Mahdar al-Jalsa al-Thaniya wa-l-Thalathin*, 537–538, 542–544; al-'Iraq, Majlis al-Nuwwab, *Mahdar al-Jalsa al-Thalitha wa-l-Thalathin*, 550–551, 555–557; al-'Iraq, Majlis al-Nuwwab, *Mahdar al-Jalsa al-Rabi'a wa-l-Thalathin*, 564–565, 569–570.

106. Al-'Iraq, Majlis al-A'yan, *Mahdar al-Jalsa al-Hadiya 'Ashara*, 152, see also 154.

107. See Clause 1(3) of the TCCDR of 1916 and Clause 1(iii) of the revised TCCDR of 1918.

108. See Dobbs's comments following Bruce, "The Sandeman Policy," 66. Compare "Annual Report on Events in Iraq During 1956," PRO, FO 371/128038/VQ1011/1, pp. 2–3.

2. FAMILY LAW AS A SITE OF STRUGGLE AND SUBORDINATION

1. Baghdad Wilayet Judicial Department, "Report on the Administration of Civil Justice from the Occupation of Baghdad to 31st December, 1917," and Baghdad Wilayet Judicial Department, "Report on the Administration of Civil Justice for the Year 1918," both in *Iraq Administration Reports: 1914–1932*, 10 vols., sources established by Robert L. Jarman (Slough, U.K.: Archive Editions, 1992), 1:527–528 and 2:575–576.

2. "Special Report by His Majesty's Government in the United Kingdom of Great Britain and Northern Ireland to the Council of the League of Nation on the Progress of Iraq During the Period 1920–1931," in *Iraq Administration Reports*, 10:76–79.

3. Toby Dodge, *Inventing Iraq: The Failure of Nation Building and a History Denied* (New York: Columbia University Press, 2003), 67.

4. Baghdad Wilayet Judicial Department, "Report on the Administration of Civil Justice from the Occupation of Baghdad to 31st December, 1917," 1:528.

5. Thomas Lyell, *The Ins and Outs of Mesopotamia* (London: A. M. Philpot, 1923), 7 and 141.

6. Ibid., 142.

7. Ibid., 144–145, 150–151.

8. Ibid., 145, 158.

9. Leila Ahmed, *Women and Gender in Islam: Historical Roots of a Modern Debate* (New Haven, Conn.: Yale University Press, 1992), 149–155.

10. "Report by His Majesty's High Commissioner on the Finance, Administration and Condition of the 'Iraq, for the Period from October 1st, 1920 to March 31st, 1922," in *Iraq Administration Reports*, 7:48.

11. Nigel G. Davidson, "The Constitution of Iraq," *Journal of Comparative Legislation and International Law* 7 (February 1925), 49–50; Philip Willard Ireland, *Iraq: A Study in Political Development* (London: J. Cape, 1937), 370–390; C. A. Hooper, *The Constitutional Law of Iraq* (Baghdad: Mackenzie & Mackenzie, 1928), 132–133 (Article 76–77).

12. "Special Report by His Majesty's Government on the Progress of Iraq During the Period 1920–1931," in *Iraq Administration Reports*, 10:78–79; Zehra F. Arat, "Turkish Women and the Republican Reconstruction of Tradition," in Fatma Müge Göçek and Shiva Balaghi, eds., *Reconstructing Gender in the Middle East* (New York: Columbia University Press, 1994), 62–67.

13. Khairi al-'Umari, *Hikayat Siyasiyya min Ta'rikh al-'Iraq al-Hadith* (Baghdad: Dar al-Qadisiyya, 1980), 122.

14. "Special Report by His Majesty's Government on the Progress of Iraq During the Period 1920–1931," 10:78–79.

15. Ibid., 10:76–79; Judges and Qadhis Law, no. 31 of 1929, in *Iraq Administration Reports*, 9:356.

16. *Iraq Government Gazette*, 13 (15 July 1923).

17. J. N. D. Anderson, "A Draft Code of Personal Law for 'Iraq," *Bulletin of the School of Oriental and African Studies* 15 (1953): 43–60; Joseph Schacht, *An Introduction*

to Islamic Law (Oxford, U.K.: Clarendon Press, 1964), 104; Linant Y. De Bellefonds, "Le Code du Statut Personnel Irakien du 30 decembre 1959," *Studia Islamica* 13 (1960), 82.

18. Extract from Council Agenda, 13 December 1931, National Archives of India (NAI), Baghdad High Commission File (BHCF), Shara Courts Laws and Regulations, 8/117, vol. 2.

19. "Iraq Police Abstract of Intelligence," no. 16, 19 April 1933, and no. 17, 27 April 1933, Public Record Office, London (PRO), Air 23/589, vol. XV. Sunni clerics also opposed the draft, but we do not have their reasons in writing.

20. *Al-Istiqlal*, 21 August 1936, 2; *al-Istiqlal*, 8 March 1938, 2; 'Ala' al-Din Kharufa, *Sharh Qanun al-Ahwal al-Shakhsiyya*, 2 vols. (Baghdad: Matba'at al-'Ani, 1962–1963), 1:23.

21. *Al-Qada'*, 1 (May 1945), 117; *al-Zaman*, 21 May 1946, 2; *al-Zaman*, 29 May 1946, 2.

22. Anderson, "A Draft Code," 43.

23. 'Abd al-Razzaq al-Hasani, *Ta'rikh al-Wizarat al-'Iraqiyya*, 10 vols., 7th ed. (Baghdad: Afaq 'Arabiyya, 1988), 8:122.

24. *Sada al-Ahali*, 29 April 1952, 2; *Liwa' al-Istiqlal*, 7 May 1952, 2; *Liwa' al-Istiqlal*, 8 May 1952, 2; *Liwa' al-Istiqlal*, 15 May 1952, 2.

25. For an English translation of many of the draft's provisions, see Anderson, "A Draft Code." A more complete Arabic version can be found in Husain 'Ali al-A'zami, *Ahkam al-Zawaj* (Baghdad: Sharikat al-Taba' wa-l-Nashr al-Ahaliyya, 1949), and Husain 'Ali al-A'zami, *Al-Wasaya wa-l-Mawarith* (Baghdad: al-Rashid, 1949).

26. Precedents for the Iraqi law proposal were the Ottoman Law of Family Rights of 1917, Egyptian legislation (mainly in the years 1920, 1923, and 1929), and the Civil Code of Iran, passed in 1928 and supplemented in 1931 and 1937, which based its articles regarding family matters on the shari'a.

27. In this chapter, as in the primary sources on which it is based, the words *Shi'i* and *Ja'fari* are used interchangeably. At the time, the word *Sunni* was frequently used as a synonym for *Hanafi*, ignoring the fact that the Kurds were Sunni *shafi'is*.

28. Al-A'zami, *Ahkam al-Zawaj*, 4. For more about al-A'zami, see Mir Basri, *A'lam al-Adab fi al-'Iraq al-Hadith*, 3 vols. (London: Dar al-Hikma, 1994–1999), 2:450.

29. Schacht, *An Introduction to Islamic Law*, 252. Muhammad Qadri Pasha was the first to attempt to organize the personal status provisions of the Hanafi school of jurisprudence into a comprehensive code in Egypt. Although his code did not gain the Egyptian authorities' formal approval, it was published by the government in 1875 and enjoyed a semiofficial status.

30. 'Abd al-Karim Rida al-Hilli, *Al-Ahkam al-Ja'fariyya fi al-Ahwal al-Shakhsiyya*, 2d ed. (Baghdad: al-Muthana, 1947), 3. For more on al-Hilli, see Hamid al-Matba'i, *Mawsu'at A'lam al-'Iraq fi al-Qarn al-'Ishrin*, 3 vols. (Baghdad: Wizarat al-Thaqafa wa-l-I'lam, 1996), 2:149. See also 'Abd al-Karim al-'Uzri, *Ta'rikh fi Dhikrayat al-'Iraq, 1930–1958* (Beirut: Markaz al-Abjadiya, 1982), 244–245.

31. See, for example, Noel Coulson and Doreen Hinchcliffe, "Women and Law Reform in Contemporary Islam," in Lois Beck and Nikki R. Keddie, eds., *Women in the Muslim World*, 37–51 (Cambridge, Mass.: Harvard University Press, 1978);

Annelies Moors, "Debating Islamic Family Law: Legal Texts and Social Practices," in Margaret L. Meriwether and Judith E. Tucker, eds., *A Social History of Women and Gender in the Modern Middle East*, 141–175 (Boulder, Colo.: Westview, 1999); Suad Joseph, ed., *Gender and Citizenship in the Middle East* (Syracuse, N.Y.: Syracuse University Press, 2000); and Judith E. Tucker, *Women, Family, and Gender in Islamic Law* (Cambridge, U.K.: Cambridge University Press, 2008).

32. Quoted in Anderson, "A Draft Code," 44; an Arabic version of this memorandum can be found in *Sada al-Ahali*, 29 April 1952, 2.

33. See Article 3 in al-A'zami, *Ahkam al-Zawaj*, 16.

34. See Articles 9, 19, and 20 in al-A'zami, *Ahkam al-Zawaj*, 24–25, 42, and Anderson, "A Draft Code," 47.

35. Al-A'zami, *Ahkam al-Zawaj*, 38; al-Hilli, *Al-Ahkam al-Ja'fariyya*, 14.

36. The 1917 Ottoman Law of Family Rights determined that as a condition of competence for marriage a man should be at least eighteen and a woman at least seventeen. The same ages were required by Turkish civil law. The Civil Code of Iran, which generally based its articles regarding family matters on the shari'a, prescribed that the marriage of girls younger than fifteen and of boys younger than eighteen was prohibited. Both the Ottoman and Iranian codes, however, left room for marriage at an earlier age. See J. N. D. Anderson, "Recent Developments in Shari'a Law III," *Muslim World* 41 (1951), 113–116; 'Ali Raza Naqvi, "The Family Law of Iran (II)," *Islamic Studies* 7 (June 1968), 149.

37. See Articles 7(1–2) and 17(2) in Anderson, "A Draft Code," 47, and al-A'zami, *Ahkam al-Zawaj*, 24, 41.

38. Compare Article 74 as given in Anderson, "A Draft Code," 54, with the discussion of this same issue in al-Hilli, *Al-Ahkam al-Ja'fariyya*, 12–13, and al-A'zami, *Ahkam al-Zawaj*, 38–40.

39. See Article 13 in al-A'zami, *Ahkam al-Zawaj*, 41.

40. Al-A'zami, *Ahkam al-Zawaj*, 220–221.

41. *Al-'Alam al-'Arabi*, 13 July 1935, 3; *'Alam al-Ghad*, 1 March 1945, 217–218; *al-Sa'a*, 8 January 1946, 1 and 3.

42. Al-'Iraq, Majlis al-Nuwwab, *Mahdar al-Jalsa al-Thamina wa-l-'Ishrin min al-Ijtima' Ghair al-I'tiyadi li-Sanat 1937* (Baghdad: Matba'at al-Hukuma, 1937), 432–433.

43. The Ottoman Law of Family Rights stated that if a woman stipulated in her marriage contract that her husband was not to take additional wife, and he did so anyway, either she or her husband's second wife was to be divorced, the contract was considered valid, and the stipulation would be recognized. See Anderson, "Recent Developments in Shari'a Law III," 122.

44. See Article 22(2) in al-A'zami, *Ahkam al-Zawaj*, 51.

45. Jamil Sidqi al-Zahawi, "Al-Mar'a wa-l-Difa' 'Anha," in 'Abd al-Hamid al-Rashudi, ed., *Al-Zahawi: Dirasat wa-Nusus* (Beirut: al-Haya, 1966), 114.

46. Sami Shawkat, *Hadhihi Ahdafuna* (Baghdad: n.p., 1939), 83–84. For more on Shawkat's perceptions of masculinity and femininity, see Peter Wien, *Iraqi Arab Nationalism* (London: Routledge, 2006), especially 78–104.

47. *The Holy Quran*, 2 vols., text, translation, and commentary by Abdullah Yusuf-Ali (Lahore, Pakistan: Shaikh Muhammad Ashraf, 1937), 1:221; see also 1:179.

48. Al-A'zami, *Ahkam al-Zawaj*, 8–9.

49. Ruth Frances Woodsmall, *Moslem Women Enter a New World* (New York: Round Table Press, 1936), 115; Naziha al-Dulaimi, *Al-Mar'a al-'Iraqiyya* (Baghdad: al-Rabita, [1950?]), 8–10, 37.

50. *Al-Zaman*, 21 June 1954, 4–5. Compare the Ottoman Law of Family Rights, Article 38, in Anderson, "Recent Developments in Shari'a Law III," 122–123.

51. See, for example, the interview with Sabiha Sheikh Dauod [*sic*], 21 February 1955, Ruth Frances Woodsmall Private Papers, Box 62, Folder 5, Sophia Smith Collection, Smith College, Northampton, Mass.

52. Doris Adams, "Current Population Trends in Iraq," *Middle East Journal* 10 (1956), 155; al-Jumhuriyya al-'Iraqiyya, Wizarat al-Dakhiliyya, Mudiriyyat al-Nufus al-'Amma, *Al-Majmu'a al-Ihsa'iyya li-Tasjil 'Am 1957*, 2 vols., 26 parts (Baghdad: Government Press, 1964), 2:16:24.

53. Chibli Mallat, "Shi'ism and Sunnism in Iraq: Revisiting the Codes," in Chibli Mallat and Jane Connors, eds., *Islamic Family Law* (London: Graham and Trotman, 1990), 83.

54. Al-Hilli, *Al-Ahkam al-Ja'fariyya*, 6.

55. Shakir Mustafa Salim, *Marsh Dwellers of the Euphrates Delta* (London: Athlone Press, 1962), 57; Mustafa Muhammad Hasanain, *Nizam al-Mas'uliyya 'ind al-'Asha'ir al-'Iraqiyya al-'Arabiyya al-Mu'asira* (Cairo: Matba'at al-Istiqlal al-Kubra, 1967), 415–416; see also Muhammad Jawad Mughniyya, "Al-Mut'a," *al-'Irfan* 37 (1950), 1096.

56. See Adams, "Current Population Trends in Iraq," 155.

57. Ahmad Fahmi, *Taqrir Hawla al-'Iraq* (Baghdad: al-Maktaba al-'Asriyya, 1926), 49; Mohammed Fadhel Jamali, *The New Iraq: Its Problem of Bedouin Education* (New York: Bureau of Publication, Teachers College, Columbia University, 1934), 77; 'Abd al-Jabbar Faris, *'Aman fi al-Furat al-Awsat* (Najaf: Matba'at al-Ra'i, 1934), 121.

58. See Articles 17–18 in Anderson, "A Draft Code," 47, and al-A'zami, *Ahkam al-Zawaj*, 29–30.

59. Al-A'zami, *Ahkam al-Zawaj*, 22–23.

60. See Articles 32–41 in al-A'zami, *Ahkam al-Zawaj*, 71, 74, 76–77, 83–84, 93–94, and Anderson, "A Draft Code," 48–49.

61. See, for example, *al-Zaman*, 6 June 1958, 5.

62. Al-A'zami, *Ahkam al-Zawaj*, 76–77; al-Hilli, *Al-Ahkam al-Ja'fariyya*, 6.

63. Al-A'zami, *Ahkam al-Zawaj*, 85; cf. Muhammad Abu Zahra, *Al-Ahwal al-Shakhsiyya* (Cairo: Dar al-Fikr al-'Arabi, 1957), 204–205.

64. Compare the 1920 Egyptian Law. See Ron Shaham, *Family and the Courts in Modern Egypt* (Leiden: Brill, 1997), esp. 70 and 115.

65. See Articles 42–51 in al-A'zami, *Ahkam al-Zawaj*, 222, 224, 227–228, 234, 239, and Anderson, "A Draft Code," 49–50.

66. Al-Hilli, *Al-Ahkam al-Ja'fariyya*, 44–45, 54; al-A'zami, *Ahkam al-Zawaj*, 105, 223.
67. See, for example, Ma'ruf al-Rusafi, *Diwan al-Rusafi*, 2 vols., 2d ed. (Baghdad: Afaq 'Arabiyya, 1986), 2:332–349; al-Zahawi, "Al-Mar'a wa-l-Difa' 'Anha," 113–114; *'Alam al-Ghad*, 1 March 1945, 217–218.
68. Saniha Amin Zaki, *Dhikrayat Tabiba 'Iraqiyya* (London: Dar al-Hikma, 2005), 284.
69. Al-Dulaimi, *Al-Mar'a al-'Iraqiyya*, 33–44.
70. Al-A'zami, *Ahkam al-Zawaj*, 72, 220.
71. See Anderson, "A Draft Code," 55; al-Hilli, *Al-Ahkam al-Ja'fariyya*, 99, 101; and al-A'zami, *Ahkam al-Zawaj*, 210–213.
72. Nazik al-Mala'ika, *Al-Tajzi'iyya fi al-Mujtama' al-'Arabi* ('Aka [Acre]: Maktab al-Aswar, 1978), 36; al-Dulaimi, *al-Mar'a al-'Iraqiyya*, 39–40; Sabiha al-Shaikh Da'ud, *Awwal al-Tariq Ila al-Nahda al-Niswiyya fi al-'Iraq* (Baghdad: al-Rabita, 1958), 176.
73. See Articles 123, 137–139, and 148 in al-A'zami, *Al-Wasaya wa-l-Mawarith*, 181–182, 195, 201.
74. Ma'ruf al-Rusafi, "Al-Zu'ama fi al-'Iraq," in Sa'id al-Badri, ed., *Ara' al-Rusafi fi al-Siyasa wa-l-Din wa-l-Ijtima'*, 2d ed. (Baghdad: al-Ma'arif, 1951), 12. I could not find any proof for the second claim.
75. Al-Zahawi, "Al-Mar'a wa-l-Difa' 'Anha," 115.
76. Mubejel Baban, interviewed by the author, London, 20 August 1997.
77. Al-A'zami, *Al-Wasaya wa-l-Mawarith*, 175, and cf. al-A'zami, *Ahkam al-Zawaj*, 72, 220.
78. The *'idda* is the period during which a divorced woman may not remarry, usually three months or three menstrual cycles from the date of the declaration or, if the woman is pregnant, until the delivery of the baby.
79. See Articles 53–56 and 61 in al-A'zami, *Ahkam al-Zawaj*, 123, 126, 128–129, 143, and Anderson, "A Draft Code," 50–51. Compare the Ottoman Law of Family Rights and the 1929 Egyptian Law in J. N. D. Anderson, "Recent Developments in Shari'a Law V," *Muslim World* 41 (1951), 274–276; Shaham, *Family and the Courts in Modern Egypt*, 102.
80. See Articles 58–60 in al-A'zami, *Ahkam al-Zawaj*, 130, 135–137, and Anderson, "A Draft Code", 51.
81. Compare, for example, *al-Hawadith*, 6 April 1946, 2, and *al-Hawadith*, 30 April 1946, 2, with *Liwa' al-Istiqlal*, 7 May 1952, 2–3. See also al-A'zami, *Ahkam al-Zawaj*, 122–129.
82. See Articles 64, 68–69, and the relevant discussion in al-A'zami, *Ahkam al-Zawaj*, 166–170. Compare al-Hilli, *Al-Ahkam al-Ja'fariyya*, 76–77.
83. See Article 44 in al-A'zami, *Ahkam al-Zawaj*, 162–163, 227–228, al-Hilli, *Al-Ahkam al-Ja'fariyya*, 46–47, and Anderson, "A Draft Code," 50.
84. See Articles 70 and 71 in al-A'zami, *Ahkam al-Zawaj*, 163–166; see also Anderson's discussion of the similarities and differences between the draft and the Ottoman and Egyptian legislation in "A Draft Code," 50–54.
85. See Articles 62–63 in al-A'zami, *Ahkam al-Zawaj*, 150–154.

86. Ibid., 118; Anderson, "A Draft Code," 50.

87. Al-A'zami, *Ahkam al-Zawaj*, 144–148; see also al-Hilli, *Al-Ahkam al-Ja'fariyya*, 67–68.

88. Amin Zaki, *Dhikrayat Tabiba 'Iraqiyya*, 284.

89. *Al-'Alam al-'Arabi*, 13 July 1935, 3; *al-Sa'a*, 8 January 1946, 3.

90. Al-Dulaimi, *Al-Mar'a al-'Iraqiyya*, 35, 37, 42–43; see also 'A. Sh., "Al-Nahda al-Niswiyya fi al-'Iraq," *al-Mu'allim al-Jadid* 18 (1955), 80.

91. Tucker, *Women, Family, and Gender in Islamic Law*, 70–71.

92. Mounira M. Charrad, *States and Women's Rights: The Making of Postcolonial Tunisia, Algeria, and Morocco* (Berkeley and Los Angeles: University of California Press, 2001).

93. Anderson discusses this letter in his article "A Draft Code of Personal Law for 'Iraq," but from a different perspective. The original document can be found in Norman Anderson Private Papers, PP MS 60, 1/5, 1950–1958, School of Oriental and African Studies Special Collections, London.

94. Amjad al-Zahawi (d. 1967) was the son of the mufti of Baghdad during the Ottoman period, a professor at the Iraqi Law School, and then the president of the Sunni Division of the Court of Cassation (1933–1946). He was a leader of the Association of the Muslim Brotherhood in Iraq and in 1951 was teaching at Madrasat al-Sulaimaniyya. Qasim al-Qaisi (d. 1955) was a member of the Sunni Division of the Court of Cassation (1922–1937) and the mufti of Baghdad from 1951 until his death. Najm al-Din al-Wa'iz (d. 1967) was a teacher at Madrasat al-Qublaniyya in 1951 and replaced al-Qaisi as the mufti of Baghdad in 1955. For more, see Basri, *A'lam al-Adab fi al-'Iraq al-Hadith*, 2:339–340, 346; and Yunis Ibrahim al-Samarra'i, *Ta'rikh 'Ulama' Baghdad* (Baghdad: Wizarat al-Awqaf, 1982), 102–106, 544–545, 686–687.

95. The full text of their letter was published in *Liwa' al-Istiqlal*, 7 May 1952, 2–3.

96. Norman Anderson Private Papers, PP MS 60, 1/5, 1950–1958; *Liwa' al-Istiqlal*, 7 May 1952, 2–3; Anderson, "A Draft Code," 49, 50, 52–53.

97. Anderson, "A Draft Code," 43; compare Mallat, "Shi'ism and Sunnism in Iraq."

98. Anderson, "A Draft Code," 43; "Special Report by His Majesty's Government on the Progress of Iraq During the Period 1920–1931," 10:76–79; Judges and Qadhis Law, No. 31 of 1929, in *Iraq Administration Reports*, 9:356.

99. Anderson, "A Draft Code," 43.

100. Muhammad Bahr al-'Ulum, *Adwa' 'Ala Qanun al-Ahwal al-Shakhsiyya al-'Iraqi* (Najaf: Matba'at al-Nu'man, 1963), 10. Although no date was mentioned, al-Hakim's comment that his opposition had undermined government efforts to introduce such a law until the time when 'Abd al-Karim Qasim was in power after the overthrow of the monarchy indicates that he was referring to the developments of May 1952 because no real effort to introduce a new law of personal status was made from this date until 1959.

101. Quoted in *Liwa' al-Istiqlal*, 15 1952, 2.

3. POLITICS, ELECTION LAW, AND EXCLUSION

1. Compare Articles 6 and 18 with Articles 36 and 42 in C. A. Hooper, *The Constitutional Law of Iraq* (Baghdad: Mackenzie & Mackenzie, 1928), 41, 59, 87–88, 93.

2. Iraq Ministry of Justice, *Compilation of Laws and Regulations Issued Between 1st January 1924 and 31st December 1925* (Baghdad: Government Press, 1926), 45–51.

3. See, for example, "Note on Proposals for the Electoral Law for Mesopotamia," written by E. L. Norton, Secretary to the Committee of Ex-Turkish Deputies on Electoral Law, India Office Library, London (IO), L/P&S 10/759, 20 August 1920; Nigel G. Davidson, "The Constitution of Iraq," *Journal of Comparative Legislation and International Law* 7 (February 1925), 47–48.

4. Janet Wallach, *Desert Queen: The Extraordinary Life of Gertrude Bell* (New York: Anchor Books, 1999), 83. See also Liora Lukitz, *A Quest in the Middle East: Gertrude Bell and the Making of Modern Iraq* (London: I. B. Tauris, 2006), 45–50; Brian Harrison, *Separate Spheres: The Opposition to Women's Suffrage in Britain* (New York: Holmes and Meier, 1978), 83, 119, and esp. 254.

5. Gertrude Bell, *The Letters of Gertrude Bell*, selected and edited by Lady Bell, 2 vols. (London: Ernest Benn, 1927), 2:478; see also Sabiha al-Shaikh Da'ud, *Awwal al-Tariq Ila al-Nahda al-Niswiyya fi al-'Iraq* (Baghdad: al-Rabita, 1958), 49–54.

6. Evelyn Baring (Lord Cromer), *Modern Egypt* (London: Macmillan, 1911), 883.

7. "Report by His Majesty's Government in the United Kingdom of Great Britain and Northern Ireland to the Council of the League of Nations on the Administration of 'Iraq for the Year 1928," in *Iraq Administration Reports: 1914–1932*, 10 vols., sources established by Robert L. Jarman (Slough, U.K.: Archive Editions, 1992), 9:130. See also "Note on the Present Education in Iraq," 30 August 1930, National Archives of India, New Delhi (NAI), Baghdad High Commission File (BHCF), Correspondence with the Ministry of Education 5/1/1, vol. II.

8. Timothy Mitchell, *Colonising Egypt* (Cambridge, U.K.: Cambridge University Press, 1991), 112.

9. Compare "Report on Rockefeller Fellowship Study, 1928–1929," Ruth Frances Woodsmall Private Papers, Box 25, p. 243, Sophia Smith Collection, Smith College, Northampton, Mass., and Permanent Mandates Commission, Tenth Session, Provisional Minutes, Eighth Meeting, held Monday, 8 November 1926, Public Records Office, London (PRO), Colonial Office (CO) 730/96, pp. 19–20, with Mona Russell, "Competing, Overlapping, and Contradictory Agendas: Egyptian Education Under British Occupation," *Comparative Studies of South Asia, Africa, and the Middle East* 21 (2001), 55.

10. The report of the Monroe Educational Inquiry Commission from 1932 pointed out not only discrimination against rural girls in Iraq, but also the limited scope of public education for girls. In 1931–1932, there were not much more than eight thousand girls in nondenominational public schools. See Paul Monroe, *Report of the Educational Inquiry Commission* (Baghdad: Government Press, 1932), 130–134.

11. Ayad al-Qazzaz, "Power Elite in Iraq, 1920–1958: A Study of the Cabinet," *The Muslim World* 61 (1971), 268. See also George L. Harris, *Iraq: Its People, Its Society, Its Culture* (New Haven, Conn.: Harf Press, 1958), 121.

12. See Da'ud, *Awwal al-Tariq*, 141–142. Hassun was no doubt inspired by the struggle for women's suffrage in neighboring countries such as Egypt, Syria, and Lebanon. See also Margot Badran, *Feminists, Islam, and Nation: Gender and the Making of Modern Egypt* (Princeton, N.J.: Princeton University Press, 1995), 207–212; and Elizabeth Thompson, *Colonial Citizens: Republican Rights, Paternal Privilege, and Gender in French Syria and Lebanon* (New York: Columbia University Press, 2000), 117–126.

13. *Al-Sha'b*, 26 March 1958, 5.

14. C. J. Edmonds, *Kurds, Turks, and Arabs* (London: Oxford University Press, 1957), 14.

15. "Women's Clubs Taboo, Report on Current Events for the Period April 15 to 30, 1934," Paul Knabenshue to the Secretary of State, 5 May 1934, U.S. National Archives, Washington, D.C. (USNA), Records of the Department of State Relating to the Internal Affairs of Iraq, 1930–1944, and Confidential U.S. State Department Central Files, Iraq 1945–1949, Internal Affairs, Decimal File 890G.00, General Conditions/29.

16. Naziha al-Dulaimi, "Rabitat al-Mar'a al-'Iraqiyya," *al-Thaqafa al-Jadida* 5 (1982), 107; Husain Jamil, *Al-Haya al-Niyabiyya fi al-'Iraq, 1925–1946: Mawqif Jama'at al-Ahali Minha* (Baghdad: al-Muthana, 1983), 186; "Al-Mithaq al-Watani li-l-Hizb al-Shuyu'i al-'Iraqi," in Fakhri Karim, ed., *Kitabat al-Rafiq Fahd*, 2d ed. (Baghdad: al-Tariq al-Jadid, 1976), 135.

17. Phebe Marr, *The Modern History of Iraq* (Boulder, Colo.: Westview, 1985), 45; Majid Khadduri, *Independent Iraq, 1932–1958: A Study in Iraqi Politics*, 2d ed. (London: Oxford University Press, 1960), 302–304.

18. Iraq Ministry of Justice, *Compilation of Laws and Regulations Issued Between 1st January 1946 and 31st December 1946* (Baghdad: Government Press, 1949), 9–21; Charles Tripp, *A History of Iraq* (Cambridge, U.K.: Cambridge University Press, 2000), 114.

19. For more, see 'Abd al-Razzaq al-Hasani, *Ta'rikh al-Wizarat al-'Iraqiyya*, 10 vols., 7th ed. (Baghdad: Afaq 'Arabiyya, 1988), 7:150–156; Tawfiq al-Suwaidi, *Mudhakkirati: Nisf Qarn min Ta'rikh al-'Iraq wa-l-Qadiya al-'Arabiyya* (Beirut: Dar al-Kitab al-'Arabi, 1969), 452–456.

20. See, for example, *al-Zaman*, 23 February 1948, 1.

21. The texts of the two proposal can be found in *al-Umma*, 14 March 1951, 2 (from which the quote comes), and *al-Sha'b*, 26 February 1951, 2.

22. See sessions 28–31 from 27 March to April 1951 in al-'Iraq, Majlis al-Nuwwab, *Al-Dawra al-Intikhabiyya al-Thaniya 'Ashara min al-Ijtima' al-I'tiyadi li-Sanat 1950* (Baghdad: Matba'at al-Hukuma, n.d.), 455, 488, 496, 498, 513.

23. See Law No. 74 of 1952 amending Electoral Law No. 11 of 1946, as quoted in the *Official Gazette*, no. 3129 (12 July 1952), in H. Beleey to A. Eden, 22 July 1952, PRO, Foreign Office (FO) 371/98734/EQ1016/28.

24. Al-Hasani, *Ta'rikh al-Wizarat*, 8:202, 294–305, 344; Khadduri, *Independent Iraq*, 305; J. Troutbeck to A. Eden, 31 October 1952 (received 5 November 1952), PRO, FO 371/98735/EQ1016/39; J. Troutbeck to A. Eden, 20 December 1952, PRO, FO 371/98736/EQ1016/88.

25. See George Grassmuck's claim in "The Electoral Process in Iraq, 1952–1958," *Middle East Journal* 14(1960), 400, and compare it with the text of the decree as given in *al-Sha'b*, 12 December 1952, 1 and 5.

26. Al-Hasani, *Ta'rikh al-Wizarat*, 8:344–345.

27. Phebe Marr, *The Modern History of Iraq*, 2d ed. (Boulder, Colo.: Westview, 2004), 73–74.

28. Sir M. Wright to Foreign Office, 26 March 1958, PRO, FO 371/134198/VQ1015/33; *al-Zaman*, 28 March 1958, 5.

29. See the protocols for the Chamber of Deputies sessions 28–31, from 27 March to 3 April 1951 (cited in note 22).

30. Quoted in *al-Hawadith*, 18 May 1946, 2.

31. Quoted in ibid., 16 April 1949, 2.

32. Quoted in ibid., 12 July 1949, 3.

33. Quoted in *al-Zaman*, 28 March 1958, 5

34. Ibid., 29 March 1958, 5.

35. *Al-Sijill*, 21 November 1946, 1.

36. *Al-Ahali*, 28 October 1952, 5.

37. "Mrs. Fadel Jamali, 3 March 1955," Ruth Woodsmall Papers, Box 62, Folder 5; Ruth Frances Woodsmall and Charlotte Johnson, *Study of the Role of Women, Their Activities, and Organizations in Lebanon, Egypt, Iraq, Jordan, and Syria, October 1954–August 1955* (New York: International Federation of Business and Professional Women, 1956), 50; *al-Zaman*, 30 October 1953, 3.

38. Sura 4, verse 1, *The Holy Quran*, 2 vols., text, translation, and commentary by Abdullah Yusuf-Ali (Lahore, Pakistan: Shaikh Muhammad Ashraf, 1937), 1:178.

39. Nihal al-Zahawi, "Al-Mar'a fi Ri'ayat al-Islam," *al-Ukhuwwa al-Islamiyya*, 27 November 1953, 27–29.

40. *Muhawarat al-Imam al-Muslih Kashif al-Ghita' al-Shaikh Muhammad al-Husain Ma'a al-Safirain al-Baritani wa-l-Amriki fi Baghdad*, 3rd ed. (Najaf: n.p., 1954), 62–76. For a fascinating discussion about the way 'A'isha was perceived by Sunni and Shi'i scholars in the premodern period, see Denise Spellberg, *Politics, Gender, and the Islamic Past: The Legacy of 'A'isha Bint Abi-Bakr* (New York: Columbia University Press, 1994), 101–149.

41. *Muhawarat al-Imam al-Muslih Kashif al-Ghita'*, 3rd ed. (Najaf: n.p., 1954), 65.

42. Al-Hasani, *Ta'rikh al-Wizarat*, 7:31–33.

43. Muhammad Mahdi Kubba, *Mudhakkirati fi Samim al-Ahdath* (Beirut: Dar al-Tali'a, 1965), 174.

44. *Al-Zaman*, 23 February 1948, 1. For more about women's participation in the *wathba*, see al-Hasani, *Ta'rikh al-Wizarat*, 7:255, 260, 268, and Kubba, *Mudhakkirati fi Samim al-Ahdath*, 229–232. One participant is especially noted for her courage.

She marched on 27 January at the head of the line of demonstrators determined to cross al-Ma'mun Bridge in the face of police fire. Her companions were hit, but she managed to cross and opened the way for others to follow. She was designated "Heroine of the Bridge" (Batalat al-Jisr) and years later was still depicted as "a role model of women's heroic struggle to free their homeland." See Hanna Batatu, *The Old Social Classes and the Revolutionary Movements of Iraq* (Princeton, N.J.: Princeton University Press, 1978), 552, 557–558, and the speech of the Iraqi representative in Maliha Jawwad, *Al-Mu'tamar al-Nisa'i al-'Alami al-Mun'aqad fi Copenhagen* (Baghdad: al-Rabita, 1954), 22.

45. Muhammad Siddiq Shanshal, "Hurriyyat al-Mar'a al-Siyasiyya wa-Haqquha al-Intikhabi," *Liwa' al-Istiqlal*, 12 November 1950, 1 and 4.

46. See Nira Yuval-Davis and Floya Anthias, "Introduction," in Nira Yuval-Davis and Floya Anthias, eds., *Women–Nation–State* (London: Macmillan, 1989), 6–10.

47. For more, see Batatu, *The Old Social Classes*, 305–310; al-Hasani, *Ta'rikh al-Wizarat*, 7:37–41.

48. Kamil al-Chadirchi, *Mudhakkirat Kamil al-Chadirchi wa-Ta'rikh al-Hizb al-Watani al-Dimuqrati* (Beirut: Dar al-Tali'a, 1970), 511 and 526.

49. "Huquq al-Mar'a al-'Iraqiyya," *Sada al-Ahali*, 29 May 1951, 1.

50. "Shumul Haqq Intikhab al-Mar'a," *Sada al-Ahali*, 12 December 1951, 1 and 4.

51. Jamil, *Al-Haya al-Niyabiyya fi al-'Iraq*, 186.

52. Batatu, *The Old Social Classes*, 513–514; "Al-Mithaq al-Watani li-l-Hizb al-Shuyu'i al-'Iraqi."

53. Yusuf Salman Yusuf, "Yawm al-Nisa' al-'Alami," in Karim, ed., *Kitabat al-Rafiq Fahd*, 407–413.

54. See Raja' al-Zanburi, "Matba'at al-Hizb, Muhakamat al-Rafiq Fahd, Awwal Tanzim Nisa'i, al-Sijn," *al-Thaqafa al-Jadida* 5 (1982), 63–65.

55. Al-Hasani, *Ta'rikh al-Wizarat*, 8:118–123.

56. Ibid.; *al-Ittihad al-Dusturi*, 22 August 1950, 1.

57. Yuval-Davis and Anthias, "Introduction," 6–10.

58. 'Abd al-Razzaq al-Hasani, *Al-Usul al-Rasmiyya li-Ta'rikh al-Wizarat al-'Iraqiyya* (Sidon, Lebanon: al-'Irfan,, 1964), 139, 141.

59. *Al-Zaman*, 18 August 1943, 2.

60. See al-Hasani, *Ta'rikh al-Wizarat*, 8:122.

61. Woodsmall and Johnson, *Study of the Role of Women*, 40–43, quote on 43.

62. Al-Jumhuriyya al-'Iraqiyya, Wizarat al-Dakhiliyya, Mudiriyyat al-Nufus al-'Amma, *Al-Majmu'a al-Ihsa'iyya li-Tasjil 'Am 1957*, 2 vols., 26 parts (Baghdad: Government Press, 1964), 2:16:14.

63. *Sada al-Ahali*, 12 December 1951, 2; *al-Zaman*, 20 June 1952, 2.

64. Nuri al-Sa'id, statement to the press, 8 November 1952, PRO, FO 371/98735/EQ1016/46.

65. Quoted in *al-Bilad*, 7 March 1956, 6, and *al-Zaman*, 7 March 1956, 4.

66. Quoted in *al-Zaman*, 7 March 1958, 1.

67. Sir M. Wright to Foreign Office, 26 March 1958, PRO, FO 371/134198/VQ1015/33; *al-Zaman*, 28 March 1958, 5.

68. Al-Jumhuriyya al-'Iraqiyya, *Al-Majmu'a al-Ihsa'iyya li-Tasjil 'Am 1957*, 2:16:14.

4. GENDER DISCOURSE AND DISCONTENT: ACTIVISM UNRAVELED

1. Doreen Ingrams, *The Awakened: Women in Iraq* (London: Third World Center, 1983). Jacqueline S. Ismael and Shereen T. Ismael's "Gender and State in Iraq," in Suad Joseph, ed., *Gender and Citizenship in the Middle East*, 185–211 (Syracuse, N.Y.: Syracuse University Press, 2000), also tends toward this approach, as does my article "The Other 'Awakening' in Iraq: The Women's Movement in the First Half of the Twentieth Century," *British Journal of Middle Eastern Studies* 31 (2004): 153–173.

2. Deborah Cobbett, "Women in Iraq," in Committee Against Repression and for Democratic Rights in Iraq, *Saddam's Iraq: Revolution or Reaction?* 120–137 (London: Zed Books, 1989). A similar tendency can be discerned in Marion Farouk-Sluglett, "Liberation or Repression? Pan-Arab Nationalism and the Women's Movement in Iraq," in Derek Hopwood, Habib Ishow, and Thomas Koszinowski, eds., *Iraq: Power and Society*, 51–73 (Reading, U.K.: Ithaca Press, 1993). Efforts to create a more inclusive picture can be found in Martina Kamp, "Abschied von der Abaya? Eine historische Interpretation zur politischen und sozio-ökonomischen Situation irakischer Frauen während der Monarchie," master's thesis, Hamburg University, 1997, and Nadje Sadig al-Ali, *Iraqi Women: Untold Stories from 1948 to the Present* (London: Zed Books, 2007).

3. I point to the existence of an "official" narrative and an "unofficial" narrative on the women's movement in my 2004 article "The Other 'Awakening' in Iraq," 170, and develop the idea systematically in a somewhat different version of this chapter: "Competing Narratives: Histories of the Women's Movement in Iraq, 1910–1958," *International Journal of Middle East Studies* 40, no. 3 (August 2008): 445–466. In her valuable book *Iraqi Women*, al-Ali also challenges Iraqi women's polarized narratives and provides a nuanced account of their experiences in the second half of the twentieth century.

4. Sabiha al-Shaikh Da'ud, *Awwal al-Tariq Ila al-Nahda al-Niswiyya fi al-'Iraq* (Baghdad: al-Rabita, 1958), 175; *al-Hawadith*, 18 June 1946, 2.

5. Hanna Batatu, *The Old Social Classes and the Revolutionary Movements of Iraq* (Princeton, N.J.: Princeton University Press, 1978), 5–361; Marion Farouk-Sluglett and Peter Sluglett, "The Transformation of Land Tenure and Rural Social Structure in Central and Southern Iraq, c. 1870–1958," *International Journal of Middle East Studies* 15 (1983): 491–505.

6. Ruth Frances Woodsmall and Charlotte Johnson, *Study of the Role of Women, Their Activities, and Organizations in Lebanon, Egypt, Iraq, Jordan, and Syria, Oc-*

tober 1954–August 1955 (New York: International Federation of Business and Professional Women, 1956), 48.

7. Sara Fadil al-Jamali, who founded the Women's Temperance and Social Welfare Society, was the American wife of Muhammad Fadil al-Jamali, who filled high posts at the Ministry of Education in the 1930s and was foreign minister in 1946, 1947, and 1952 and prime minister between 1953 and 1954; Asiya Tawfiq Wahbi, president of the women's branch of the Child Protection (or Welfare) Society during the 1940s, was married to Tawfiq Wahbi, who was at different times the minister of economics, minister of education, and minister social affairs; 'Ismat Sabah al-Sa'id, vice president of the women's branch of the Red Crescent in the mid-1940s, was Nuri al-Sa'id's daughter-in-law; Zakiyya Pachachi, chairperson of the Iraqi Women's Union in the 1940s, came from a family that had produced several prime ministers, ministers, and others who had attained key roles in Iraq's government.

8. Members were also young, urban dwellers, primarily students, and single women. See Batatu, *The Old Social Classes*, 1205; Majid Khadduri, *Republican 'Iraq* (London: Oxford University Press, 1969), 121; Mubejel Baban, interviewed by the author, London, 20 August 1997; Bushra Perto, interviewed by the author, London, 18 August 1997. Both Baban and Perto were senior members of the League for the Defense of Women's Rights under the monarchy.

9. Yusuf Salman Yusuf, "Yawm al-Nisa' al-'Alami," in Kakhri Karim, ed., *Kitabat al-Rafiq Fahd*, 2d ed., 407–413 (Baghdad: al-Tariq al-Jadid, 1976); Naziha al-Dulaimi, *Al-Mar'a al-'Iraqiyya* (Baghdad: al-Rabita, [1950?]), 46–47; Naziha al-Dulaimi, "Rabitat al-Mar'a al-'Iraqiyya," *al-Thaqafa al-Jadida* 5 (1982), 112.

10. For Da'ud's institutional affiliations, see *Sada al-Ahali*, 5 July 1951, 2; Da'ud, *Awwal al-Tariq*, 179; *al-Zaman*, 28 June 1946, 2; and *al-Zaman*, 27 June 1948, 2. The Iraqi Women's Union's narrative also found its way into period newspapers and periodicals. See, for example, 'A. Sh., "Al-Nahda al-Niswiyya fi al-'Iraq," *al-Mu'allim al-Jadid* 18 (1955), 78–85; Suad al-Umari, "Participation of Women in Community Life in Iraq," *International Women's News* 50 (June 1956): 535–536. This narrative can also be learned from interviews conducted by Ruth Woodsmall and Charlotte Johnson in 1955 with union members. These interviews are cataloged in the Ruth Frances Woodsmall Private Papers, Box 62, Folder 5, Sophia Smith Collection, Smith College, Northampton, Mass.

11. Al-Dulaimi, *Al-Mar'a al-'Iraqiyya*; al-Dulaimi, "Rabitat al-Mar'a al-'Iraqiyya." The League for the Defense of Women's Rights narrative can also be learned from the speech of its representative at the 1953 international women's conference in Copenhagen, from the post-1958 press, and from my interviews with other league leaders, especially Mubejel Baban and Bushra Perto (cited in note 8). See Maliha Jawwad, *Al-Mu'tamar al-Nisa'i al-'Alami al-Mun'aqad fi Copenhagen* (Baghdad: al-Rabita, 1954). In addition, references may be found in the book of another leading Communist activist, Su'ad Khairi, *Thawrat 14 Tammuz* (Beirut: Dar Ibn Khaldun, 1980), 74–76.

12. Da'ud, *Awwal al-Tariq*, 130–134; al-Dulaimi, "Rabitat al-Mar'a al-'Iraqiyya," 106.

13. Scholars studying the emergence of Egyptian feminism are now reconsidering Amin's role. See, for example, Beth Baron, *The Women's Awakening in Egypt: Culture, Society, and the Press* (New Haven, Conn.: Yale University Press, 1994); Margot Badran, *Feminists, Islam, and Nation: Gender and the Making of Modern Egypt* (Princeton, N.J.: Princeton University Press, 1995); Leila Ahmed, *Women and Gender in Islam: Historical Roots of a Modern Debate* (New Haven, Conn.: Yale University Press, 1992).

14. Khidir al-'Abbasi, *Tahrir al-Mar'a Baina Sha'irain al-Zahawi wa-l-Rusafi* (Baghdad: Matba'at al-Umma, [1953?]), 5, 25, 39–47; Jamil Sidqi al-Zahawi, *Diwan Jamil Sidqi al-Zahawi* (Beirut: al-'Awda, 1972), 316–328; Hilal Naji, *Al-Zahawi wa-Diwanihi al-Mafqud* (Cairo: Dar al-'Arab, 1963), 162–165.

15. For the full text of this article, see Jamil Sidqi al-Zahawi, "Al-Mar'a wa-l-Difa' 'Anha," in 'Abd al-Hamid al-Rashudi, ed., *Al-Zahawi: Dirasat wa-Nusus*, 112–117 (Beirut: al-Haya, 1966). For more about the reactions to the article, see al-'Abbasi, *Tahrir al-Mar'a*, 26–38, and Khairi al-'Umari, *Hikayat Siyasiyya min Ta'rikh al-'Iraq al-Hadith* (Baghdad: Dar al-Qadisiyya, 1980), 96–99.

16. Da'ud, *Awwal al-Tariq*, 157, 162, 204–205; 'Abd al-Rahman Sulaiman al-Darbandi, *Dirasat 'an al-Mar'a al-'Iraqiyya al-Mu'asira*, 2 vols. (Baghdad: Dar al-Basri, 1968), 1:46; al-'Abbasi, *Tahrir al-Mar'a*, 19–20; 'Abd al-Razzaq al-Hilali, *Ta'rikh al-Ta'lim fi al-'Iraq fi al-'Ahd al-'Uthmani, 1638–1917* (Baghdad: Sharikat al-Taba' wa-l-Nashr al-Ahaliyya, 1959), 158–161. For more about al-Zahawi, see Dina Rizk Khoury, "Looking at the Modern: A Biography of an Iraqi Modernist," in Mary Ann Fay, ed., *Auto/Biography and the Construction of Identity in the Middle East*, 109–124 (New York: Palgrave, 2001).

17. For example, 'Abd al-Razzaq al-Hilali, "Al-Sha'ir al-Failasuf Jamil Sidqi al-Zahawi," in *Diwan Jamil Sidqi al-Zahawi*, Qaf–Ha' [Arabic letters in place of page numbers] (Beirut: al-'Awda, 1972); Yusuf 'Izz al-Din, *Al-Shi'r al-'Iraqi al-Hadith* (Cairo: al-Ma'arif, 1977), 103, 141–143.

18. Da'ud, *Awwal al-Tariq*, 134; al-Dulaimi, "Rabitat al-Mar'a al-'Iraqiyya," 106.

19. Da'ud, *Awwal al-Tariq*, 130–133; al-Dulaimi, "Rabitat al-Mar'a al-'Iraqiyya," 106.

20. Ma'ruf al-Rusafi, *Diwan al-Rusafi*, 2 vols., 2d ed. (Baghdad: Afaq 'Arabiyya, 1986), 2:71–75; see also Yousif Izzidien [Yusuf 'Izz al-Din], "The Emancipation of Iraqi Women: Women and Their Influence on Iraqi Life and Poetry," *Bulletin of the College of Arts, Baghdad University* 1 (1959), 35–37.

21. Al-Rusafi, *Diwan al-Rusafi*, 2:350–358.

22. Da'ud, *Awwal al-Tariq*, 130–131; al-'Umari, *Hikayat Siyasiyya*, 101–102; "Intelligence Report No. 7," 1 April 1922, National Archives of India, New Delhi (NAI), Baghdad High Commission File (BHCF), Internal Intelligence Reports 19/1, vol. III. For more about al-Rusafi and al-Zahawi, see Wiebke Walther, "From Women's Problems to Women as Images in Modern Iraqi Poetry," *Die Welt des Islams* 36 (1996): 219–241.

23. Da'ud, *Awwal al-Tariq*, 128–130, 137–138.

24. Ibid., 136–137, 242; "Special Report on the Progress of Iraq During the Period 1920–1931," in *Iraq Administration Reports: 1914–1932*, 10 vols., sources established by Robert L. Jarman (Slough, U.K.: Archive Editions, 1992), 10:232.

25. Al-Dulaimi, "Rabitat al-Mar'a al-'Iraqiyya," 106; Khairi, *Thawrat 14 Tammuz*, 74–75; *Tariq al-Sha'b*, 1 April 1979.

26. In both Batatu, *The Old Social Classes*, 394–398, and al-'Umari, *Hikayat Siyasiyya*, esp. 105–106, 126–128.

27. See Baron, *The Women's Awakening in Egypt*; Badran, *Feminists, Islam, and Nation*, 14–16; Deniz Kandiyoti, "End of Empire: Islam, Nationalism, and Women in Turkey," in Deniz Kandiyoti, ed., *Women, Islam, and the State* (London: Macmillan, 1991), 26–27; and Parvin Paidar, *Women and the Political Process in Twentieth-Century Iran* (Cambridge, U.K.: Cambridge University Press, 1995), 48–49, 92.

28. Da'ud, *Awwal al-Tariq*, 48–49.

29. *Al-Lisan* 1 (1919), 183–184.

30. Da'ud, *Awwal al-Tariq*, 55; "Intelligence Report No. 22," 1 October 1921, NAI, BHCF, Internal Intelligence Reports 19/1, vol. II.

31. Da'ud incorrectly dated that meeting as being in May 1918. Compare Da'ud, *Awwal al-Tariq*, 49–51, with Gertrude Bell, *The Letters of Gertrude Bell*, 2 vols., selected and edited by Lady Bell (London: Ernest Benn, 1927), 2:457.

32. Da'ud, *Awwal al-Tariq*, 27–35. See also Jawwad, *Al-Mu'tamar al-Nisa'i al-'Alami*, 21; *al-Fikr al-Jadid*, 10 March 1973, 4.

33. Da'ud, *Awwal al-Tariq*, 27–35; *al-Fikr al-Jadid*, 10 March 1973, 4. For more about women's participation in the revolt, see Rufa'il Butti, "Al-Mar'a al-'Iraqiyya al-Haditha," *al-Kitab* 4 (November 1947), 1877; *al-'Arusa*, 11 July 1928, 9; al-Darbandi, *Dirasat*, 2:250–251; 'Ali al-Khaqani, "Sha'irat fi Thawrat al-'Ishrin," in Muhammad 'Ali Kamal al-Din, ed., *Thawrat al-'Ishrin fi Dhikraha al-Khamsin*, 353–375 (Najaf: Dar al-Tadamun, 1971).

34. Compare Da'ud, *Awwal al-Tariq*, 85–92, with al-Dulaimi, "Rabitat al-Mar'a al-'Iraqiyya," 106.

35. Da'ud, *Awwal al-Tariq*, 85–87; al-'Umari, *Hikayat Siyasiyya*, 117–118; *al-'Arusa*, 4 July 1928, 3; Batatu, *The Old Social Classes*, 323.

36. Da'ud, *Awwal al-Tariq*, 87–89; *al-'Arusa*, 4 July 1928, 3; and *al-Istiqlal*, 3 February 1923, 2, as quoted in *Kashaf Mawdu'at al-Mar'a fi Jaridat al-Istiqlal: 1920–1960* (Baghdad: n.p., 1980), 33.

37. Da'ud, *Awwal al-Tariq*, 89 and 119.

38. E. S. Stevens, "The Woman [sic] Movement in Iraq," *The Near East and India* 10 (October 1929), 400.

39. See quotes from Da'ud's article published in *al-Bilad* on 30 October 1929 (and not October 1930, as she mistakenly claimed) in her book *Awwal al-Tariq*, 86, and in al-'Umari, *Hikayat Siyasiyya*, 120–121.

40. See, for example, al-'Abbasi, *Tahrir al-Mar'a*, 48–50.

41. Da'ud, *Awwal al-Tariq*, 85.

42. Stevens, "The Woman [sic] Movement," 400.

43. Ibid.; Da'ud, *Awwal al-Tariq*, 92; al-'Umari, *Hikayat Siyasiyya*, 118.

44. Da'ud, *Awwal al-Tariq*, 87–88, 141–142, 204–205.

45. Al-Dulaimi, "Rabitat al-Mar'a al-'Iraqiyya," 106.

46. Da'ud, *Awwal al-Tariq*, 52, 55–56; "Intelligence Report No. 7."

47. Da'ud, *Awwal al-Tariq*, 51–82, 120–124, 136–137; al-Dulaimi, "Rabitat al-Mar'a al-'Iraqiyya," 106; *al-Fikr al-Jadid*, 24 March 1973, 4.

48. Al-Dulaimi, "Rabitat al-Mar'a al-'Iraqiyya," 107.

49. Batatu, *The Old Social Classes*, 405–409.

50. Ibid., 406.

51. "Iraq Police, Abstract of Intelligence," Basra, no. 4, 25 January 1930, NAI, BHCF.

52. Da'ud, *Awwal al-Tariq*, 205–208. See also al-Darbandi, *Dirasat*, 1:162–164.

53. See note 7 on Sara Fadil al-Jamali.

54. Da'ud, *Awwal al-Tariq*, 181; Hind Tahsin Kadry, *Women's Education in Iraq* (Baghdad: n.p., 1958), 26; Woodsmall and Johnson, *Study of the Role of Women*, 48–49; "Women's Activities," Woodsmall Private Papers, Box 62, Folder 6.

55. Da'ud, *Awwal al-Tariq*, 177.

56. Al-Dulaimi, "Rabitat al-Mar'a al-'Iraqiyya," 107.

57. Woodsmall and Johnson, *Study of the Role of Women*, 48; al-Darbandi, *Dirasat*, 1:227.

58. *Al-Istiqlal*, 7 February 1936, 1, 3; *al-Istiqlal*, 16 February 1936, 3.

59. Al-Dulaimi, "Rabitat al-Mar'a al-'Iraqiyya," 107; Da'ud, *Awwal al-Tariq*, 156, 158–159.

60. According to Da'ud, the change occurred in 1942, but according to al-Dulaimi in 1943.

61. Da'ud, *Awwal al-Tariq*, 173–174.

62. Al-Dulaimi, "Rabitat al-Mar'a al-'Iraqiyya," 108–109.

63. Quoted in Woodsmall and Johnson, *Study of the Role of Women*, 48.

64. Da'ud, *Awwal al-Tariq*, 175–181; see also "Women's Activities."

65. Al-Dulaimi, "Rabitat al-Mar'a al-'Iraqiyya," 108–109.

66. Ibid.; Da'ud, *Awwal al-Tariq*, 175; *Al-Mu'tamar al-Nisa'i al-'Arabi* (Cairo: Dar al-Ma'arif, 1944), 214–219, 268–271; Woodsmall and Johnson, *Study of the Role of Women*, 48. The precise date of the union's formation is difficult to ascertain; however, the union celebrated its first anniversary in June 1946. See *al-Hawadith*, 18 June 1946, 2.

67. Da'ud, *Awwal al-Tariq*, 175; *al-Hawadith*, 18 June 1946, 2.

68. *Al-Hawadith*, 18 June 1946, 2.

69. Al-Dulaimi, "Rabitat al-Mar'a al-'Iraqiyya", 109.

70. Woodsmall and Johnson, *Study of the Role of Women*, 48.

71. 'A. Sh., "Al-Nahda al-Niswiyya fi al-'Iraq," 80.

72. Da'ud, *Awwal al-Tariq*, 144–147, 169–70, 176–177, 232, 235–237; 'A. Sh., "Al-Nahda al-Niswiyya fi al-'Iraq," 79–81. See also Woodsmall and Johnson, *Study of the Role of Women*, 39, 49; *al-Zaman*, 8 September 1947, 2; *al-Zaman*, 23 May 1948, 2; *al-*

Zaman, 12 July 1953, 4; *al-Zaman*, 6 November 1956, 4; *al-Zaman*, 16 October 1957, 2; and *Liwa' al-Istiqlal*, 22 June 1949, 2.

73. Al-Dulaimi, "Rabitat al-Mar'a al-'Iraqiyya," 107, 109; al-Dulaimi, *Al-Mar'a al-'Iraqiyya*, 48–50; Ellen Fleischmann, "The Other 'Awakening': The Emergence of Women's Movements in the Modern Middle East, 1900–1940," in Margaret L. Meriwether and Judith E. Tucker, eds., *A Social History of Women and Gender in the Modern Middle East* (Boulder, Colo.: Westview, 1999), 102.

74. Al-Umari, "Participation of Women."

75. *Al-Zaman*, 28 June 1946, 2; Doreen Warriner, *Land Reform and Development in the Middle East* (London: Royal Institute of International Affairs, 1957), 181.

76. *Liwa' al-Istiqlal*, 22 June 1949, 2; *al-Hawadith*, 9 July 1949, 2.

77. 'A. Sh., "Al-Nahda," 84–85.

78. In the mid-1950s, the Iraqi government admitted that accurate statistics concerning births, deaths, and infant mortality were unavailable and noted that even estimates could not be made. See al-'Iraq, Wizarat al-Iqtisad, al-Da'ira al-Ra'isiyya li-l-Ihsa', *Al-Majmu'a al-Ihsa'iyya al-Sanawiyya al-'Amma, 1955* (Baghdad: Matba'at al-Zahra', 1956), 229.

79. "Dr. Laimana Zaki" (interview), 10 February 1955, Woodsmall Papers, Box 62, Folder 5.

80. Uriel Dann, *Iraq Under Qassem: A Political History, 1958–1963* (Jerusalem: Israel Universities Press, 1969), 117; Batatu, *The Old Social Classes*, 705, 882–883; Farouk-Sluglett, "Liberation or Repression?" 64.

81. Raja' al-Zanburi, "Matba'at al-Hizb, Muhakamat al-Rafiq Fahd, Awwal Tanzim Nisa'i, al-Sijn," *al-Thaqafa al-Jadida* 5 (1982): 56–81.

82. Al-Dulaimi, "Rabitat al-Mar'a al-'Iraqiyya," 110; *Sada al-Ahali*, 8 October 1951, 2–3.

83. Al-Dulaimi, "Rabitat al-Mar'a al-'Iraqiyya," 110. See also al-Ali, *Iraqi Women*, 86–87.

84. Baha' al-Din Nuri, *Mudhakirat Baha' al-Din Nuri* (London: Dar al-Hikma,, 2001), 144.

85. Bushra Perto, interviewed by the author, London, 18 August 1997.

86. Jawwad, *Al-Mu'tamar al-Nisa'i al-'Alami*, 23.

87. Al-Dulaimi, "Rabitat al-Mar'a al-'Iraqiyya," 111–113; al-Dulaimi, *Al-Mar'a al-'Iraqiyya*, 46–47; Jawwad, *Al-Mu'tamar al-Nisa'i al-'Alami*, 19–23; "Al-Conference al-Awwal li-Rabitat al-Difa' 'An Huquq al-Mar'a 10/3/1955," *al-Thaqafa al-Jadida* 5 (1982): 122–123; Mubejel Baban and Bushra Perto, interviewed by the author, London, 18 and 20 August 1997.

88. Fleischmann, summing up scholarly works on the development of women's movements in the Middle East, points out these themes in "The Other 'Awakening,'" 89–139.

89. See Roger T. Stearn, "Ingrams, Doreen Constance (1906–1997)," *Oxford Dictionary of National Biography* (Oxford, U.K.: Oxford University Press), 2004, available at http://www.oxforddnb.com/view/article/67156.

90. Ingrams, *The Awakened*; Eric Davis, *Memories of State: Politics, History, and Collective Identity* (Berkeley and Los Angeles: University of California Press, 2005), 148–199; Tariq Nafi' al-Hamdani, "Al-Haraka al-Niswiyya," in *Hadarat al-'Iraq*, 13:181–208 (Baghdad: Dar al-Huriyya li-l-Tiba'a, 1985).

91. Ismael and Ismael, "Gender and State in Iraq," 193; Dann, *Iraq Under Qassem*, 321.

92. General Federation of Iraqi Women, *"The Iraqi Woman['s] Association" and the Role of the Iraqi Communist Party in Emptying It of Its Social Essence* (Baghdad: n.p., 1980).

93. Ingrams, *The Awakened*, 111.

94. Cobbett, "Women in Iraq," 120.

95. Fran Hazelton (former secretary of CARDRI), e-mail message to the author, 24 January 2008.

5. CHALLENGING THE GOVERNMENT'S GENDER DISCOURSE

1. 'Abd al-Razzaq al-Hasani, *Ta'rikh al-Wizarat al-'Iraqiyya*, 10 vols., 7th ed. (Baghdad: Afaq 'Arabiyya, 1988), 9:150; Ruth Frances Woodsmall and Charlotte Johnson, *Study of the Role of Women, Their Activities, and Organizations in Lebanon, Egypt, Iraq, Jordan, and Syria, October 1954–August 1955* (New York: International Federation of Business and Professional Women, 1956), 49.

2. Sabiha al-Shaikh Da'ud, *Awwal al-Tariq Ila al-Nahda al-Niswiyya fi al-'Iraq* (Baghdad: al-Rabita, 1958), 175.

3. Da'ud, *Awwal al-Tariq*, 61–62, 76–79, 176, 211–220; *Sada al-Ahali*, 12 December 1951, 2–3; 'A. Sh., "Al-Nahda al-Niswiyya fi al-'Iraq," *al-Mu'allim al-Jadid* 18 (1955), 79–81; *Al-Mu'tamar al-Nisa'i al-'Arabi* (Cairo: Dar al-Ma'arif, 1944), 270; see also excerpts from journals published by the Iraqi Women's Union or by its organizations in United Nations, Department of Social Affairs, Division of Social Affairs, *Iraq: January 1948–June 1953* (New York: United Nations, 1953), esp. 5 and 11.

4. The book was published right before the 1958 coup, but it was already in advanced stages of preparation at the beginning of 1955. See Miss Sabiha Sheikh Daoud, 21 February 1955, Ruth Frances Woodsmall Private Papers, Box 62, Folder 5, Sophia Smith Collection, Smith College, Northampton, Mass.

5. Da'ud, *Awwal al-Tariq*, 223–229.

6. Ibid., 175–176.

7. *Al-Zaman*, 21 June 1954, 4–5.

8. 'A. Sh., "al-Nahda al-Niswiyya fi al-'Iraq," 80; *al-Zaman*, 21 June 1954, 4–5; Da'ud, *Awwal al-Tariq*, 176, 223–229.

9. Husain 'Ali al-A'zami, *Ahkam al-Zawaj* (Baghdad: Sharikat al-Taba' wa-l-Nashr al-Ahaliyya, 1949), 210–213.

10. Ibid., 29–30.

11. Ibid., 123, 126, 128–129.

12. Al-Hasani, *Ta'rikh al-Wizarat al-'Iraqiyya*, 8:118–123.

13. Ibid.; *al-Ittihad al-Dusturi*, 22 August 1950, 1.

14. Al-'Iraq, Wizarat al-Ma'arif, *Ta'rikh Biladika wa-Umatika fi Khadirihi*, 3rd ed. (Baghdad: Sharikat al-Tijara wa-l-Tiba'a, 1952), 14 and 129; this is a textbook for sixth-grade pupils.

15. *Al-Ittihad al-Dusturi*, 22 August 1950, 1.

16. Lila Abu-Lughod, ed., *Remaking Women: Feminism and Modernity in the Middle East* (Princeton, N.J.: Princeton University Press, 1998).

17. See the 22 April 1951 memorandum by the Iraqi Women's Union in *Sada al-Ahali*, 12 December 1951, 2–3, and the 23 February 1958 memorandum in *al-Sha'b*, 24 February 1958, 4, or in *al-Zaman*, 26 February 1958, 3.

18. See the memorandum quoted in *al-Bilad*, 7 March 1956, 5, as well as the memos quoted in *Sada al-Ahali*, 12 December 1951, 2–3, and *al-Zaman*, 20 June 1952, 2.

19. *Sada al-Ahali*, 12 December 1951, 2–3; *al-Bilad*, 7 March 1956, 5; *al-Zaman*, 26 February 1958, 3.

20. Iraqi Women's Union, memo, 22 April 1951 (cited in note 17).

21. Quoted in *al-Zaman*, 26 February 1958, 3.

22. Quoted in ibid., 3.

23. See, for example, *al-Zaman*, 26 February 1958, 3.

24. *Al-Bilad*, 12 March 1956, 5.

25. *Al-Zaman*, 26 February 1958, 3.

26. Quoted in *al-Sha'b*, 20 October 1953, 3.

27. Ibid.

28. *Sada al-Ahali*, 12 December 1951, 2–3.

29. See al-Hasani, *Ta'rikh al-Wizarat*, 1:353.

30. *Al-Zaman*, 22 February 1958, 4; *al-Sha'b*, 24 February 1958, 4–5; *al-Zaman*, 26 February 1958, 3.

31. Quoted in *al-Zaman*, 7 March 1958, 1.

32. *Al-Zaman*, 9 March 1958, 4.

33. Ibid.; *al-Zaman*, 8 March 1958, 4.

34. Quoted in *al-Sha'b*, 26 March 1958, 8. The way Wahbi portrays these events indicates that they may well have been inspired by the actions of Egyptian feminists a few years earlier. In February 1951, Egyptian feminists, headed by Duriya Shafiq, forced their way into the Egyptian Parliament. They demanded to meet with the heads of Parliament and agreed to disperse only after receiving a promise that efforts would be made to give women political rights. See Duriya Shafiq, *Al-Mar'a al-Misriyya* (Cairo: al-Adab, 1955), 201–208; Cynthia Nelson, *Doria Shafik, Egyptian Feminist: A Woman Apart* (Gainesville: University Press of Florida, 1996), 168–172.

35. *Al-Sha'b*, 26 March 1958, 8. I have been unable to find any indication of a continuation of the union's campaign after this date.

36. *Al-Zaman*, 28 March 1958, 5; Sir M. Wright to Foreign Office, 26 March 1958, Public Record Office, London (PRO), Foreign Office (FO) 371/134198/VQ1015/33.

37. Naziha al-Dulaimi, *Al-Mar'a al-'Iraqiyya* (Baghdad: al-Rabita, [1950?]), 46–47; Maliha Jawwad, *Al-Mu'tamar al-Nisa'i al-'Alami al-Mun'aqad fi Copenhagen* (Baghdad: al-Rabita, 1954), 23.

38. *Al-Bilad*, 22 August 1959; Naziha al-Dulaimi, "Rabitat al-Mar'a al-'Iraqiyya," *al-Thaqafa al-Jadida* 5 (1982), 110; *al-Zaman*, 26 September 2001, 8.

39. Al-Dulaimi, *Al-Mar'a al-'Iraqiyya*, 13, 11–12, 16, 22–23, 28–30.

40. Ibid., 8–10, 15–16, 20, 34–42.

41. Ibid., 34–42.

42. Ibid., 50.

43. Mubejel Baban, interviewed by the author, London, 20 August 1997.

44. Al-Dulaimi, *Al-Mar'a al-'Iraqiyya*, 46–47.

45. For the quote, see Jawwad, *Al-Mu'tamar al-Nisa'i al-'Alami*, 23; see also al-Dulaimi, "Rabitat al-Mar'a al-'Iraqiyya," 112.

46. Al-Dulaimi, "Rabitat al-Mar'a al-'Iraqiyya," 111–113; Mubejel Baban, interviewed by author, London, 20 August 1997.

47. Al-Dulaimi, "Rabitat al-Mar'a al-'Iraqiyya," 111.

48. Mubejel Baban, interviewed by the author, London, 20 August 1997.

49. Su'ad Khairi, *Thawrat 14 Tammuz* (Beirut: Dar Ibn Khaldun, 1980), 173.

50. *Al-Waqa'i' al-'Iraqiyya* 3 (3 August 1958), 7; *al-Waqa'i' al-'Iraqiyya* 489 (23 February 1961), 1.

51. See, for example, Naziha al-Dulaimi's speech in *Iraq Times*, 9 March 1960, 1.

52. See the law and the attached memorandum in *al-Waqa'i' al-'Iraqiyya* 280 (30 December 1959), 8.

53. *Al-Waqa'i' al-'Iraqiyya* 280 (30 December 1959), 1–8; a detailed analysis of the law can be found in J. N. D. Anderson, "A Law of Personal Status for Iraq," *International and Comparative Law Quarterly* 9 (October 1960): 542–563.

54. *Al-Thawra*, 7 March 1960, as quoted in Anderson, "A Law of Personal Status for Iraq," 561–563.

55. See, for example, *Iraq Times*, 10 March 1960, 1; *al-Thawra*, 7 March 1960, as quoted in Anderson, "A Law of Personal Status for Iraq," 561–563; Amal Rassam, "Political Ideology and Women in Iraq: Legislation and Cultural Constraints," in Joseph G. Jabbra and Nancy W. Jabbra, eds., *Women and Development in the Middle East and North Africa*, 82–95 (Leiden: E. J. Brill, 1992); Suad Joseph, "Elite Strategies for State Building: Women, Family, Religion, and the State in Iraq and Lebanon," in Deniz Kandiyoti, ed., *Women, Islam, and the State*, 176–200 (London: Macmillan Press, 1991); Nadje Sadig al-Ali, *Iraqi Women: Untold Stories from 1948 to the Present* (London: Zed Books, 2007); Achim Rohde, *Facing Dictatorship: State–Society Relations in Ba'thist Iraq* (London: Routledge, 2010); and Noga Efrati, "Negotiating Rights in Iraq: Women and the Personal Status Law," *Middle East Journal* 59, no. 4 (Autumn 2005): 577–595.

EPILOGUE: PAST MEETS PRESENT

1. Hind Makiya and Sawsan El Barak, "Iraq's Overlooked Women," *Washington Post*, 30 November 2003, B7; Raja Habib Khuzai and Songul Chapouk, "Iraq's Hidden Treasure," *New York Times*, 3 December 2003, available at http://www.nytimes.com/2003/12/03/opinion/iraq-s-hidden-treasure.html; Nadje al-Ali and Nicola Pratt, "Women in Iraq: Beyond the Rhetoric," *Middle East Research and Information Project* 239 (2006), 2.
2. See, for example, *al-Zaman*, 14 January 2004, available at http://www.azzaman.com/index.asp?fname=2004\01\01-13\999.htm&storytitle; *al-Ilaf*, 15 January 2004, available at http://www.elaph.com/web/webform/SearchArticle.aspx?ArticleId=1074183249870127800; *al-Zaman*, 21 January 2004, available at http://www.azzaman.com/index.asp?fname=2004\01\01-20\998.htm&storytitle.
3. Larry Diamond, *Squandered Victory: The American Occupation and the Bungled Effort to Bring Democracy to Iraq* (New York: Times Books, 2005), 145 and 156.
4. For the English text of the TAL, see http://govinfo.library.unt.edu/cpa-iraq/government/TAL.html.
5. In other words, the lists of candidates had to look like this: "man, man, woman," and so on. The assumption was that many small parties would participate in the elections, and if a party received only five mandates, four men would enter Parliament, but only one woman. It turned out that only large parties were elected, and most women candidates entered.
6. Ed Wong, "Iraqi Constitution Draft Includes Curbs to Women's Rights," *New York Times*, 20 July 2005, available at http://www.nytimes.com/2005/07/20/international/middleeast/20women.html#; Abdul Hamid el-Zibari, "Iraqi Women Organize a Sit-In for Their Constitutional Rights," *Peyamner News Agency*, 10 August 2005, available at http://www.peyamner.com/print.php?id=18553&lang=english; Catherine E. Morris, "Iraqi Women Leaders Call for Equal Rights Under Constitution," *Peyamner News Agency*, 10 August 2005, available at http://www.peyamner.com/print.php?id=18548&lang=english.
7. See the official text of the Iraqi Constitution, Article 49(4), available at http://www.uniraq.org/documents/iraqi_constitution.pdf.
8. See, for example, Emily Flynn Vencat, "'This is My Mission': An Activist for Women in Iraq on the Challenges Ahead," *Newsweek*, 6 November 2005, available at http://www.krg.org/articles/detail.asp?lngnr=12&smap=&rnr=77&anr=7312; Azhar al-Shaikhli, interview in *al-Ilaf*, 26 February 2007, available at http://www.elaph.com/Web/Webform/SearchArticle.aspx?ArticleId=214305&sectionarchive=AkhbarKhasa.
9. See, for example, *Weekly Gazette of the Republic of Iraq*, 13 August 1958, 37.
10. "Al-Dustur al-Mu'qat," in *Al-Mawsu'a al-Qanuniyya al-'Iraqiyya*, 9–18 (Beirut: al-Dar al-'Arabiyya li-l-Mawsu'at, n.d.). For an English translation, see http://www.niqash.org/content.php?contentTypeID=291&id=2306&lang=0.

11. Phebe Marr, *The Modern History of Iraq*, 2d ed. (Boulder, Colo.: Westview, 2004), 180–181.

12. Manal Yunis 'Abd al-Razzaq al-Alusi, *Al-Mar'a wa-l-Tatawwur al-Siyasi fi al-Watan al-'Arabi* (Baghdad: Dar al-Shu'un al-Thaqafiyya al-'Amma, 1989), 196.

13. See, for example, Elizabeth Palmer, "Iraqi Women Crowd Ballot in Election," *CBS Evening News*, 6 March 2010.

14. Woodrow Wilson International Center for Scholars, Conflict Prevention Project, Middle East Project, and Women Waging Peace, *Winning the Peace Conference Report: Women's Role in Post-Conflict Iraq*, supplemental material (Washington, D.C.: Woodrow Wilson International Center for Scholars, April 2003), 8 and 16. See also Kathryn Mikha'il, "Al-Mar'a al-Rifiyya," *'Iraq al-Ghad*, 29 July, 2005, available at http://www.Iraqoftomorrow.org/viewarticle.php?id=31591&pg=iraqa ndtheworld; *al-Zaman*, 8 August, 2005, 3.

15. See Amatzia Baram, "Neo-Tribalism in Iraq: Saddam Hussein's Tribal Policies 1991–1996," *International Journal of Middle East Studies* 29 (1997): 1–31; Faleh A. Jabar and Hosham Dawod, eds., *Tribes and Power: Nationalism and Ethnicity in the Middle East* (London: Saqi, 2003), esp. part 2, p. 2; Charles Tripp, *A History of Iraq* (Cambridge, U.K.: Cambridge University Press, 2000), 265; Marr, *The Modern History of Iraq*, 262–263. For the decision, see *Tariq al-Sha'b* 8 (March 1990), 6; Suha Omar, "Women: Honour, Shame, and Dictatorship," in Fran Hazelton, ed., *Iraq Since the Gulf War: Prospects for Democracy* (London: Zed Books, 1994), 64.

16. "Nashitat: Al-Mukallafun bi-Kitabat al-Dustur Mutalabun bi-l-I'timad 'ala al-Qawanin al-Dawliyya," *al-Zaman*, 4 August 2005, at http://www.azzaman.com/index.asp?fname=2005\08\08-03\973.htm&storytitle.

17. See reports from al-'Amara by Donald Macintyre in *The Independent*, 24 April 2003, and by Glen Owen in the *London Times*, 24 April 2003.

18. Toby Dodge, *Inventing Iraq: The Failure of Nation Building and a History Denied* (New York: Columbia University Press, 2003), 168.

19. James Glanz, "Thanks to Guards, Iraq Oil Pipeline Is Up and Running, On and Off," *New York Times*, 3 September 2005, available at http://www.nytimes.com/2005/09/03/international/middleeast/03oil.html; Dumeetha Luthra, "Tribal Justice Takes Hold," *BBC News*, 2 February 2004, available at http://news.bbc.co.uk/2/hi/middle_east/3449869.stm; Rory Carroll, "Women Battle for Rights in New Iraq," *The Guardian*, 15 August 2005, available at http://www.guardian.co.uk/world/2005/aug/15/iraq.gender.

20. Woodrow Wilson International Center for Scholars et al., *Winning the Peace Conference Report*, 8 and 16; "Iraq: Fears Grow for Women's Rights as Deadline Looms for Constitution Draft," IRINNews.org, 28 July 2005; *'Iraq al-Ghad*, 29 July 2005, available at http://www.Iraqoftomorrow.org/viewarticle.php?id=31591&pg=iraqa ndtheworld; *al-Zaman*, 4 August 2005; *al-Zaman*, 8 August 2005.

21. See Article 45(2), Iraqi Constitution, available at http://www.uniraq.org/documents/iraqi_constitution.pdf.

22. See Amatzia Baram, "Iraq 2003–2009: The U.S. Between Baghdad, al-Qaʿidah, and the Tribal *Sahwah*," unpublished paper, June 2009, available at http://iraq. haifa.ac.il/index.php/articles/19-iraq-2003–2009-the-us-between-baghdad-al-qaidah-and-the-tribal-sahwah.html; al-Maktab al-Iʿlami li-Raʾis al-Wuzaraʾ, "Bayan Suhufi," 8 October 2008, available at http://cabinet.iq/ArticleShow. aspx?id=664&lang=A; Ahmad al-Saʿdawi, "A State Governed by Law and Tribes," *Niqash*, 24 July 2008, available at http://www.niqash.org/content.php?contentTy peID=75&id=2254&lang=0.

23. Saleem al-Wazzan, "Abuse of Women Continues," *Niqash*, 29 July 2010, available at http://www.niqash.org/content.php?contentTypeID=74&id=2728&lang=0.

24. Although one article provided that sanity and maturity are essential to the capacity to marry, another stated that this capacity becomes automatic when one reaches the age of eighteen.

25. For more about post-1958 developments in Iraq's Personal Status Law, see Noga Efrati, "Negotiating Rights in Iraq: Women and the Personal Status Law," *Middle East Journal* 59, no. 4 (Autumn 2005): 577–595.

26. Ibid.

27. For the full text of the decision, see *al-Ilaf*, 15 January 2004, available at http://www. elaph.com/web/webform/SearchArticle.aspx?ArticleId=1074183249870127800, or Mawsuʿat al-Nahrain (Qararat Hukumiyya), available at http://nahrain.com/d/ law/024.html. See also Nathan Brown, "Debating Islam in Post-Baathist Iraq," March 2005, available at http://www.carnegieendowment.org/files/PO13.Brown. FINAL2.pdf#search=%22Brown%20post-Baathist%22.

28. "Al-Dustur al-ʿIraqi: Al-Nuqat al-ʿAliqa," *al-Sharq al-Awsat*, 8 August 2005, available at http://www.aawsat.com/details.asp?section=4&issueno=9750&article= 316518&search; "Al-Qadaya al-Mutabaqqiya fi al-Dustur," *Wikalat Karbalaʾ li-l-Anbaʾ*, 16 August 2005, available at http://208.78.41.208/artc.php?id=2434.

29. Nathan Brown, "Constitution of Iraq Draft Bill of Rights," 27 July 2005, available at http://www.carnegieendowment.org/files/BillofRights. pdf#search=%22Constitution%20of%20Iraq%20Draft%20Bill%20of%20 Rights%22.

30. Quoted in Dexter Filkins and James Glanz, "New U.S. Envoy Will Press Iraqis on Their Charter," *New York Times*, 26 July 2005, available at http://query.nytimes. com/gst/fullpage.html?res=9C01E0D6123FF935A15754C0A9639C8B63&pagewa nted=all.

31. See official text of the Iraqi Constitution available at http://www.parliament.iq/ Iraqi_Council_of_Representatives.php?name=singal9asdasdas9dasda8w9wervw 8vw854wvw5w0v98457475v38937456033t64tg34t64gi4dow7wnf4w4y4t386b5 w6576i75page&pa=showpage&pid=3.

32. Quoted in "US: Charter Most Progressive Document in the Muslim World," *Peyamner News Agency*, 29 August 2005, originally downloaded from http://www. peyamner.com/print.php?id=20178&lang=english, but now available at http:// www.lebanonwire.com/0805/05082825AFP.asp.

33. Juan Cole, "Struggles Over Personal Status and Family Law in Post-Baathist Iraq," in Kenneth M. Cuno and Manisha Desai, eds., *Family, Gender, and Law in a Globalizing Middle East and South Asia* (Syracuse, N.Y.: Syracuse University Press, 2009), 124.

34. Ellen Knickmeyer, "Kurds Fault U.S. on Iraqi Charter," *Washington Post Foreign Service*, 21 August 2005, available at http://web.krg.org/articles/detail.asp?rnr=2 4&lngnr=12&anr=5452&smap=; Dexter Filkins, "Secular Iraqis Say New Charter May Curb Rights," *New York Times*, 24 August 2005, available at http://www.nytimes.com/2005/08/24/international/middleeast/24iraq.html.

35. Quoted in Pamela Constable, "Iraqi Women Decry Move to Cut Rights," *Washington Post Foreign Service*, 16 January, 2004, A12. See also Ed Wong, "Iraqi Constitution Draft Includes Curbs to Women's Rights," *New York Times*, 20 July 2005, available at http://www.nytimes.com/2005/07/20/international/middleeast/20women.html.

36. Quoted in *al-Sharq al-Awsat*, 15 August 2005, available at http://www.aawsat.com/details.asp?section=4&article=317698&issueno=9757.

37. Nadje Sadig al-Ali, *Iraqi Women: Untold Stories from 1948 to the Present* (London: Zed Books, 2007), 240–246, 253–259; Nadje al-Ali and Nicola Pratt, "Women Organizing and the Conflict in Iraq Since 2003," *Feminist Review* 88 (2008): 74–85. See also "'Iraqiyyat Yatazahrn fi Baghdad," *al-Sharq al-Awsat*, 10 August 2005, available at http://www.aawsat.com/details.asp?section=4&issueno=9752&article =316863&search; Faranz Fassihi, "Iraqi Shiite Women Push Islamic Law on Gender Roles," *Wall Street Journal*, 9 March 2005, A1; Catherine Philp, "Iraq's Women of Power Who Tolerate Wife-Beating and Promote Polygamy," *Times Online*, 31 March 2005, available at http://www.timesonline.co.uk/tol/news/world/iraq/article440798.ece.

38. Compare Brown, "Debating Islam in Post-Baathist Iraq."

39. Cole, "Struggles Over Personal Status and Family Law in Post-Baathist Iraq," 124.

40. Al-Ali and Pratt, "Women in Iraq," 23.

BIBLIOGRAPHY

ARCHIVAL MATERIAL

Public Record Office, London (PRO)

Air 23	Air Ministry, Royal Air Force, Overseas Commands
CO 696	Colonial Office, Iraq Sessional Papers
FO 371	Foreign Office, Political Correspondence
FO 624	Foreign Office, Baghdad Embassy

India Office Library, London (IO)

L/P&S 10	Files of the Political and Secret Departments
L/P&S 12	Files of the Political and Secret Departments

National Archives of India, New Delhi (NAI)

BHCF	Baghdad High Commission File

U.S. National Archives, Washington, D.C. (USNA)

Records of the Department of State Relating to the Internal Affairs of Iraq, 1930–1944, and Confidential U.S. State Department Central Files, Iraq, 1945–1949, Internal Affairs. Decimal File 890G

OFFICIAL PUBLICATIONS

Iraq

Al-'Iraq. Majlis al-A'yan. *Mahdar al-Jalsa al-Hadiya 'Ashara min al-Ijtima' al-'Adi li-Sanat 1950–1951.* Baghdad: Matba'at al-Hukuma, 1951.

Al-'Iraq. Majlis al-Nuwwab. *Al-Dawra al-Intikhabiyya al-Thaniya 'Ashara min al-Ijtima' al-I'tiyadi li-Sanat 1950*. Baghdad: Matba'at al-Hukuma, n.d.

——. *Mahdar al-Jalsa al-Rabi'a wa-l-Thalathin min al-Ijtima' al-I'tiyadi li-Sanat 1950*. Baghdad: Matba'at al-Hukuma, 1951.

——. *Mahdar al-Jalsa al-Thalitha wa-l-Thalathin min al-Ijtima' al-I'tiyadi li-Sanat 1950*. Baghdad: Matba'at al-Hukuma, 1951.

——. *Mahdar al-Jalsa al-Thamina wa-l-'Ishrin min al-Ijtima' Ghair al-I'tiyadi li-Sanat 1937*. Baghdad: Matba'at al-Hukuma, 1937.

——. *Mahdar al-Jalsa al-Thaniya wa-l-Thalathin min al-Ijtima' al-I'tiyadi li-Sanat 1950*. Baghdad: Matba'at al-Hukuma, 1951.

Iraq Ministry of Economics. Principal Bureau of Statistics. *Statistical Abstract, 1950*. Baghdad: Government Press, 1952.

Iraq Ministry of Justice. *Compilation of Laws and Regulations Issued Between 1st January 1924 and 31st December 1925*. Baghdad: Government Press, 1926.

——. *Compilation of Laws and Regulations Issued Between 1st January 1946 and 31st December 1946*. Baghdad: Government Press, 1949.

Al-'Iraq. Wizarat al-Iqtisad. Al-Da'ira al-Ra'isiyya li-l-Ihsa'. *Al-Majmu'a al-Ihsa'iyya al-Sanawiyya al-'Amma, 1955*. Baghdad: Matba'at al-Zahra', 1956.

Al-'Iraq. Wizarat al-Ma'arif. *Ta'rikh Biladika wa-Umatika fi Khadirihi*. 3rd ed. Baghdad: Sharikat al-Tijara wa-l-Tiba'a, 1952.

Al-Jumhuriyya al-'Iraqiyya. Wizarat al-Dakhiliyya. Mudiriyyat al-Nufus al-'Amma. *Al-Majmu'a al-Ihsa'iyya li-Tasjil 'am 1957*. 2 vols. 26 parts. Baghdad: Government Press, 1964.

Al-Waqa'i' al-'Iraqiyya.

Great Britain

Great Britain. General Officer Commanding-in-Chief, Mesopotamia Expeditionary Force. *The Baghdad Penal Code*. Baghdad: n.p., 1918.

DISSERTATIONS

Amin, Mudhaffar Abdullah. "Jama'at al-Ahali: Its Origin, Ideology, and Role in Iraqi Politics, 1932–1946." 2 vols. Ph.D. diss., University of Durham, 1980.

Kamp, Martina. "Abschied von der Abaya? Eine historische Interpretation zur politischen und sozio-ökonomischen Situation irakischer Frauen während der Monarchie." Master's thesis, Hamburg University, 1997.

PRIVATE PAPERS

H. R. P. Dickson Papers. St. Antony's College, Oxford, U.K.

Norman Anderson Private Papers. School of Oriental and African Studies, Special Collections, London.

Ruth Frances Woodsmall Private Papers. Sophia Smith Collection, Smith College, Northampton, Mass.

PERIODICALS

Al-Ahali
Al-Akhbar
Al-'Alam al-'Arabi
'Alam al-Ghad
Al-'Arusa
Al-Bilad
Al-Fikr al-Jadid
The Guardian
Al-Hawadith
Al-Ilaf
The Independent
'Iraq al-Ghad
Iraq Government Gazette
Al-Istiqlal
Al-Ittihad al-Dusturi
Al-Kitab
Al-Lisan
Liwa' al-Istiqlal
London Times
Lughat al-'Arab
Newsweek
New York Times
Peyamner News Agency
Al-Qada'
Al-Sa'a
Al-Sabah
Sada al-Ahali
Al-Sha'b
Al-Sharq al-Awsat
Al-Sijill
Tariq al-Sha'b
Al-Thawra
Al-Ukhuwwa al-Islamiyya
Al-Umma
Wall Street Journal
Washington Post
Weekly Gazette of the Republic of Iraq
Wikalat Karbala' li-l-Anba'
Al-Zaman

PUBLISHED WORKS IN ARABIC

Books

Al-'Abbasi, Khidir. *Tahrir al-Mar'a Baina Sha'irain al-Zahawi wa-l-Rusafi*. Baghdad: Matba'at al-Umma, [1953?].

Abu Zahra, Muhammad. *Al-Ahwal al-Shakhsiyya*. Cairo: Dar al-Fikr al-'Arabi, 1957.

Al-Alusi, Manal Yunis 'Abd al-Razzaq. *Al-Mar'a wa-l-Tatawwur al-Siyasi fi al-Watan al-'Arabi*. Baghdad: Dar al-Shu'un al-Thaqafiyya al-'Amma, 1989.

Amin Zaki, Saniha. *Dhikrayat Tabiba 'Iraqiyya*. London: Dar al-Hikma, 2005.

Al-'Attar, 'Arif Rashid. *Al-Ijram fi al-Khalis*. Baghdad: al-Ma'arif, 1963.

Al-A'zami, Husain 'Ali. *Ahkam al-Zawaj*. Baghdad: Sharikat al-Taba' wa-l-Nashr al-Ahaliyya, 1949.

——. *Al-Wasaya wa-l-Mawarith*. Baghdad: al-Rashid, 1949.

Al-Badri, Sa'id, ed. *Ara' al-Rusafi fi al-Siyasa wa-l-Din wa-l-Ijtima'*. 2d ed. Baghdad: al-Ma'arif, 1951.

Bahr al-'Ulum, Muhammad. *Adwa' 'Ala Qanun al-Ahwal al-Shakhsiyyai al-'Iraqi*. Najaf: Matba'at al-Nu'man, 1963.

Basri, Mir. *A'lam al-Adab fi al-'Iraq al-Hadith*. 3 vols. London: Dar al-Hikma, 1994–1999.

Al-Chadirchi, Kamil. *Mudhakkirat Kamil al-Chadirchi wa-Ta'rikh al-Hizb al-Watani al-Dimuqrati*. Beirut: Dar al-Tali'a, 1970.

Al-Darbandi, 'Abd al-Rahman Sulaiman. *Dirasat 'an al-Mar'a al-'Iraqiyya al-Mu'asira*. 2 vols. Baghdad: Dar al-Basri, 1968.

Da'ud, Sabiha al-Shaikh. *Awwal al-Tariq Ila al-Nahda al-Niswiyya fi al-'Iraq*. Baghdad: al-Rabita, 1958.

Al-Dulaimi, Naziha. *Al-Mar'a al-'Iraqiyya*. Baghdad: al-Rabita, [1950?].

Fahmi, Ahmad. *Taqrir Hawla al-'Iraq*. Baghdad: al-Maktaba al-'Asriyya, 1926.

Faris, 'Abd al-Jabbar. *'Aman fi al-Furat al-Awsat*. Najaf: Matba'at al-Ra'i, 1934.

Al-Fir'awn, Fariq al-Muzhir. *Al-Qada' al-'Asha'iri*. Baghdad: Matba'at al-Najah, 1941.

Hasanain, Mustafa Muhammad. *Nizam al-Mas'uliyya 'ind al-'Asha'ir al-'Iraqiyya al-'Arabiyya al-Mu'asira*. Cairo: Matba'at al-Istiqlal al-Kubra, 1967.

Al-Hasani, 'Abd al-Razzaq. *Ta'rikh al-Wizarat al-'Iraqiyya*. 10 vols. 7th ed. Baghdad: Afaq 'Arabiyya, 1988.

——. *Al-Usul al-Rasmiyya li-Ta'rikh al-Wizarat al-'Iraqiyya*. Sidon, Lebanon: al-'Irfan, 1964.

Al-Hilali, 'Abd al-Razzaq. *Ta'rikh al-Ta'lim fi al-'Iraq fi al-'Ahd al-'Uthmani 1638–1917*. Baghdad: Sharikat al-Taba' wa-l-Nashr al-Ahaliyya, 1959.

Al-Hilli, 'Abd al-Karim Rida. *Al-Ahkam al-Ja'fariyya fi al-Ahwal al-Shakhsiyya*. 2d ed. Baghdad: al-Muthana, 1947.

'Izz al-Din, Yusuf. *Al-Shi'r al-'Iraqi al-Hadith*. Cairo: al-Ma'arif, 1977.

Al-Jalali, Muhammad al-Baqir. *Mujaz Ta'rikh 'Asha'ir al-'Amara*. Baghdad: al-Najah, 1947.

Jamil, Husain. *Al-Haya al-Niyabiyya fi al-'Iraq, 1925–1946: Mawqif Jama'at al-Ahali Minha*. Baghdad: al-Muthana, 1983.

Jamil, Makki. *Ta'liqat 'ala Nizam Da'awi al-'Asha'ir wa-Ta'dilatihi*. Baghdad: Matba'at al-Karah, 1935.

Jawwad, Maliha. *Al-Mu'tamar al-Nisa'i al-'Alami al-Mun'aqad fi Copenhagen*. Baghdad: al-Rabita, 1954.

Karim, Fakhri, ed. *Kitabat al-Rafiq Fahd*. 2d ed. Baghdad: al-Tariq al-Jadid, 1976.

Kashaf Mawdu'at al-Mar'a fi Jaridat al-Istiqlal: 1920–1960. Baghdad: n.p., 1980.

Khairi, Su'ad. *Thawrat 14 Tammuz*. Beirut: Dar Ibn Khaldun, 1980.

Kharufa, 'Ala' al-Din. *Sharh Qanun al-Ahwal al-Shakhsiyya*. 2 vols. Baghdad: Matba'at al-'Ani, 1962–1963.

Khayyat, Ja'far. *Al-Qarya al-'Iraqiyya*. Beirut: Dar al-Kashshaf, 1950.

Kubba, Muhammad Mahdi. *Mudhakkirati fi Samim al-Ahdath*. Beirut: Dar al-Tali'a, 1965.

Al-Mala'ika, Nazik. *Diwan Nazik al-Mala'ika*. 2 vols. Beirut: Dar al-'Awda, 1986.

——. *Al-Tajzi'iyya fi al-Mujtama' al-'Arabi*. 'Aka (Acre): Maktab al-Aswar, 1978.

Al-Matba'i, Hamid. *Mawsu'at A'lam al-'Iraq fi al-Qarn al-'Ishrin*. 3 vols. Baghdad: Wizarat al-Thaqafa wa-l-I'lam, 1996.

Muhawarat al-Imam al-Muslih Kashif al-Ghita' al-Shaikh Muhammad al-Husain Ma'a al-Safirain al-Baritani wa-l-Amriki fi Baghdad. 3rd ed. Najaf: n.p., 1954.

Al-Mu'tamar al-Nisa'i al-'Arabi. Cairo: Dar al-Ma'arif, 1944.

Naji, Hilal. *Al-Zahawi wa-Diwanihi al-Mafqud*. Cairo: Dar al-'Arab, 1963.

Nuri, Baha' al-Din. *Mudhakirat Baha' al-Din Nuri*. London: Dar al-Hikma, 2001.

Rabitat al-Difa' 'an Huquq al-Mar'a. *Al-Mu'tamar al-Awal li-Rabitat al-Difa' 'an Huquq al-Mar'a*. Baghdad: Dar Baghdad, 1959.

Al-Rashudi, 'Abd al-Hamid, ed. *Al-Zahawi: Dirasat wa-Nusus*. Beirut: al-Haya, 1966.

Al-Rusafi, Ma'ruf. *Diwan al-Rusafi*. 2 vols. 2d ed. Baghdad: Afaq 'Arabiyya, 1986.

Al-Samarra'i, Yunis Ibrahim. *Ta'rikh 'Ulama' Baghdad*. Baghdad: Wizarat al-Awqaf, 1982.

Shafiq, Duriya. *Al-Mar'a al-Misriyya*. Cairo: al-Adab, 1955.

Shawkat, Sami. *Hadhihi Ahdafuna*. Baghdad: n.p., 1939.

Al-Suwaidi, Tawfiq. *Mudhakkirati: Nisf Qarn min Ta'rikh al-'Iraq wa-l-Qadiya al-'Arabiyya*. Beirut: Dar al-Kitab al-'Arabi, 1969.

Al-'Umari, Khairi. *Hikayat Siyasiyya min Ta'rikh al-'Iraq al-Hadith*. Baghdad: Dar al-Qadisiyya, 1980.

Al-'Uzri, 'Abd al-Karim. *Ta'rikh fi Dhikrayat al-'Iraq, 1930–1958*. Beirut: Markaz al-Abjadiya, 1982.

Al-Wardi, 'Ali. *Dirasa fi Tabi'at al-Mujtama' al-'Iraqi*. Baghdad: Matba'at al-'Ani, 1965.

Al-Zahawi, Jamil Sidqi. *Diwan Jamil Sidqi al-Zahawi*. Beirut: al-'Awda, 1972.

Articles

'A. Sh. "Al-Nahda al-Niswiyya fi al-'Iraq." *Al-Mu'allim al-Jadid* 18 (1955): 77–85.

Butti, Rufa'il. "Al-Mar'a al-'Iraqiyya al-Haditha." *Al-Kitab* 4 (November 1947): 1874–1879.

"Al-Conference al-Awwal li-Rabitat al-Difa' 'An Huquq al-Mar'a 10/3/1955." *Al-Thaqafa al-Jadida* 5 (1982): 122–123.

Al-Dulaimi, Naziha. "Rabitat al-Mar'a al-'Iraqiyya." *Al-Thaqafa al-Jadida* 5 (1982): 104–116.

"Al-Dustur al-Mu'qat." In *Al-Mawsu'a al-Qanuniyya al-'Iraqiyya*, 9–18. Beirut: al-Dar al-'Arabiyya li-l-Mawsu'at, n.d.

Al-Hamdani, Tariq Nafi'. "Al-Haraka al-Niswiyya." In *Hadarat al-'Iraq*, 13:181–208. Baghdad: Dar al-Huriyya li-l-Tiba'a, 1985.

Al-Hilali, 'Abd al-Razzaq. "Al-Sha'ir al-Failasuf Jamil Sidqi al-Zahawi." In *Diwan Jamil Sidqi al-Zahawi*, Qaf–Ha' [Arabic letters for page numbers]. Beirut: al-'Awda, 1972.

Al-Khalidi, Kazim Baji. "'Ashirat al-Mushallab wa-l-Nahwa." *Al-Turath al-Sha'bi* 2 (1978): 65–72.

Al-Khaqani, 'Ali. "Sha'irat fi Thawrat al-'Ishrin." In Muhammad 'Ali Kamal al-Din, ed., *Thawrat al-'Ishrin fi Dhikraha al-Khamsin*, 353–375. Najaf: Dar al-Tadamun, 1971.

"Al-Mithaq al-Watani li-l-Hizb al-Shuyu'i al-'Iraqi." In Fakhri Karim, ed., *Kitabat al-Rafiq Fahd*, 2d ed., 123–137. Baghdad: al-Tariq al-Jadid, 1976.

Mughniyya, Muhammad Jawad. "Al-Mut'a." *Al-'Irfan* 37 (1950): 1095–1096.

Al-Rusafi, Ma'ruf. "Al-Zu'ama fi al-'Iraq." In Sa'id al-Badri, ed., *Ara' al-Rusafi fi al-Siyasa wa-l-Din wa-l-Ijtima'*, 2d ed., 9–15. Baghdad: al-Ma'arif, 1951.

Yusuf, Yusuf Salman. "Yawm al-Nisa' al-'Alami." In Fakhri Karim, ed., *Kitabat al-Rafiq Fahd*, 2d ed., 407–413. Baghdad: al-Tariq al-Jadid, 1976.

Al-Zahawi, Jamil Sidqi. "Al-Mar'a wa-l-Difa' 'Anha." In 'Abd al-Hamid al-Rashudi, ed., *Al-Zahawi: Dirasat wa-Nusus*, 112–117. Beirut: al-Haya, 1966.

Al-Zanburi, Raja'. "Matba'at al-Hizb, Muhakamat al-Rafiq Fahd, Awwal Tanzim Nisa'i, al-Sijn." *Al-Thaqafa al-Jadida* 5 (1982): 56–81.

PUBLISHED WORKS IN OTHER LANGUAGES

Books

Abdullah, Thabit A. J. *A Short History of Iraq*. London: Pearson-Longman, 2003.

Abu-Lughod, Lila, ed. *Remaking Women: Feminism and Modernity in the Middle East.* Princeton, N.J.: Princeton University Press, 1998.

Ahmed, Leila. *Women and Gender in Islam: Historical Roots of a Modern Debate.* New Haven, Conn.: Yale University Press, 1992.

Al-Ali, Nadje Sadig. *Iraqi Women: Untold Stories from 1948 to the Present*. London: Zed Books, 2007.

Al-Ali, Nadje and Nicola Pratt. *What Kind of Liberation? Women and the Occupation of Iraq*. Berkeley and Los Angeles: University of California Press, 2009.

The Arab Bulletin: Bulletin of the Arab Bureau in Cairo, 1916–1919. 4 vols. Buckinghamshire, U.K.: Archives Editions, 1986.

Badran, Margot. *Feminists, Islam, and Nation: Gender and the Making of Modern Egypt.* Princeton, N.J.: Princeton University Press, 1995.

Baring, Evelyn (Lord Cromer). *Modern Egypt.* London: Macmillan, 1911.

Baron, Beth. *The Women's Awakening in Egypt: Culture, Society, and the Press.* New Haven, Conn.: Yale University Press, 1994.

Batatu, Hanna. *The Old Social Classes and the Revolutionary Movements of Iraq.* Princeton, N.J.: Princeton University Press, 1978.

Beck, Lois and Nikki Keddie, eds. *Women in the Muslim World.* Cambridge, Mass.: Harvard University Press, 1978.

Bell, Gertrude. *The Letters of Gertrude Bell.* 2 vols. Selected and edited by Lady Bell. London: Ernest Benn, 1927.

Bullard, Reader. *The Camels Must Go: An Autobiography.* London: Faber and Faber, 1961.

Charrad, Mounira M. *States and Women's Rights: The Making of Postcolonial Tunisia, Algeria, and Morocco.* Berkeley and Los Angeles: University of California Press, 2001.

Dann, Uriel. *Iraq Under Qassem: A Political History, 1958–1963.* Jerusalem: Israel Universities Press, 1969.

Davis, Eric. *Memories of State: Politics, History, and Collective Identity.* Berkeley and Los Angeles: University of California Press, 2005.

Diamond, Larry. *Squandered Victory: The American Occupation and the Bungled Effort to Bring Democracy to Iraq.* New York: Times Books, 2005.

Dodge, Toby. *Inventing Iraq: The Failure of Nation Building and a History Denied.* New York: Columbia University Press, 2003.

Edmonds, C. J. *Kurds, Turks, and Arabs.* London: Oxford University Press, 1957.

Eppel, Michael. *The Palestine Conflict in the History of Modern Iraq: Dynamics of Involvement, 1928–1948.* London: Frank Cass, 1994.

Farouk-Sluglett, Marion and Peter Sluglett. *Iraq Since 1958.* 3d ed. London: I. B. Tauris, 2001.

Fleischmann, Ellen. *The Nation and Its "New" Women: The Palestinian Women's Movement, 1920–1948.* Berkeley and Los Angeles: University of California Press, 2003.

Fulanain [S. E. Hedgcock and M. E. Hedgecock]. *Haji Rikkan: Marsh Arab.* London: Chatto & Windus, 1927.

General Federation of Iraqi Women. *"The Iraqi Woman['s] Association" and the Role of the Iraqi Communist Party in Emptying It of Its Social Essence.* Baghdad: n.p., 1980.

Göçek, Fatma Müge and Shiva Balaghi, eds. *Reconstructing Gender in the Middle East: Tradition, Identity, and Power.* New York: Columbia University Press, 1994.

Haj, Samira. *The Making of Iraq 1900–1963: Capital, Power, and Ideology.* Albany: State University of New York Press, 1997.

Hall, Stuart, ed. *Representation: Cultural Representations and Signifying Practices.* London: Sage, 1997.

Hall, Stuart and Bram Gieben, eds. *Formations of Modernity*. Cambridge, U.K.: Polity Press, 1992.

Harris, George L. *Iraq: Its People, Its Society, Its Culture*. New Haven, Conn.: Harf, 1958.

Harrison, Brian. *Separate Spheres: The Opposition to Women's Suffrage in Britain*. New York: Holmes and Meier, 1978.

The Holy Quran. 2 vols. Text, translation, and commentary by Abdullah Yusuf-Ali. Lahore, Pakistan: Shaikh Muhammad Ashraf, 1937.

Hooper, C. A. *The Constitutional Law of Iraq*. Baghdad: Mackenzie & Mackenzie, 1928.

Howarth, David. *Discourse*. Philadelphia: Open University Press, 2000.

Ingrams, Doreen. *The Awakened: Women in Iraq*. London: Third World Center, 1983.

Iraq Administration Reports: 1914–1932. 10 vols. Sources established by Robert L. Jarman. Slough, U.K.: Archive Editions, 1992.

Ireland, Philip Willard. *Iraq: A Study in Political Development*. London: J. Cape, 1937.

Jabar, Faleh A. and Hosham Dawod, eds. *Tribes and Power: Nationalism and Ethnicity in the Middle East*. London: Saqi, 2003.

Jamali, Mohammed Fadhel. *The New Iraq: Its Problem of Bedouin Education*. New York: Bureau of Publication, Teachers College, Columbia University, 1934.

Joseph, Suad, ed. *Gender and Citizenship in the Middle East*. Syracuse, N.Y.: Syracuse University Press, 2000.

Kadry, Hind Tahsin. *Women's Education in Iraq*. Baghdad: n.p., 1958.

Kandiyoti, Deniz, ed. *Women, Islam, and the State*. London: Macmillan Press, 1991.

Keddie, Nikki R. *Women in the Middle East: Past and Present*. Princeton, N.J.: Princeton University Press, 2007.

Keddie, Nikki R. and Beth Baron, eds. *Women in Middle Eastern History: Shifting Boundaries in Sex and Gender*. New Haven, Conn.: Yale University Press, 1991.

Khadduri, Majid. *Independent Iraq, 1932–1958: A Study in Iraqi Politics*. 2d ed. London: Oxford University Press, 1960.

——. *Republican 'Iraq*. London: Oxford University Press, 1969.

Longrigg, Stephen H. *Iraq, 1900 to 1950: A Political, Social, and Economic History*. London: Oxford University Press, 1953.

Lukitz, Liora. *A Quest in the Middle East: Gertrude Bell and the Making of Modern Iraq*. London: I. B. Tauris, 2006.

Lyell, Thomas. *The Ins and Outs of Mesopotamia*. London: A. M. Philpot, 1923.

Main, Ernest. *Iraq: From Mandate to Independence*. London: Allen and Unwin, 1935.

Mann, James Saumarez. *An Administrator in the Making: James Saumarez Mann, 1893–1920*. Edited by his father. London: Longmans, Green, 1921.

Marr, Phebe. *The Modern History of Iraq*. Boulder, Colo.: Westview, 1985.

——. *The Modern History of Iraq*. 2d ed. Boulder, Colo.: Westview, 2004.

Meriwether, Margaret L. and Judith E. Tucker, eds. *A Social History of Women and Gender in the Modern Middle East*. Boulder, Colo.: Westview, 1999.

Mitchell, Timothy. *Colonising Egypt*. Cambridge, U.K.: Cambridge University Press, 1991.

Monroe, Paul. *Report of the Educational Inquiry Commission*. Baghdad: Government Press, 1932.

Nakash, Yitzhak. *The Shi'is of Iraq*. Princeton, N.J.: Princeton University Press, 1994.

Nelson, Cynthia. *Doria Shafik, Egyptian Feminist: A Woman Apart*. Gainesville: University Press of Florida, 1996.

Paidar, Parvin. *Women and the Political Process in Twentieth-Century Iran*. Cambridge, U.K.: Cambridge University Press, 1995.

Roded, Ruth. *Women in Islam and the Middle East: A Reader*. 2d ed. London: I. B. Tauris, 2008.

——. *Women in Islamic Biographical Collections: From Ibn Sa'd to Who's Who*. Boulder, Colo.: Lynne Rienner, 1994.

Rohde, Achim. *Facing Dictatorship: State–Society Relations in Ba'thist Iraq*. London: Routledge, 2010.

Salim, Shakir Mustafa. *Marsh Dwellers of the Euphrates Delta*. London: Athlone Press, 1962.

Sanasarian, Eliz. *The Women's Rights Movement in Iran: Mutiny, Appeasement, and Repression, from 1900 to Khomeini*. New York: Praeger, 1982.

Schacht, Joseph. *An Introduction to Islamic Law*. Oxford, U.K.: Clarendon Press, 1964.

Shaham, Ron. *Family and the Courts in Modern Egypt*. Leiden: Brill, 1997.

Simon, Reeva S. *Iraq Between the Two World Wars: The Creation and Implementation of a Nationalist Ideology*. New York: Columbia University Press, 1986.

Sluglett, Peter. *Britain in Iraq 1914–1932*. New York: Columbia University Press, 2007.

Spellberg, Denise. *Politics, Gender, and the Islamic Past: The Legacy of 'A'isha Bint Abi-Bakr*. New York: Columbia University Press, 1994.

Stevens, E. S. *By Tigris and Euphrates*. London: Hurst and Blackett, 1923.

Thompson, Elizabeth. *Colonial Citizens: Republican Rights, Paternal Privilege, and Gender in French Syria and Lebanon*. New York: Columbia University Press, 2000.

Tripp, Charles. *A History of Iraq*. Cambridge, U.K.: Cambridge University Press, 2000.

Tucker, Judith E., ed. *Arab Women: Old Boundaries, New Frontiers*. Bloomington: Indiana University Press, 1993.

——. *Women, Family, and Gender in Islamic Law*. Cambridge, U.K.: Cambridge University Press, 2008.

——. *Women in Nineteenth-Century Egypt*. Cambridge, U.K.: Cambridge University Press, 1985.

United Nations. Department of Social Affairs. Division of Social Affairs. *Iraq: January 1948–June 1953*. New York: United Nations, 1953.

Wallach, Janet. *Desert Queen: The Extraordinary Life of Gertrude Bell*. New York: Anchor Books, 1999.

Warriner, Doreen. *Land Reform and Development in the Middle East*. London: Royal Institute of International Affairs, 1957.

Wien, Peter. *Iraqi Arab Nationalism*. London: Routledge, 2006.

Wilson, Arnold T. *Loyalties, Mesopotamia, 1914–1917: A Personal and Historical Record*. 2 vols. London: Oxford University Press, 1936.

Al Witry, Hashim. *Health Services in Iraq*. Jerusalem: A. Duncker, 1944.

Woodrow Wilson International Center for Scholars, Conflict Prevention Project, Middle East Project, and Women Waging Peace. *Winning the Peace Conference Re-*

port: *Women's Role in Post-Conflict Iraq*. Supplemental material. Washington, D.C.: Woodrow Wilson International Center for Scholars, April 2003.

Woodsmall, Ruth Frances. *Moslem Women Enter a New World*. New York: Round Table Press, 1936.

Woodsmall, Ruth Frances and Charlotte Johnson. *Study of the Role of Women, Their Activities, and Organizations in Lebanon, Egypt, Iraq, Jordan, and Syria, October 1954–August 1955*. New York: International Federation of Business and Professional Women, 1956.

Yuval-Davis, Nira and Floya Anthias, eds. *Women–Nation–State*. London: Macmillan, 1989.

Zuhur, Sharifa D. *Iraq, Women's Empowerment, and Public Policy*. Carlisle, Pa.: Strategic Studies Institute, 2006.

Articles

Adams, Doris G. "Current Population Trends in Iraq." *Middle East Journal* 10 (1956): 151–165.

Ahmed, Leila. "Feminism and Feminist Movements in the Middle East, a Preliminary Exploration: Turkey, Egypt, Algeria, People's Democratic Republic of Yemen." *Women's Studies International Forum* 5 (1982): 153–168.

Al-Ali, Nadje and Nicola Pratt. "Women in Iraq: Beyond the Rhetoric." *Middle East Research and Information Project* 239 (2006): 18–23.

——. "Women Organizing and the Conflict in Iraq Since 2003." *Feminist Review* 88 (2008): 74–85.

Anderson, J. N. D. "Changes in the Law of Personal Status in Iraq." *International and Comparative Law Quarterly* 12 (1963): 1026–1031.

——. "A Draft Code of Personal Law for 'Iraq." *Bulletin of the School of Oriental and African Studies* 15 (1953): 43–60.

——. "A Law of Personal Status for Iraq." *International and Comparative Law Quarterly* 9 (October 1960): 542–563.

——. "Recent Developments in Shari'a Law III." *Muslim World* 41 (1951): 113–126.

——. "Recent Developments in Shari'a Law IV." *Muslim World* 41 (1951): 186–198.

——. "Recent Developments in Shari'a Law V." *Muslim World* 41 (1951): 271–288.

Arat, Zehra F. "Turkish Women and the Republican Reconstruction of Tradition." In Fatma Müge Göçek and Shiva Balaghi, eds., *Reconstructing Gender in the Middle East*, 57–78. New York: Columbia University Press, 1994.

Baram, Amatzia. "Iraq 2003–2009: The U.S. Between Baghdad, al-Qa'idah, and the Tribal *Sahwah*." Unpublished paper, June 2009. Available at http://iraq.haifa.ac.il/index.php/articles/19-iraq-2003–2009-the-us-between-baghdad-al-qaidah-and-the-tribal-sahwah.html.

——. "Neo-Tribalism in Iraq: Saddam Hussein's Tribal Policies 1991–1996." *International Journal of Middle East Studies* 29 (1997): 1–31.

Baron, Beth. "A Field Matures: Recent Literature on Women in the Middle East." *Middle Eastern Studies* 32 (1996): 172–186.

Bashkin, Orit. "Representations of Women in the Writings of the Intelligentsia in Hashemite Iraq, 1921–1958." *Journal of Middle East Women's Studies* 4, no. 1 (Winter 2008): 53–82.

Brown, Lucy and David Romano. "Women in Post-Saddam Iraq: One Step Forward or Two Steps Back?" *NWSA Journal* 18, no. 3 (Fall 2006): 51–70.

Brown, Nathan. "Constitution of Iraq Draft Bill of Rights." 27 July 2005. Available at http://www.carnegieendowment.org/files/BillofRights.pdf#search= %22Constitution%20of%20Iraq%20Draft%20Bill%20of%20Rights%22.

——. "Debating Islam in Post-Baathist Iraq." March 2005. Available at http://www. carnegieendowment.org/files/PO13.Brown.FINAL2.pdf#search=%22Brown%20 post-Baathist%22.

Bruce, C. E. "The Sandeman Policy as Applied to Tribal Problems of Today." *Journal of the Royal Central Asian Society* 19 (1932): 45–67.

Cobbett, Deborah. "Women in Iraq." In Committee Against Repression and for Democratic Rights in Iraq, *Saddam's Iraq: Revolution or Reaction?* 120–137. London: Zed Books, 1989.

Cole, Juan. "Struggles Over Personal Status and Family Law in Post-Baathist Iraq." In Kenneth M. Cuno and Manisha Desai, eds., *Family, Gender, and Law in a Globalizing Middle East and South Asia*, 105–125. Syracuse, N.Y.: Syracuse University Press, 2009.

Coleman, Isobel. "Women, Islam, and the New Iraq." *Foreign Affairs* 85 (January–February 2006): 24–38.

Coulson, Noel and Doreen Hinchcliffe. "Women and Law Reform in Contemporary Islam." In Lois Beck and Nikki R. Keddie, eds., *Women in the Muslim World*, 37–51. Cambridge, Mass.: Harvard University Press, 1978.

Davidson, Nigel G. "The Constitution of Iraq." *Journal of Comparative Legislation and International Law* 7 (February 1925): 41–52.

De Bellefonds, Linant Y. "Le Code du Statut Personnel Irakien du 30 decembre 1959." *Studia Islamica* 13 (1960): 79–135.

D. N. "One Year Ago in Iraq." *Women of the Whole World* 2 (1964): 30–31.

Efrati, Noga. "Competing Narratives: Histories of the Women's Movement in Iraq, 1910–1958." *International Journal of Middle East Studies* 40, no. 3 (August 2008): 445–466.

——. "The *Effendiyya*: Where Have All the Women Gone?" *International Journal of Middle East Studies* 43, no.1 (May 2011): 375–377.

——. "Gender, Tribe, and the British Construction of Iraq." In Zach Levey and Elie Podeh, eds., *Britain and the Middle East*, 152–165. Eastbourne, U.K.: Sussex Academic Press, 2008.

——. "Negotiating Rights in Iraq: Women and the Personal Status Law." *Middle East Journal* 59, no. 4 (Autumn 2005): 577–595.

——. "The Other 'Awakening' in Iraq: The Women's Movement in the First Half of the Twentieth Century." *British Journal of Middle Eastern Studies* 31 (2004): 153–173.

Farouk-Sluglett, Marion. "Liberation or Repression? Pan-Arab Nationalism and the Women's Movement in Iraq." In Derek Hopwood, Habib Ishow, and Thomas Koszinowski, eds., *Iraq: Power and Society*, 51–73. Reading, U.K.: Ithaca, 1993.

Farouk-Sluglett, Marion and Peter Sluglett. "The Transformation of Land Tenure and Rural Social Structure in Central and Southern Iraq, c. 1870–1958." *International Journal of Middle East Studies* 15 (1983): 491–505.

Fleischmann, Ellen. "The Other 'Awakening': The Emergence of Women's Movements in the Modern Middle East, 1900–1940." In Margaret L. Meriwether and Judith E. Tucker, eds., *A Social History of Women and Gender in the Modern Middle East*, 89–134. Boulder, Colo.: Westview, 1999.

Grassmuck, George. "The Electoral Process in Iraq, 1952–1958." *Middle East Journal* 14 (1960): 397–415.

Hall, Stuart. "The Work of Representation." In Stuart Hall, ed., *Representation: Cultural Representations and Signifying Practices*, 13–74. London: Sage, 1997.

——. "The West and the Rest: Discourse and Power." In Stuart Hall and Bram Gieben, eds., *Formations of Modernity*, 275–332. Cambridge, U.K.: Polity Press, 1992.

Hassan, M. S. "Growth and Structure of Iraq's Population, 1867–1947." *Bulletin of Oxford University, Institute of Economics and Statistics* 20 (1958): 339–352.

Hatem, Mervat F. "Modernization, the State, and the Family in Middle East Women's Studies." In Margaret L. Meriwether and Judith E. Tucker, eds., *A Social History of Women and Gender in the Modern Middle East*, 63–87. Boulder, Colo.: Westview, 1999.

Ismael, Jacqueline S. and Shereen T. Ismael. "Gender and State in Iraq." In Suad Joseph, ed., *Gender and Citizenship in the Middle East*, 185–211. Syracuse, N.Y.: Syracuse University Press, 2000.

——. "Iraqi Women Under Occupation: From Tribalism to Neo-Feudalism." *International Journal of Contemporary Iraqi Studies* 1 (2007): 247–268.

Izzidein, Yousif [Yusuf ʿIzz al-Din]. "The Emancipation of Iraqi Women: Women and Their Influence on Iraqi Life and Poetry." *Bulletin of the College of Arts, Baghdad University* 1 (1959): 33–41.

Joseph, Suad. "Elite Strategies for State Building: Women, Family, Religion, and the State in Iraq and Lebanon." In Deniz Kandiyoti, ed., *Women, Islam, and the State*, 176–200. London: Macmillan Press, 1991.

Jwaideh, Albertine. "Midhat Pasha and the Land System of Lower Iraq." *St. Antony's Papers: Middle East Affairs* 3 (1963): 106–136.

Kandiyoti, Deniz. "End of Empire: Islam, Nationalism, and Women in Turkey." In Deniz Kandiyoti, ed., *Women, Islam, and the State*, 22–47. London: Macmillan, 1991.

Keddie, Nikki R. "Problems in the Study of Middle Eastern Women." *International Journal of Middle East Studies* 10 (1979): 225–240.

Khoury, Dina Rizk. "Looking at the Modern: A Biography of an Iraqi Modernist." In Mary Ann Fay, ed., *Auto/Biography and the Construction of Identity in the Middle East*, 109–124. New York: Palgrave, 2001.

Kishtainy, Khalid. "Women in Art and Literature." In Doreen Ingrams, *The Awakened: Women in Iraq*, 131–154. London: Third World Center, 1983.

Mallat, Chibli. "Shi'ism and Sunnism in Iraq: Revisiting the Codes." In Chibli Mallat and Jane Connors, eds., *Islamic Family Law*, 71–91. London: Graham and Trotman, 1990.

Meriwether, Margaret L. and Judith E. Tucker. "Introduction." In Margaret L. Meriwether and Judith E. Tucker, eds., *A Social History of Women and Gender in the Modern Middle East*, 1–24. Boulder, Colo.: Westview, 1999.

Moors, Annelies. "Debating Islamic Family Law: Legal Texts and Social Practices." In Margaret L. Meriwether and Judith E. Tucker, eds., *A Social History of Women and Gender in the Modern Middle East*, 141–174. Boulder, Colo.: Westview, 1999.

Naqvi, 'Ali Raza. "The Family Law of Iran (II)." *Islamic Studies* 7 (June 1968): 129–163.

Omar, Suha. "Women: Honour, Shame, and Dictatorship." In Fran Hazelton, ed., *Iraq Since the Gulf War: Prospects for Democracy*, 60–71. London: Zed Books, 1994.

Panel Discussion: Women in the Middle East: Progress or Regress? Special issue, *MERIA Journal* 10 (June 2006).

Pool, David. "From Elite to Class: The Transformation of Iraqi Leadership, 1920–1939." *International Journal of Middle East Studies* 12 (1980): 331–350.

Al-Qazzaz, Ayad. "Power Elite in Iraq, 1920–1958: A Study of the Cabinet." *The Muslim World* 61 (1971): 267–283.

Rassam, Amal. "Political Ideology and Women in Iraq: Legislation and Cultural Constraints." In Joseph G. Jabbra and Nancy W. Jabbra, eds., *Women and Development in the Middle East and North Africa*, 82–95. Leiden: E. J. Brill, 1992.

Russell, Mona. "Competing, Overlapping, and Contradictory Agendas: Egyptian Education Under British Occupation." *Comparative Studies of South Asia, Africa, and the Middle East* 21 (2001): 50–60.

Al-Sa'dawi, Ahmad. "A State Governed by Law and Tribes." *Niqash*, 24 July 2008.

Sirman, Nükhet. "Feminism in Turkey: A Short History." *New Perspectives on Turkey* 3 (Fall 1989): 1–34.

Spivak, Gayatry Chakravorty. "Can the Subaltern Speak? " In Cary Nelson and Laurence Grossberg, eds., *Marxism and the Interpretation of Culture*, 217–313. Urbana: University of Illinois Press, 1988.

Stearn, Roger T. "Ingrams, Doreen Constance (1906–1997)." In *Oxford Dictionary of National Biography*. Oxford, U.K.: Oxford University Press, 2004. Available at http://www.oxforddnb.com/view/article/67156.

Stevens, E. S. "The Woman [*sic*] Movement in Iraq." *The Near East and India* 10 (October 1929): 400–401.

Tucker, Judith E. "Problems in the Historiography of Women in the Middle East: The Case of Nineteenth-Century Egypt." *International Journal of Middle East Studies* 15 (1983): 321–336.

Al-Umari, Suad. "Participation of Women in Community Life in Iraq." *International Women's News* 50 (June 1956): 535–536.

Walther, Wiebke. "From Women's Problems to Women as Images in Modern Iraqi Poetry." *Die Welt des Islams* 36 (1996): 219–241.

Al-Wazzan, Saleem. "Abuse of Women Continues." *Niqash*, 29 July 2010.

Yuval-Davis, Nira and Floya Anthias. "Introduction." In Nira Yuval-Davis and Floya Anthias, eds., *Women–Nation–State*, 1–15. London: Macmillan, 1989.

INDEX

'Abd al-Ilah (regent, later crown prince of Iraq), 11, 12, 17, 90
'Abd al-Nasir, Gamal, 16, 18
'Abduh, Muhammad, 64
Abu-Lughod, Lila, 176n7
Afnan, Badi'a, 120
Afnan, Husain, 120
agrarian reform, 160
agriculture: Law Governing Rights and Duties of Cultivators, 10, 45; nomadic tribes and, 44; peasant women (fallahat), 46–47, 155; reform under republican government, 160, See also land ownership
al-Ahali (newspaper), 95
al-Ahali group, 10, 13, 90
Ahmed, Leila, xii, 65, 176n6, 177n12
'Ai'sha, 97–98, 116, 195n40
Al 'Abd al-'Abbas, Khawwam, 93
Al Fir'awn, Fariq al-Muzhir, 34, 35, 36, 183n58
al-Ali, Nadje Sadig, 172, 175n1, 197nn2, 3, 209n37
'Aliya (Queen of Iraq), 114
Amin, Mudhaffar Abdullah, 184n77
Anderson, J.N.D, 84, 188n25, 192n94
Anglo-Iraqi Treaty (1930), 9, 14, 91, 142, 158
Anthias, Floya, 106

Arab Union, formation of, 18–19, 92, 108
'Arif, 'Abd al-Salam, 19
al-'Askari, Fakhriyya, 120
al-'Askari, Ja'far, 7, 120, 178n13
Association of Liberals (Jam'iyyat al-Ahrar), 124
Aston, C.C., 34
Atatürk, Mustafa Kamal, 10
al-A'zami, Husain 'Ali: about, 58; on annulment of marriage, 61; on child custody, 72; on consent to marriage, 61; on divorce, 77; on draft Code of Personal Status, 58, 59, 61, 62, 64, 67, 68, 69, 71, 72, 73, 77, 78; on "exchange marriage", 68; on inheritance, 73; on marriage, 61, 78; on marriage of minors, 61, 62; on obedience of wife, 70; on polygamy, 64; on witnesses for validity of marriage, 67; on women's roles, 71

Baban, Mubejel, 73, 157, 198nn3, 11
Badran, Margot, 176n6, 194n12
Baghdad: under Ottoman Empire, 4; urban migration to, 10, 15–16, 113; women of, 119–120
Baghdad Pact (1955), 17–18
Baghdad Penal Code, 22, 24, 28, 37, 38, 39–40

Bakr Sidqi coup, 10, 11, 109–110
Balaghi, Shiva, 176n7
Baram, Amitzia, 207n15, 208n22
Baring, Evelyn (Lord Cromer), 88, 106
Baron, Beth, 176n7
Bashkin, Orit, 175n3
al-Bassam, Sadiq, 94
Batatu, Hanna, 12, 118, 124
Ba'th Party, 18, 165
Ba'th regime, Ingrams on, 135, 165
Beck, Lois, 176n7
Bell, Gertrude, 23, 25–26, 87–88, 96, 119, 120
al-Bilad (newspaper), 117
blood feuds, 23, 34, 35, 43, 162
Bonham-Carter, Edgar, 25, 26, 27, 28, 52, 55
Bremer, Paul, 164
British occupation: Baghdad Pact (1955),
    17–18; Cairo Conference (1921), 6; elec-
    toral system, 8–9; governance methods
    for Iraq, 4–5, 25–30; history of, 2–3,
    4–7, 9; Iraqi Constitution under, 8, 22;
    land policy under, 5, 21, 44–45; per-
    sonal status matters under, xiv, 51–56,
    172; Portsmouth Agreement, 14, 91;
    reoccupation of Iraq, 11–14, 40, 47, 126;
    revolt of 1920, 6, 55, 119–120, 133; Treaty
    of 1922, 7–8; Treaty of 1930, 9, 14, 91,
    142, 158; Treaty of 1948, 14; Tribal and
    Criminal and Civil Disputes Regulation
    (TCCDR), xii, xiii, xv, 5, 20–30, 32, 34,
    36–37, 52, 167
Bush, George W., 164, 171, 172
Butti, Rufa'il, 117, 183n61

CAABU. See Council for the Advancement
    of Arab-British Understanding
Cairo Conference (1921), 6
Cairo Women's Conference (1944), 128
CARDRI. See Committee Against Repres-
    sion and for Democratic Rights in Iraq
al-Chadirchi, Kamil, 13
Chamber of Deputies, women's "occupa-
    tion" of (1958), 149–153

Chapuk, Songul, 166
Charrad, Mounira, 79, 80
child custody, 52–53, 67, 71–72, 79–80, 129,
    140, 161, 168
child marriage, 61–63, 66, 67, 79, 155
Child Protection Society (Jam'iyyat
    Himayat al-Atfal), 112, 125, 127, 128,
    129–130, 198n2
cities, migration to, 15–16, 113
Civil Code of Iran, 188n26
Cobbett, Deborah, 112, 134, 135–136, 197n2
Code of Personal Status. See Draft Code of
    Personal Status
Cole, Juan, 171
"colonial feminism", 54–55
Committee Against Repression and for
    Democratic Rights in Iraq (CARDRI),
    135–136
consent to marriage, Draft Code of Personal
    Status, 60–63, 79
Constitution of Iraq. See Iraqi Constitution
Constitutional Union Party (CUP) (Hizb al-
    Ittihad al-Dusturi), 15, 105, 106, 139, 142
Cornwallis, Kinahan, 24, 26, 39
Council for the Advancement of Arab-Brit-
    ish Understanding (CAABU), 134
Cox, Sir Percy, 6
crimes of "honor", 24, 26, 37, 42, 48, 50, 162,
    See also honor murders
Cromer, Lord (Evelyn Baring), 88, 106
CUP. See Constitutional Union Party

Damascus Eastern Arab Women's Confer-
    ence (1930), 126
Da'ud, Ahmad al-Shaikh, 119
Da'ud, Sabiha al-Shaikh: on 1930s and
    women's movement, 124–125; about,
    114–115, 116, 200n31, 201n60, 203n4;
    criticism of TCCDR, 138–139; on "dou-
    ble servitude", 138; on education, 117;
    formation of women's societies, 127–
    128; on al-Husri, 117; on Iraqi Women's
    Society, 128, 129; on Laila, 122; on

League for the Defense of Women's Rights, 135; on *mahr*, 139; on male figures' impact on women's movement, 117; on marriage, 139; on postwar years and, 127; on rural women, 138–139; on al-Rusafi, 116; on Women's Awakening Club, 120, 121, 122; on women's education, 123; on Women's League Against Nazism and Fascism (LANF), 126; on al-Zahawi, 116

Davidson, Nigel, 27, 55

discourse, xii, 177n13

dispute settlements, women and in tribal custom, 23–24, 28, 34–35

divorce, 74–80, 81–85, 156; absence of husband, 76, 82; child custody, 71–72, 79–80, 140, 161, 168; conditional divorce, 141; husband's rights, 74–75, 77, 78, 79, 82, 156, 161; impotence and, 75, 76; Iraqi Women's Union on, 77, 129, 140, 141; irrevocable repudiation, 75, 141; *khul'*, 76, 77, 82; Personal Status Law on, 161, 168; Qur'an on, 54; revocable repudiation, 74–75; separation, 76, 77, 82; suspended divorce, 141; waiting period (*'idda*), 74, 75, 191n78; wife's options, 75–77, 161; Women's Iraqi Union on, 140

Dobbs, Agnes Esme, 120

Dobbs, Sir Henry, 7, 21, 24, 26, 30, 32, 36, 44, 50, 120

Dodge, Toby, 25, 26

Draft Code of Personal Status, 56–80, 140–141; about, 56–59; child custody, 71–72, 79–80; consent to marriage, 60–63, 79; defeat of, 85; divorce, 74–80, 81–85, 140; on forced marriage, 141; gender relations and roles in marriage, 67–80; government justification for legislation, 59–60; inheritance, 73–74; *mahr*, 61, 66, 67–69, 75, 76, 139; maintenance, 69–71, 76, 141; marriage, 60–80, 140; marriage of minor children, 61, 62, 66, 67, 79, 141, 155; matrimonial guardianship, 60–63;

opposition to, 81–85; option of puberty (*khiyar al-bulugh*), 61–62, 67; polygamy, 63–65, 156; registration of marriage contract, 66–67, 139–140; temporary marriage (*mut'a*), 65–66, 80; Women's Iraqi Union on, 140–141

Drower, Edwin M., 25, 26, 28, 120

Duka, Zakariyya Elias, 124

al-Dulaimi, Naziha: on 1930s and women's movement, 125; about, 43, 115, 154, 201n60; on birth of women's movement, 115; on child custody, 72; criticism of women's organizations, 129–130; on divorce, 72, 77; on "double servitude", 47, 138, 155; on economic independence of women, 70, 157; formation of women's societies, 128, 131; on founding of the League for the Defense of Women's Rights, 130, 131; on Iraqi Women's Union, 128, 129–130; on *Laila*, 122–123; on League for the Defense of Women's Rights, 130, 131, 154; on male figures' impact on women's movement, 117, 118; on marriage, 155–156; on personal status, 155–156, 157; political appointment, 160; on polygamy, 64–65, 156; postwar years, 128; publication date of book, 185n86; on repression of 1947, 128; on rural women, 43–44, 47, 138; on al-Rusafi, 116; on status of women, 70, 138; on Women's Awakening Club, 120; on women's education, 123; on women's health, 154–155; on Women's League Against Nazism and Fascism (LANF), 126–127; on Women's Liberation, 131; on al-Zahawi, 116

Edmonds, C.J., 89–90

education: illiteracy in mid-1950s, 16; Monroe Educational Inquiry Commission, 31, 46, 193n10; Ottoman Empire and, 2, *See also* women's education

efendiyya, use of term, 177n15

Egypt: Baghdad Pact and, 18; feminism in, 199n13, 204n34; Suez crisis (1956), 17, 18; United Arab Republic, 18; women's suffrage in, 194n12

Electoral Law, postinvasion changes, 164

Electoral Law for the Chamber of Deputies (1924), 8–9, 87, 89, 90, 142

electoral system, 86–110; 1950s, 91–92; elections of 1953, 92; elections of 1954, 92; electoral equality, 87–88; exclusion of women, 87–92; history of, 87–92; opposition to women's suffrage, 92–98; post-World War II, 90–91; under British occupation, 8–9, 87–88, *See also* women's suffrage

Eppel, Michael, 179n19

Fahd (Yusuf Salman Yusuf), 12, 14, 16, 43, 103–104, 114, 130

Faisal I (King of Iraq), 6–7, 10, 32

Faisal II (King of Iraq), 11, 17, 90

fallahin. See peasants

family law, xiv, 51–85; Article 41 (Baghdad Penal Code), 28, 37, 160; Article 41 (Iraqi Constitution 2005), 169, 170; Draft Code of Personal Status, 56–80; Ottoman Law of Family Rights of 1917, 188n26, 189n43; Personal Status Law (1959), ix, xiv, 160–161, 167, 168–171; Resolution 137, 169, 170, 171; under British occupation, 51–56, 155; under Husain regime, 167, *See also* Draft Code of Personal Status

Farouk-Sluglett, Marion, 178n13, 197n2

fasl marriage, 23, 162, 167, 168

Fatima Khan, 90

Fleischmann, Ellen, 176nn6, 8, 202n88

forced marriage, 42, 62, 63, 67, 79, 141, 156, 168

Foucault, Michel, xii

Fulanain (pseudonym), 180n15

gender relations and roles, in marriage, 67–80

Ghazi bin Faisal (King of Iraq), 10, 11

Göçek, Fatma Müge, 176n7

Grassmuck, George, 195n25

Great Britain, electoral equality in, 87–88

Hadid, Muhammad, 13

Haj, Samira, 185n29

Haji Rikkan, 26, 28–29

al-Hakim, 'Abd al-'Aziz, 168, 171

al-Hakim, Grand Ayatulla Muhsin, 84–85, 171, 192n100

Hall, Stuart, xii–xiii, 177n14

Hamandi, Ja'far, 31, 180n17

Hamuda, Na'ima Sultan, 119, 120

Hanafi, use of term, 188n27

Hanafi doctrine, 58, 59, 61, 68, 71, 72, 76, 81, 82, 139, 188n29

Hanbali doctrine, 139

Haqqi, Zakiyya Isma'il, 170

Hasanain, Mustafa Muhammad, 181n17, 183n58

al-Hasani, 'Abd al-Razzaq, 92

Hashemite monarchy: about, xii; Faisal I, 6–7, 10, 32; Faisal II, 11, 17, 90; Ghazi bin Faisal, 10, 11; history of, 6–11, 14–15; land ownership during, 45; overthrow of, 19, 92, 132; reoccupation of Iraq, 11–14, 40, 47, 126

al-Hashimi, Rafiqa, 120

al-Hashimi, Yasin, 120

Hassun, Paulina, 89, 120, 122, 194n12

Hatem, Mervat F., 177n9

al-Hawadith (newspaper), 93

health service, for peasant women, 46, 154–155

Hedgcock, Monica Grace, 23–24, 28, 29, 180n15

Hedgcock, Stuart Edwin, 23–24, 26, 28, 29, 180n15

"Heroine of the Bridge", 196n44

Higher Women's Council, 164

al-Hilli, 'Abd al-Karim Rida: about, 58; on child custody, 72; on divorce, 77; on Draft Code of Personal Status, 58, 61,

62, 68, 69, 72, 77, 78; on "exchange marriage", 68; on marriage, 61, 78; on marriage of minors, 61, 62; on obedience of wife, 70

Hizb al-Ittihad al-Dusturi. *See* Constitutional Union Party

al-Hizb al-Watani al-Dimuqrati. *See* National Democratic Party

honor murders, legal system and, 23, 26, 27, 28, 29, 31, 37, 42–43, 48, 50, 155

Houses of the People Society (*Jam'iyyat Buyut al-Umma*), 112, 127–128

Howarth, David, 177*n*13

Husain, Saddam, 135, 166–168

al-Husri, Jamila, 120

al-Husri, Sati', 7, 117, 120m, 123

Huzaima (Queen of Iraq), 125

ICP. *See* Iraqi Communist Party

IGC. *See* Iraqi Governing Council

illiteracy, 16, 46, 118–119

Independence Party. *See* Istiqlal Party

India, tribal jurisdiction in, 21

infant mortality, 16, 46, 202*n*78

Ingrams, Doreen, 112, 134–135, 175*n*3, 197*n*1

inheritance, 73–74, 161

Interim Constitution of 1970, 165

International Alliance of Women, 129

intifada (1952), 16–17, 91, 107, 132

Iran, Civil Code, 188*n*26

Iraq Petroleum Company, 15

Iraqi Communist Party (ICP): early history of, 10–12; in late 1940's, 16; on League for the Defense of Women's Rights, 131–132; platform of, 12, 179*n*16; repression of 1947, 16; Women's Committee, 130; women's movement and, 43, 90, 99, 123, 130

Iraqi Constituent Assembly, 7

Iraqi Constitution (1925), xiv, 6, 7, 8, 30, 55, 86, 87; and tribal jurisdiction, 22, 30, 32, 36; electoral system, 87–92; shari'a courts, 55, 56, 81,

Iraqi Constitution (1958), 92, 94, 108–109, 149, 150, 151, 152, 162, 165

Iraqi Constitution (1970), 165

Iraqi Constitution (2005), 164, 165, 167, 169, 170, 172

Iraqi Governing Council (IGC), ix, 164, 168

Iraqi modern history, 1–19; Anglo-Iraqi Treaty (1930), 9, 14, 91, 142, 158; Arab Union, 18–19, 92, 108; Baghdad Pact (1955), 17–18; Bakr Sidqi coup, 10, 109–110; Ba'th regime, 135, 165; British occupation, xiii-xiv, 2–3, 4–7, 9, 172; British reoccupation, 11–14, 40, 47, 126; elections in, 92; electoral system, 86–110; Husain regime, 135, 166–168; independence, 10, 40–41; intifada (1952), 16–17, 91, 107, 132; al-Kailani, Rashid 'Ali coup, 11, 40, 47, 48, 126; Ottoman Empire, 1–2; Personal Status Law (1959), ix, xiv, 160–161, 167, 168–171; Portsmouth Agreement, 14, 91; post-2003, 163–173; repression of 1947, 128, 133, 137; republican government, 160–162; Resolution 137 (2003), 169, 170, 171; revolt of 1920, 6, 55, 119–120; Suez crisis (1956), 17, 18; Treaty of 1922, 7–8; Treaty of 1930, 9, 14, 91, 142, 158; Treaty of 1948, 14; United States' effect on, 171–172; U.S. occupation of, ix-x, xv-xvi, 164; *wathba* (1948), 14, 91, 100, 130–131, 195*n*44; World War II, 11–12, *See also* Hashemite monarchy

Iraqi Parliament: Iraqi Women's Union petitions to, 129, 140; postinvasion inclusion of women's quota in representation, 164, 206*n*5; women in, xiv, 164; women's "occupation" of Chamber of Deputies, 149–153

Iraqi Women's League (after 1958) (*Rabitat al-Mar'a al-'Iraqiyya*), 160, 168

Iraqi Women's Union (*al-Ittihad al-Nisa'i al-'Iraqi*): 1950s petitions to Parliament, 129, 140, 144–145; 1956 demands, 145–146; on child custody, 129, 140;

Iraqi Women's Union (*continued*)
components of, 112–113, 127, 128; criticism of League, 157; Da'ud on, 128; demise of, 132, 137; on divorce, 77, 129, 140, 141; al-Dulaimi on, 128, 129–130; formation of, 127, 128; goals of, 138, 139, 153; *Laila*, 89, 122, 125; on marriage, 65, 139–140; and the modern woman's image, 146–148; and the notion of "gradual modernization", 142–146; on personal status, 139, 140, 141; petitions of 1950s, 91; on polygamy, 65, 139; postwar years and, 127–129; quest for reforms, 138–141; on registration of marriage contract, 140–141; social welfare works, 129–130, 133, 138; on TCCDR, 141; Week of Women's Rights (1953), 95, 142, 147; women's occupation of Chamber of Deputies (1958), 149–153; on women's rights, 99, 102, 129, 142–143; on women's suffrage, 143–145
al-'Irs, Farhan, 93
al-Islah (Reform) Party, 93
Islamic law: Bonham-Carter on, 52, 53; codification of, 59–60; Draft Code of Personal Status, 56–80; family law, 51–85, 155; Lyell on, 53–55, *See also* shari'a courts
Ismael, Jacqueline S., 175*n*3, 197*n*1
Ismael, Shereen T., 175*n*3, 197*n*1
Istiqlal Party (Independence Party), 13, 18, 93, 99–101, 179*n*17, 184*n*78
al-Ittihad al-Nisa'i al-'Iraqi. See Iraqi Women's Union

Jabr, Salih, 14
Ja'fari, use of term, 188*n*27
Ja'fari doctrine, 3, 58, 59, 61, 68, 71, 75, 76, 82, 178*n*4
al-Jamali, Muhammad Fadil, 17, 31, 141, 181*n*17, 198*n*2
al-Jamali, Sara Fadil, 125, 127, 198*n*2
Jamil, Makki, 184*n*77

Jam'iyyat al-Ahrar. See Association of Liberals
Jam'iyyat al-Aukht al-Muslima. See Muslim Sisters' Society
Jam'iyyat al-Hilal al-Ahmar. See Red Crescent Society
Jam'iyyat al-Islah al-Sha'bi. See Popular Reform Association
Jam'iyyat al-Ittihad al-Nisa'i. See Women's Union Society
Jam'iyyat al-Rabita al-Nisa'iyya. See Women's League Society
Jam'iyyat Buyut al-Umma. See Houses of the People Society
Jam'iyyat Himayat al-Atfal. See Child Protection Society
Jam'iyyat Mukafahat al-'Ilal al-Ijtima'iyya. See Temperance and Social Welfare Society
Jam'iyyat Mukafahat al-Muskirat. See Temperance Society
Jam'iyyat Mukafahat al-Naziyya wa-l-Fashiyya. See Women's League Against Nazism and Fascism
Jam'iyyat Tahrir al-Mar'a. See Women's Liberation Organization
Jawdat, 'Ali, 120
Jawdat, Fatima, 120
Jordan, Arab Union, 18–19, 92, 108
Joseph, Suad, 176*n*7
Judges and Qadhis Law (1929), 56

al-Kailani, Rashid 'Ali coup, 11, 40, 47, 48, 126
Kamp, Martina, 175*n*3, 197*n*2
Kandiyoti, Deniz, 176*n*6
Kashif al-Ghita', Muhammad Husain, 97, 98, 106
Keddie, Nikki, 176*n*7, 177*n*9
Khadduri, Rose, 128
Khairi, Su'ad, 198*n*11
al-Khalidi, Kazim Baji, 182*n*54
Khalilzad, Zalmay, 169–170, 171

al-Khatib, 'Abd al-Hamid, 124

Khidir, Zahra, 118–119

Khoury, Dina Rizk, 199n16

Kurds: armed revolt of, 4; Fatimah Khan, 90; history of, 4; ICP Party platform, 12; Kurdish politicians (post 2003), 169–171; political figures of Kurdish origin, 117

Laila (magazine), 89, 122, 125

Land Law of 1858, 2, 5, 44

land ownership: Land Law of 1858, 2, 5, 44; Land Settlement Law (1932), 10; Law Governing Rights and Duties of Cultivators (1933), 10, 45; peasants and agriculture and, 10, 15; under British occupation, 5, 44–45; under monarchy, 10, 15; under Ottoman Empire, 2; by women, 23

Land Settlement Law (1932), 10

LANF (League Against Nazism and Fascism). *See* Women's League Against Nazism and Fascism

Law Governing Rights and Duties of Cultivators (1933), 10, 45

League for the Defense of Women's Rights (*Rabitat al-Difa' 'an Huquq al-Mar'a*): in 1950s, 132, 135, 153–159; Ba'th regime, 135; change through legislation, 157; Cobbett on, 135–136; Da'ud on, 135; al-Dulaimi on, 130, 131, 154; goals of, 153–154, 156–157; history of, 73, 113, 130, 131–132, 135, 137, 159; on inheritance, 73; narrative of women's movement, xv, 112, 133, 136, 198n11; quest for new order, 153–159

League of Nations, Iraqi membership in, 7, 9

Lebanon, women's suffrage in, 194n12

legal system: Baghdad Penal Code, 22, 24, 28, 37, 38, 39–40; blood feuds, 23, 34, 35, 43, 162; British reluctance to intervene in crimes against women, 26–30; capital punishment, 27, 37–38; civil courts, 8, 24, 26; crimes against women, 23, 24, 26–37; customary law, xiii, 20, 29, 138, 155, 156; Draft Code of Personal Status, 56–80; election law and exclusion, 86–110; family law, xiv, 51–85, 155; *fasl* marriage, 23, 162, 167, 168; honor murders, 23, 26, 27, 28, 29, 31, 37, 42–43, 48, 50, 155; Judges and Qadhis Law (1929), 56; marriage customs, 23, 24, 34–36; *nahwa*, 24, 31, 33–34, 35, 36, 39, 162, 168; personal status, 51–80; religious courts, 8; return to tribal customs under Husain regime, 166–167; on sexual morals, 23, 24, 26, 33, 34; Shara' Courts Law (1923), 56; shari'a courts, 8; Spiritual Councils, 8; Tribal and Criminal and Civil Disputes Regulation (TCCDR), xii, xv, 26–50; tribal jurisdiction and, 21; tribal *majlis*, 22, 24, 26, 27; under British occupation, 5–6, 8, 172; urban crime, 22; urban-rural power distribution in, 37–39

Levey, Zach, 180n10

literacy, 16, 46

Lyell, Thomas, 53–55, 65

Mahdi Kubba, Muhammad, 13

Mahmud, Ma'ida Najib, 128

Mahmud, Nur al-Din, 16

mahr, 42, 61, 66, 67–69, 76, 139, 155, 161

al-Malai'ika, Nazik, 42, 72, 140

malaria, 16, 46, 155

Maliki doctrine, 76, 80, 82

al-Maliki, Nuri, 167

Marr, Phebe, 6

marriage: adultery, 34, 37; consent to, 60–63, 79, 208n24; *darura*, 62; "disobedience" of wife, 69, 70; divorce, 74–80, 140, 156, 161, 168; Draft Code of Personal Status, 60–67; al-Dulaimi on, 155–156; eloping, 34; "exchange marriage", 68; extramarital relations, 34, 37;

marriage (*continued*)
  fasl marriage, 23, 162, 167, 168; forced marriage, 42, 62, 63, 67, 79, 141, 156, 168; gender relations and role in, 67–80; *mahr*, 42, 61, 66, 67–69, 75, 76, 155, 161; maintenance responsibility of husband, 67–69, 76, 141; *maslaha*, 59, 62; matrimonial guardianship, 60–63; minimum age for, 63, 79, 161, 208n24; of minor girls, 61, 62, 66, 67, 79, 141, 155; *nahwa*, 24, 31, 33–34, 35, 36, 39, 162, 168; option of puberty (*khiyar al-bulugh*), 61–62, 67; Ottoman Law of Family Rights of 1917, 188n26, 189n43; Personal Status Law on, 161, 167, 168–171; polygamy, 54, 63–65, 156; Qur'an on, 54; registration of marriage contract, 66–67, 139–140; repudiation of, 75, 141, 161; al-Rusafi on, 116; separation, 76, 77, 82; sexual relations with minors, 62; temporary marriage (*mut'a*), 65–66, 80; of upper-class women, 156; waiting period ('*idda*), 74, 191n78; Women's Iraqi Union on, 139, 140, *See also* marriage customs
marriage contract: Draft Code of Personal Status, 60–67; al-Dulaimi on, 157; Ottoman Law of Family Rights of 1917, 188n26, 189n43; registration of, 66–67, 139–140
marriage customs: Draft Code of Personal Status, 67; *fasl* marriage, 23, 162, 167, 168; forced marriage, 42, 62, 63, 67, 79, 141, 156, 168; legal system and, 23, 24, 34–36; *mahr*, 42, 61, 66, 67–69, 75, 76, 155, 161; *mut'a* (temporary marriage), 65–66, 80; *nahwa*, 24, 31, 33–34, 35, 36, 39, 162, 168
Marxists, 118, 124
Meriwether, Margaret, xi-xii, 176n8, 177n9
middle class: army and, 18; women's movement and, 113
Midfa'i, Jamil, 92

military academies, Ottoman Empire and, 2
minimum age for marriage, 63, 79, 161, 208n24
minors: child custody, 71–72, 79–80, 140, 161, 168; marriage of, 61, 62, 66, 67, 79, 141, 155; sexual relations with, 62
Mitchell, Timothy, 88
The Modern Woman (*al-Mar'a al-Haditha*) (magazine), 125
modernization, "gradual modernization", 105–110, 141–159
Monroe Educational Inquiry Commission, 31, 46, 193n10
mortality rates, 16, 46, 202n78
The Mother and Child (*al-Umm wa-l-Tifl*) (magazine), 125
al-Mudarris, Fahmi, 183n61
al-Mukhtar, Tawfiq, 94
Musaddiq, Muhammad, 16
Muslim Sisters' Society (*Jam'iyyat al-Aukht al-Muslima*), 95
mut'a (temporary marriage), 65–66, 80

Nadi al-Nahda al-Nisa'iyya. See Women's Awakening Club
al-nahwa, 24, 31, 33–34, 35, 36, 39, 162, 168
al-Na'ini, Husain, 117
National Assembly, 164, 165
National Democratic Party (NDP), 12, 18, 99, 101–103, 179n18
National Front, 18
NDP. *See* National Democratic Party
Nelson, Cynthia, 176n6, 204n34
Nuri, Baha' al-Din, 16, 131

oil industry, nationalization of, 16
Ottoman Empire, Iraq under, 1–2
Ottoman Land Law of 1858, 2, 5, 44
Ottoman Law of Family Rights of 1917, 188n26, 189n43
Ottoman Vilayet Law of 1864, 1

Pachachi, Adnan, 164

Pachachi, Zakiyya, 198*n*2

Paidar, Parvin, xii, 176*n*6, 177*nn*9, 12

Pasha, Midhat, 1, 2

Pasha, Muhammad Qadri, 188*n*29

peasant women (*fallahat*): agriculture, 46–47, 155; "double servitude" of, 47, 138, 155; duties of, 46–47; education for, 31, 46; health concerns of, 46, 154–155; plight of, 43, 45–46; treatment of, 47, *See also* rural women

peasants (*fallahin*): Law Governing Rights and Duties of Cultivators, 10; women, 43, 45–46

personal status: Article 41 (Baghdad Penal Code), 28, 37, 160; Article 41 (Iraqi Constitution 2005), 169, 170; Charrad on, 79; Draft Code of Personal Status, 56–80; al-Dulaimi on, 155–156, 157; Iraqi Women's Union on, 139, 140, 141; Lyell on, 54; Personal Status Law (1959), ix, xiv, 160–161, 167, 168–171; Resolution 137 (2003), 169, 170, 171; Shara' Courts Law (1923), 56; shari'a courts, 55; state-tribe alliances and, 79; under British rule, 51–56, 172; under Husain regime, 167; Women's Iraqi Union on, 139, 140, *See also* family law

Personal Status Law (1959), ix, xiv, 160–161, 167, 168–171; 1978 amendment, 168, 170; abolition of, 169, 170; Resolution 137 (2003), 169, 170, 171

Perto, Bushra, 131–132, 198*nn*3, 11

Podeh, Elie, 180*n*10

political process: who can hold elected office, 87, 88, 93; women in Parliament, 164, 206*n*5; women's participation in, xiv, 90, 164

political rights for women, 86–110; education and, 101, 107; Hashemite period, xiv ; Iraqi Women's Union on, 141–142; al-Istiqlal position on, 99–100; modern woman's image, 146–148; postinvasion Iraq, 163–165; al-Sa'id on, 106–109;

Shi'is on, 97; United Nations and, 144; women's "occupation" of Chamber of Deputies (1958), 149–153, *See also* women's movement

polygamy: Draft Code of Personal Status, 63–65, 156; Qur'anic sanction of, 54, 64; Women's Iraqi Union on, 139

Popular Reform Association (*Jam'iyyat al-Islah al-Sha'bi*), 10–11, 179*n*14

Portsmouth Agreement, 14, 91

Pratt, Nicola, 172, 175*n*1, 209*n*37

property rights. *See* land ownership

public health in Iraq, 155

qadis, 52, 56, 83

Qadri Pasha, Mohamad, 58

al-Qai'da, tribal fighters against, 167

al-Qaisi, Qasim, 81, 192*n*94

Qasim, 'Abd al-Karim, 14, 18, 115, 135, 161, 192*n*100

Rabitat al-Difa' 'an Huquq al-Mar'a. See League for the Defense of Women's Rights

Rabitat al-Mar'a al-'Iraqiyya. See Iraqi Women's League

al-Rahhal, Amina, 126

al-Rahhal, Husain, 118, 126

Ra'uf, 'Afifa, 128, 131

The Red Crescent (al-Hilal al-Ahmar) (magazine), 125

Red Crescent Society (*Jam'iyyat al-Hilal al-Ahmar*), 112, 125, 127, 128, 198*n*2

Reform (al-Islah) Party, 93

Repression of 1947, 128, 133, 137

repudiation of marriage, 75, 141, 161, *See also* divorce

Resolution 137 (2003), 169, 170, 171

retribalization of women, 166–167

Revolutionary Command Council, 166

Rikkan, Haji, 28

Rivett Carnac, H.G., 26, 27

Roded, Ruth, 177*nn*9, 11

rural women: Da'ud on, 138–139; "double servitude" of, 47, 138, 155; al-Dulaimi on, 43–44, 47, 138; medical services for, 46; mortality rates for, 46, 202n78; "tribalization" of, 30, 37, 43–44, 47, *See also* peasant women

al-Rusafi, Ma'ruf, 42, 115, 116, 138, 139

Sada al-Ahali (newspaper), 102

al-Sadr, Muhammad Sadiq, 81, 82, 83

al-Sa'dun, 'Abd al-Karim, 38

al-Sa'dun, 'Abd al-Muhsin, 30, 38, 39

al-Sa'dun, 'Abdulla Falih, 38, 39

Sa'dun case, 38–40, 183n68

al-Sahifa (periodical), 118

al-Sa'id, 'Ismat Sabah, 198n2

al-Sa'id, Nai'ma, 106, 120

al-Sa'id, Nuri: about, 7, 178n13, 198n2; government following British reoccupation, 47; government of 1946, 14; on "gradual modernization", 105–108, 109, 142, 148; period from 1948 to 1958, 15–19, 48, 49, 92, 139, 142; on personal status laws, 48, 49, 57; on TCCDR, 48, 49; Treaty of 1930, 9; on women's political rights, 106–109, 149–153

Salim, Shakir Mustafa, 35, 65

al-Samarra'i Fa'iq, 13

Sanasarian, Eliz, 176n6

Sandeman, Sir Robert, 21

al-Sani', 'Abdulla, murder of, 38–40, 183n68

Schacht, Joseph, 58

schools. *See* education

secular education, Ottoman Empire and, 2

Shafi'i doctrine, 188n27

Shafiq, Duriya, 204n34

shaikhs: land ownership and, 5, 21, 44–45; under British occupation, 5, 21

Shanshal, Muhammad Siddiq, 13, 100

Shara' Courts Law (1923), 56

Shara' Procedure Law (1937), 63

shari'a courts, 3, 8, 52, 139

Shawkat, Sami, 64, 93, 189n46

sheikhs. *See* shaikhs

Shi'i Ja'fari doctrine, 58, 59, 61, 68, 71, 75, 76, 82

Shi'is: Draft Code of Personal Status, 58; exclusion from government positions, 3; history of, 3; on inheritance, 73; legal system of, 3–4; in modern politics, 14, 17; *mut'a* (temporary marriage), 65–66; under British occupation, 6; under Ottoman Empire, 3–4; use of term, 188n27; wife maintenance, 69

al-Sijill (newspaper), 94

Sirman, Nükhet, 176n6

Sluglett, Peter, 178n13, 183nn61, 63

Spellberg, Denise, 195n40

Spivak, Gayatry, 27

Stevens, E.S., 120, 121–122

Suez crisis (1956), 17, 18

Sulaiman, Hikmat, 10

Sunni, use of term, 188n27

Sunni Hanafi doctrine, 58, 59, 61, 68, 71, 72, 76, 81, 82, 139

Sunni Maliki doctrine, 76, 80, 82

Sunni Shafi'i doctrine, 188n27

Sunnis: Draft Code of Personal Status, 58; on inheritance, 73; under British occupation, 6; under Ottoman Empire, 3–4; wife maintenance, 69

al-Suwaidi, Naji, 24, 30, 31

al-Suwaidi, Tawfiq, 14, 90

Syria: United Arab Republic, 18; women's suffrage in, 194n12

TAL. *See* Transitional Administrative Law

TCCDR. *See* Tribal and Criminal and Civil Disputes Regulation

Temperance and Social Welfare Society (*Jam'iyyat Mukafahat al-'Ilal al-Ijtima'iyya*), 112

Temperance Society (*Jam'iyyat Mukafahat al-Muskirat*), 125, 127

temporary marriage (*mut'a*), 65–66, 80

Thabit, A.J. Abdullah, 178

Thompson, Elizabeth, 176n6, 194n12

Transitional Administrative Law (TAL), 164

Treaty of Sèvres, 4

Tribal and Criminal and Civil Disputes Regulation (TCCDR): 1951 amendment of, 47–50, 186n105; abolition of, 25, 28, 160; British mandate and, 5, 20–26, 40–41; crimes against women, 24, 50; crimes involving honor, 24, 30–37, 42–43, 48, 50; Hedgcock, Monica Grace and Stuart Edwin, on, 29; history of, xii, 20–23, 40–41; intellectual opposition to, 30–32, 44; land ownership and, 45; negotiating "tribal law", 30–37; opposition to, xv, 32, 41–42, 43–44; oppression of women and, 44; revision of, 28, 30, 31; al-Sa'id government and, 48–49; shaikh's challenges to, 32–37; Tribal Code to replace, 32–37; tribal jurisdiction and, 21; urban-rural power distribution in, 37–39, 155

tribal fighters, against al-Qai'da, 167

tribal *majlis*, 22, 24, 26, 27

tribalization of women: under British occupation and mandate, 21–30, 37–40; "independent" Iraq and, 40–44; republican government and, 160; retribalization since 2003?, 166–167; rural women, 30, 37, 43–44, 47

Tripp, Charles, 178, 178nn6, 9, 185n90, 195n18, 207n15

Tucker, Judith E., xi–xii, 78, 176nn7, 8, 177n9

Turkish law, matters of personal status, 55–56

'ulama', xiv, 4, 52, 53, 56, 57, 65, 75, 83, 84, 105

al-'Ulum, Muhammad Bahr, 192n100

al-'Umari, Arshad, 14

al-'Umari, Khairi, 187n13, 199nn15, 22, 200nn26, 35, 39, 201n43, 202n74

United Arab Republic, formation of, 18, 108

United National Front, 18

United States: assessment of impact on Iraq, 171–172; rhetoric regarding Iraqi politics in 2010, 165–166

urban migration, 15–16, 113

U.S. invasion, status of Iraqi women under, ix–x, xv–xvi, 163–173

veiling of women, 116, 118

Vilayet Law of 1864, 1

Wahbi, Asiya Tawfiq, 65, 139, 151, 198n2, 204n34

Wahbi, Tawfiq, 198n2

al-Wa'iz, Najm al-Din, 81, 192n94

wathba (1948), 14, 91, 100, 130–131, 194n44

Wazir, 'Abd al-Masih, 120

Wazir, 'Abd al-Masih, Mari, 120

Week of Virtue (1953), 95

Week of Women's Rights (1953), 95, 142, 147

Wilson, Arnold T., 23

women: Constitutional Union Party on, 105, 106; depicted in *Haji Rikkan*, 28–29; divorce options of, 75–77, 161; "double servitude" of, 44–47, 138, 155; Duka on, 124; economic independence of, 70, 157; election law and exclusion, 86–110; gender relations in marriage, 67–80; "independent" Iraq and, 40–44; inheritance by, 73–74, 161; in Iraqi Parliament, 164, 206n5; Iraqi Women's Union on modern woman's image, 146–148; Kashif al-Ghita' on, 97, 98; marginalization of, 29; modern woman's image, 146–148; murder of, 23, 27, 29, 31, 33, 37, 42, 43, 155; "obedience" of, 69–70; personal status of, 51–80; Qur'an on, 95, 97; role of, 67–80, 142; subordination of, 78; travel by, 69–70; treatment by legal system, 23–24; treatment of, 47; Tribal and Criminal and Civil Disputes Regulation (TCCDR), 20, 50; "tribalization" of rural women, 30, 37, 43–44, 47;

women (*continued*)

tribalization under British occupation and mandate, 21–30, 37–40; working outside the home, 70, 71, 156; al-Zahawi on, 95–96, *See also* marriage; peasant women; political rights for women; rural women; women's education; women's movement; women's suffrage

"women's awakening", 134

Women's Awakening Club (*Nadi al-Nahda al-Nisa'iyya*), 64, 120–122

Women's Committee (ICP), 130

women's education: Da'ud on, 117, 123; al-Dulaimi on, 123; goals of, 88–89; al-Husri on, 117; al-Istiqlal platform on, 100; Khidir on, 118–119; Monroe Educational Inquiry Commission, 31, 46, 193n10; political rights and, 100, 101, 107; for tribal women, 31, 46

Women's International Democratic Federation, 132

Women's League Against Nazism and Fascism (LANF) (*Jam'iyyat Mukafahat al-Naziyya wa-l-Fashiyya*), 126

Women's League Society (*Jam'iyyat al-Rabita al-Nisa'iyya*), 113, 114, 126, 128, 131, 132, 133, 137

Women's Liberation Organization (*Jam'iyyat Tahrir al-Mara*), 131, 137

women's magazines, 125

women's movement, xv, 111–136; Article 41 (Baghdad Penal Code), 28, 37, 160; Article 41 (Iraqi Constitution 2005), 169, 170; Cairo Women's Conference (1944), 128; competing narratives of, 115, 128–129, 133–136, 197n3; Damascus Eastern Arab Women's Conference (1930), 126; history: 1910–1932, 115–123; history: 1930s to end of World War II, 123–127; history: postwar, 127–133;

post-2003 struggle, 163–173; published works on, 176n6; repression of 1947, 128, 133, 137; retribalization of women since, 166–167, 2003; revolt of 1920 as defining moment in, 119–120; Week of Women's Rights (1953), 95, 142, 147; women's magazines, 125; women's "occupation" of Chamber of Deputies (1958), 149–153; women's organizations, 125, *See also* Iraqi Women's Union; League for the Defense of Women's Rights; political rights for women; women's suffrage

women's suffrage: efforts to change women's exclusion in Iraq, 91–92; first voting by women, 165; in Great Britain, 87–88; Iraqi Community Party and, 99, 103–104; Iraqi Women's Union on, 143–145; Istiqlal Party and, 99–101; National Democratic Party and, 99, 101–103; in neighboring countries, 194n12; opposition to, 92–98; supporters of, xv, 98–104

Women's Temperance and Social Welfare Society, 112, 125, 127, 128, 198n2

Women's Union Society (*Jam'iyyat al-Ittihad al-Nisa'i*), 137

Woodsmall, Ruth, 107, 127

working-class women, 123

The Young Iraqi Woman (*Fatat al-'Iraq*) (magazine), 125

Youth Club (*Nadi al-Shabiba*), 124

Yusuf, Yusuf Salman. *See* Fahd

Yuval-Davis, Nira, 106

al-Zahawi, Amjad, 81, 95, 192n94

al-Zahawi, Asma', 64, 120, 121m, 122

al-Zahawi, Jamil Sidqi, 63–64, 73, 115, 116

al-Zahawi, Nihal, 95–96, 106